SIGHT AND EMBODIMENT
IN THE MIDDLE AGES

SIGHT AND EMBODIMENT IN THE MIDDLE AGES

Suzannah Biernoff

BD
214
.B54
2002

First published 2002 by
PALGRAVE MACMILLAN
Houndmills, Basingstoke, Hampshire RG21 6XS and
175 Fifth Avenue, New York, N.Y. 10010
Companies and representatives throughout the world

PALGRAVE MACMILLAN is the global academic imprint of the Palgrave Macmillan division of St. Martin's Press, LLC and of Palgrave Macmillan Ltd. Macmillan® is a registered trademark in the United States, United Kingdom and other countries. Palgrave is a registered trademark in the European Union and other countries.

ISBN 0–333–96120–X hardback

This book is printed on paper suitable for recycling and made from fully managed and sustained forest sources.

A catalogue record for this book is available from the British Library.

Library of Congress Cataloging-in-Publication Data

Biernoff, Suzannah.
    Sight and embodiment in the Middle Ages / Suzannah Biernoff.
        p.   cm.—(New Middle Ages)
    Includes bibliographical references and index.
    ISBN 0–333–96120–X
    1. Vision—History—To 1500.   2. Body, Human (Philosophy)—
History—To 1500.   3. Vision—Religious aspects—Christianity—
History of doctrines—Middle Ages, 600–1500.   4. Body, Human—
Religious aspects—Christianity—History of doctrines—Middle Ages,
600–1500.   I. Title.   II. New Middle Ages (Palgrave Macmillan
(Firm))
    BD214 .B54   2002
    152.14'09'02—dc21   2001056045

10   9   8   7   6   5   4   3   2   1
11   10   09   08   07   06   05   04   03   02

Printed and bound in Great Britain by
Antony Rowe Ltd, Chippenham and Eastbourne

For David

CONTENTS

LIST OF FIGURES

ACKNOWLEDGEMENTS

This book has its origins in my PhD dissertation. Of the many people who shaped and supported its development, thanks are due in particular to Susan Best. As a supervisor, colleague and friend she has been both inspirational and instrumental, and my work has benefited enormously from her ideas and intellectual rigour.

My speculations were nourished and tested in several reading groups: thanks especially to Nicky Teffer and Anne Douglas for many stimulating conversations. Jill Bennett, Jane Chance and Miri Rubin provided valuable feedback and contributed to the development and clarification of my ideas. I am also indebted to David Mann, to the editorial team at Palgrave, and to several anonymous readers whose critical attention to the manuscript improved it in style and substance. Jo North provided copy-editing expertise; Lara Biernoff made intelligent and sensitive comments on early drafts; John Swettenham talked me through the final stages; and Hildy kept me smiling through the task of proofreading and indexing.

I was assisted in my research by an Australian Postgraduate Research Award, and have received generous support, in the final stage of the project, from Chelsea College of Art and Design in London. The following individuals and organisations have kindly given permission for their photographs to be reproduced in this book: The British Library (Figs 1.1, 1.2 and 3.1); the Master and Fellows of St John's College, Cambridge (Fig. 2.1); Bibliothèque Nationale de France (Fig. 6.1); Ministero per i Beni e le Attività Culturali, Firenze (Fig. 6.2); the Beinecke Rare Book and Manuscript Library, Yale University (Fig. 6.3); and Abtei Frauenwörth, Chiemsee (Fig. 6.4).

Finally, for her good company and innumerable kindnesses, I am deeply grateful to my mother Diana Biernoff.

INTRODUCTION:
MEDIEVAL VISION IN PERSPECTIVE

> ... 'the optical unconscious' now appears as a new dark continent ripe
> for exploration.[1]
>
> *Martin Jay*

The recent proliferation of books and articles devoted to vision and
visuality has prompted speculation of a 'pictorial turn' or 'paradigm
shift in the cultural imaginary of our age'.[2] Yet despite this interest, and
the expanding body of scholarship it has produced, the medieval period
has remained curiously under-represented. To quote Jeffrey Hamburger,
'the relation between medieval and modern modes of vision remains
vexed, in large measure because, the history of optics and perspective
aside, it remains virtually unexamined'.[3] This book will, I hope, enable
such historical comparisons to be made. But before we turn our attention
to the Middle Ages, it seems salutary to reflect on the visuality of modern
historiography. Where medieval vision is concerned, I believe we are
dealing less with a scholarly oversight than with an historical blind spot.
There are at least three plausible reasons why historians and theorists
of vision may have neglected medieval texts or images. The first has
to do with the critical apparatus available to the contemporary theorist.
Recent work on visuality has been dominated by a Lacanian paradigm
in which the visual *gestalt*—the mirror image for example—signifies the
bounded subject of modern culture. It is not surprising that psychoanalytic theory encounters its historical limits in the pre-modern
period, where subject–object relations (mediated by vision) are more
indeterminate, and where bodies (or at least *fleshly* bodies) are more
fluid.[4]

Secondly, the history of vision has for the most part been written as the
story of the progressive 'rationalisation' of sight. Irrespective of whether
such enlightenment is celebrated or disparaged, the narrative itself requires
a 'dark' age, as the counterpoint to reason's illuminating rays. This, in the

briefest terms, is our blind spot, the anti-visual and unseen other of modern ocularcentrism. If, in the footsteps of Rosalind Krauss and Martin Jay, we set out to explore the 'dark continent' of the optical unconscious, medieval vision would demand a further descent, behind or beneath that partially mapped continent of modern visuality.

A certain symmetry between *pre*-modern and *post*-modern is implicit in this periodisation of vision. The current fascination with the 'underside' of Western ocularcentrism—its repressions and exclusions—has grown out of post-modern concerns, and there has been a tendency to find echoes of this post-modern sensibility in the distant rather than immediate historical past. The most famous example is Umberto Eco's claim that we live in 'the new Middle Ages'.[5] More specifically but in a similar vein, Michael Camille likens medieval visual culture to that of the late twentieth century, seeing in both the signs of 'deep, unsettled questioning as to the function of the visual in society'.[6] And Michael Ann Holly compares Michel Foucault's 'violation' of historical perspective to the 'medieval treatment of space'. In contrast to the 'dogmatic and doctrinaire' perspectivism of the Renaissance (and by extension the grand narratives of modernity), medieval spatiality could, she speculates, 'be construed as creatively liberating'.[7]

It is not my intention to argue for or against such connections. They are, however, a salient reminder that writing history is a narcissistic pursuit: what intrigues us about the past has everything to do with the present. More directly related to the concerns and scope of this book is the dialectical shape of the narrative I have described. It is hard, within a structure of historical polarities, to imagine how religion and science, or ocularphobia and ocularcentrism might coexist; yet they assuredly do in the later Middle Ages (for the purposes of this study, the twelfth to fourteenth centuries).

A third possible explanation for the apparent obscurity of medieval vision is that the narrative contours of this history have tended to be pegged to visible landmarks: inventions that literally alter, extend or transform human sight; or stylistic changes in the visual arts. If vision has a history, then it must be sought in the realm of the visible, or so the reasoning goes.[8] Nowhere is this assumption more apparent than in the prominence given in accounts of visual history to the 'rediscovery' of single point perspective in Renaissance Italy, and the associated 'rebirth' of pictorial naturalism.[9] If, as one author has claimed, these developments mark the 'awakening of sight' then medieval vision is an oxymoron.[10]

Mitigating against this perception of an anti-ocular Middle Ages is a marked increase, from around 1200, in the production and use of religious images. What for Huizinga was a sign of a culture in decline—a reification of thought—other medievalists have interpreted as evidence of a new 'need to see'.[11] As Gothic churches were being adorned with painted altarpieces, crucifixes, fresco cycles and liturgical objects, devotional practices were becoming increasingly focused on the visual perception of the sacred as well as techniques of interior visualisation. An emphasis on private devotion from the thirteenth century onwards provided the impetus for the production of illuminated manuscripts, small, affordable devotional paintings and sculptures, and the construction of family chapels. The later Middle Ages also saw the popularisation of 'indulgence images' associated with the remission of sin, and a proliferation of miracle working images.[12] Vision had become a predominant and structuring element of devotional practice, both private and cultic. Yet from a secular perspective—from the perspective, that is, of the distancing and objectifying gaze of modern ocularcentrism—these developments are imperceptible.

Clearly there is no simple correspondence between the history of visual art and the history of vision. Once this is acknowledged, it becomes necessary to ask what basis there is for the privileging of the visible in the history of vision. Can we reconstruct historical viewers—*how* people looked—from *what* they looked at? In short, must a history of vision necessarily be a history of image making and reception? This is a salient question for art historians, and indeed anyone interested in studying or teaching visual culture (where *visual* culture is so often assumed to be *visible*). It is worth dwelling for a moment on the invisibility of vision; its existence, so to speak, outside the visible frame.

In the Middle Ages, vision was a way of relating to oneself, to the sensible world including other animate beings, and to God. As such, it exceeded both viewing subjects and visible objects, as well as determining their mode of interaction. There were, of course, competing models of vision, as well as conventional distinctions and analogies between different levels or kinds of sight: corporeal, intellectual and spiritual vision being a common tripartite classification. It is difficult, given this complexity, to offer a single, succinct definition of vision. If one characteristic were to be singled out as definitive for the purposes of this study, it would have to be the dynamic, reciprocal nature of medieval vision, as it was imagined and enacted across a range of discourses and practices. The eye was simultaneously receptive, passive, vulnerable to sensations; and active: roaming, grasping or piercing its objects. Sight was at once an extension of the sensitive soul towards an object, and the passage of sensible forms through the eye and into the brain. A medieval definition of vision, then, is clearly incompatible with a methodology that would treat either viewing subjects or visible objects as autonomous entities, or their relationship as unidirectional.

Medieval vision is most visible in its traversal of people and things, where it is translated into corporeal processes or abstracted into the language of geometrical optics. These effects and principles are, on occasion, rendered in pictures—in Chapter 6, for example, Christ's body becomes the focus (and visible record) of ocular desire. More often, however, the imaging and imagining of vision occurs in texts, ranging from courtly romances to source material for sermons, scholastic philosophy and, of course, scientific writings on optics. In consequence, a certain disregard for disciplinary boundaries has been inescapable. Where attitudes to vision were contested or in conflict, I have highlighted the disparity between various bodies of knowledge. At other times the inclusiveness and eclecticism of medieval visuality has been emphasised. In sum, the object of this inquiry is not a particular set of visual artefacts delimited by space or time, but the multiple configurations of a complex visual culture. It is a topic that, to be sure, intersects fundamentally with the concerns of art history, but it cannot be contained within the traditional methodological frames of that discipline.

Finally, something must be said of the relationship between vision and visuality. The term 'visuality' is generally used to signal the cultural constructedness of vision, to prise open the notion of 'natural' (and therefore singular, historically constant) sight to a multiplicity of visual practices, discourses and cultures. In this sense visuality extends beyond the ordinary notion of vision as a physical (if psychologically 'mediated') phenomenon. Peter de Bolla comments that visuality is 'the name we might give to a figurative spacing that opens up, controls, or legislates the terrain upon which a large number of concepts are articulated'.[13] In this expanded field, visuality is implicated in social formations and ideologies; it could be expected to have political as well as discursive effects, and to structure or circumscribe how we know and interact with each other and the world. Let me briefly elaborate on these points—the intertwining of nature and culture, and the expanded field of visuality—in relation to the content and scope of this book.

In keeping with the definition of visuality given above, I have taken it as given that looking is a cultural practice as well as a physiological process; and that vision is always mediated by discourses about vision. On the other hand, my contention that looking in the Middle Ages entailed a *physical* encounter between bodies, needs to be differentiated from arguments about the poetics or metaphorics of sight. We do not think of metaphors or allegories as having corporeal effects; and if they do (one may, for example, 'feel' another's eyes on one's face or body) those 'imagined' effects are distinguished from 'real' events. In the Middle Ages, however, a lascivious gaze was said to be equivalent to sin, and a look could literally be venomous: these were no mere figures of speech. Conversely, the ardent contemplation of Christ's wounds—increasingly represented in devotional images—could effect not only an emotional transformation, but in some cases bodily signs of identification with the Saviour. Where modern science ascribes such phenomena to the subjective operations of the human psyche, medieval theories of vision offered compelling physiological explanations for many of these optical effects.

Many of our contemporary visual metaphors in fact correspond to earlier scientific axioms. The notion of a 'piercing gaze', a 'sharp look', a 'clear eye' or 'fleeting glance', and a host of words related to knowledge and understanding ('insight', intellectual 'blindness' and 'clarity' to name but a few) all had a very literal meaning in the Middle Ages. Aside from these vernacular examples, Teresa Brennan has argued that psychoanalytic accounts of sight refigure extramission (the theory that rays or optical pneuma emitted by the eye are responsible for vision) as a psychical force.[14] In such instances one might say that medieval vision has become part of modern visuality. What was a *physical* phenomenon in the Middle Ages is now a potent symbol; a *psychical effect*.[15]

Of modern theorists, Maurice Merleau-Ponty's insistence on the mind's incarnation (in a generalised 'flesh' that exceeds individual bodies), and his metaphor of perceptual intertwining perhaps bring us closest to the reciprocal, corporeal flux of medieval vision.[16] Central to Merleau-Ponty's phenomenology is the imbrication of physical, psychical and socio-historical aspects of perception, as well as the interlacing of vision and the visible.[17] Yet these metaphors—intertwining, imbrication, intercorporeity—convey an idea of differentiation as well as inseparability.[18] Here, too, I have attempted to hold on to this paradox, by maintaining a distinction between vision as an organising metaphor, and vision as a physical event, while acknowledging their convolution. By allowing this space between sight and its discursive or visual manifestations it is possible to think of nature and culture as mutually constituting, and of both nature *and* culture as historically mutable.[19]

With regard to the second distinctive feature of visuality—its seemingly boundless analytical scope—it has been necessary to impose limits on what is already a wide-ranging topic. It would have been possible, for example, to ask whether medieval vision, in its scientific, theological, literary and devotional aspects, was related to broader social and religious changes. I have not actively pursued such links. The various models and modalities of medieval vision are not, in other words, interpreted here as the effects of social, economic or political determinants.[20] What *can* be said of the period around 1200 is that the developments discussed in these pages constitute new domains of visuality. Optical science, with its legitimation of sense-based knowledge, is in this respect continuous with the contemporaneous humanisation of Christ, and the veritable explosion in the production of religious art during the thirteenth century.[21] Each of these developments speaks of a heightened attentiveness to human emotions and experiences, and an increased *visual* engagement with the natural and social world; whether in terms of scientific curiosity, or a worldly (rather than other-worldly) religious sensibility.

To what extent were these cultural practices and ideas about vision shared by the many millions of people living in England or France or Italy in the twelfth and thirteenth centuries? How much can we infer from an altarpiece, a treatise on optics, a devotional handbook, or a poem about love at first sight? Are we limited to talking about a discourse of vision— a body of knowledge, a repertoire of literary motifs—shared by an educated elite, or can we speak more generally about medieval visual culture? These kinds of questions can only ever be answered speculatively, but there are reasons to think that the ideas discussed here had a life beyond the cloister and the university. In the first place, many of the texts I have used cut across the nominal boundary between 'high' and 'low' culture. Sermons, for example, functioned as 'a kind of mass communication' allowing intellectual trends and new scientific theories to be disseminated to a wide audience.[22] What is more, the influence clearly flowed both ways: ancient beliefs about the evil eye and the sexuality of sight find their way into the visual theories of medieval theologians, philosophers and medical authors. I would not claim that all of these sources represent common knowledge or consensus. But the repetition of metaphors, images, desires and anxieties through different texts—destined for quite different audiences—suggests that vision was a rich and contested discursive terrain in the later Middle Ages.

The concerns and questions I have sketched out so far form the broad historical and theoretical parameters of this book. What remains, by way of an introduction, is to consider in more detail the existing perspectives on medieval vision.

In modernity's shadow

I have said that the history of vision has been written as a story of the progressive rationalisation (even liberation) of sight in Western culture: a story in which the pre-modern period is darkened by modernity's shadow. One particularly influential version of this historical narrative contrasts modern ocularcentrism to medieval ocularphobia.[23] The most notable proponents of this argument, Lucien Febvre and Robert Mandrou, claimed that it was not until the seventeenth or eighteenth century that the 'anti-ocular' culture of the late Middle Ages was replaced by the modern hierarchy of the senses, with vision in first place.[24] Febvre argued that:

> The sixteenth century did not see first: it heard and smelled, it sniffed the air and caught sounds. It was only later, as the seventeenth century was approaching, that it seriously and actively became engaged with geometry, focusing attention on the world of forms with Kepler (1571–1630) and Desargues of Lyon (1593–1662). It was then that *vision* was unleashed in the world of science as it was in the world of physical sensations, and the world of beauty as well.[25]

Two common assumptions are encapsulated in this passage. First, that the modern rationalisation of sight is the historical antithesis of a pre-modern 'dark' ages: a period in which religious (as opposed to secular and scientific) and irrational (as opposed to rational) forces held sway. For Febvre, however, medieval visuality is not merely shaped or, more accurately, distorted by a religious sensibility. He is describing a culture in which sight is actively repressed, and with it, the possibility of scientific observation as well as aesthetic appreciation. In this respect, Febvre's account is extreme. Other commentators, as we shall see, retain the discursive outline of the rationalisation of sight while explaining the 'irrationality' of medieval vision in terms of a primitive or child-like visual consciousness rather than a repressive ocularphobia.

The second assumption I want to highlight is that the primacy of sight is synonymous with geometrical optics. While Febvre seizes upon seventeenth-century optics, others have proposed an earlier date. The formulation and application of single-point perspective in the fifteenth century has long been imbued with almost mythical significance: supposedly marking the momentous shift from symbolism to naturalism, from 'reading' pictures to truly *seeing* them.[26] If, as David Michael Levin has claimed, 'The Renaissance "rediscovery" of linear perspective codified, and at the same time promoted, a new historical style of vision',[27] then pre-perspectival, pre-Renaissance habits of vision must be qualitatively different.

Levin's approach to the history of vision is fairly representative of that taken by intellectual historians, as well as historians of art, in locating the beginning of the modern era in the Renaissance. The Middle Ages is thereby relegated to the 'other' side of the divide, the 'pre-modern'. As Levin writes in his introduction to *The Opening of Vision*:

The 'modern' world begins, in the story I want to tell about the West, with the Renaissance. It is to the people of the Renaissance that we owe the beginnings of modern science and technology, an unprecedented expansion of trade and commerce, the glorious vision of humanism, and a mighty challenge to the mediaeval authority of faith, announced in the name of a self-validating rationality.[28]

It is in this supposedly secular climate of scientific inquiry and intellectual humanism that Renaissance art is born, corresponding to what Levin describes as 'the triumphant, rapturous, almost delirious awakening of sight to the vision of a geometrical, completely rational world'.[29] But if sight is thus 'awakened', how did people *see* prior to the Renaissance? Levin's alternative to modern ocularcentrism—which he regards as egocentric, distancing and ultimately destructive—is inspired by Heidegger and Merleau-Ponty. If the 'modern' gaze assumes a God's-eye view on a world unfurled in its passivity before us, the pre-modern, mystico-religious gaze is defined in terms of Heidegger's notion of 'beholdenness'.[30] For Levin, this term signifies the awareness that we inhabit a world in which we are always already beheld. In theological language, we are 'in *God's* picture'.[31] But if this decentring of the human subject before an omnipotent and omnipresent divine gaze could be construed as a form of blindness—in that the human subject is first and foremost an object of the divine gaze— Levin also points towards a more inclusive understanding of 'primordial beholdenness' in which 'to behold is to be *held* by what one sees'.[32] In other words, 'beholdenness' implies a relationship, between subject and object, of reciprocity and mutual dependency: one is 'held' by objects (and not only by God), just as one beholds them, and is beholden to them.

Whereas Levin advocates the 'recollection' of this pre-modern ontology of sight as an antidote to modern ocularcentrism,[33] the art historians Samuel Edgerton and Ernst Gombrich are more committed to a model of historical progress. To them, the spatial discontinuity characteristic of medieval art looks like the product of an infantile or primitive perceptual consciousness. Edgerton's insights into the medieval mind are inspired by Piaget's theory of spatial development in children:

> Within the history of Western civilization, at least, the 'phylogeny' of linear perspective from the Middle Ages through the Renaissance has clear enough parallels to the 'ontogenetic' mental growth of a modern child learning to perceive an abstractly structured visual space and to think of pictures in linear perspective.[34]

Gombrich suggests a similar parallel between 'primitive image making', a category in which he includes medieval art, and 'the imagery of the blind and the insane'.[35] Underpinning these claims is the correlation of mathematical perspective and modern sight, where 'modern' denotes scientific, rational and objective. Conversely, the absence of mathematical perspective in representational art of the Middle Ages is read as symptomatic of an immature, deficient or in some way distorted spatial and perceptual orientation.[36]

Umberto Eco, writing about the shift from symbolism to naturalism in twelfth- and thirteenth-century thought, borrows Lewis Mumford's term 'neurotic' to characterise the twelfth-century conception of the world.[37] 'There was something missing in the twelfth century', he writes, 'and in the symbolical mentality as a whole, which caused this absorption of concrete reality into a universe of symbols.'[38] This missing element, in Eco's view, 'was any conception, however slight, that nature had a structure of itself and was intelligible in itself'.[39] The suggestion, here, is that invisible essences took precedence over visible appearances, that sensible objects pointed beyond themselves to spiritual or moral truths. But Eco goes a step further, arguing that the symbolic outlook amounts to the flight from a 'hostile reality' marked by a lack of social cohesion and individual insecurity. Cultural 'neurosis', in this scenario, takes the form of a retreat from nature into a *super*natural world of order and unity.[40]

When the idea of naturalism in the visual arts is added to this equation, the gap between medieval consciousness and the real is pushed even further apart. Edgerton's conflation of pictorial and perceptual 'styles' is a case in point. Here too, medieval vision is defined in opposition to realism or naturalism, though for Edgerton the emergence of this mode of representation is sought and found at the level of material culture, rather than in philosophical treatises. The chronological gap between Eco (writing about thirteenth-century aesthetics) and Edgerton (concerned primarily with Renaissance painting) exemplifies the difficulty of lining up historical changes across the different domains of visuality.[41] Aside from this difference though, Edgerton's analysis is consistent with the neurotic paradigm. Working backwards from a normative conception of Renaissance perspectivism, he writes:

> Unlike the Renaissance painter depicting his scene in perspective, the medieval artist viewed his world quite subjectively. He saw each element in his composition separately and independently, and thus paid little attention to anything in the way of a systematic spatial relationship between objects. He was absorbed within the visual world he was representing rather than, as with the perspective painter, standing without it, observing from a single, removed viewpoint.[42]

Edgerton's medieval artist is characterised by an inability to distance himself, spatially and psychologically, from his surroundings.[43] It is this perceptual proximity between subject and object, or rather the subject's absorption in each individual object, that precludes any objective view of the world.[44] Where Eco had posited a flight from the real, Edgerton invokes a distorting subjectivism, comparing the medieval artist's apparent lack of an objective, external viewpoint to the creative efforts of a child: 'Instead of looking at things from a single, detached vantage, the young artist tends to see everything egocentrically.'[45] This analogy between the medieval artist and the 'egocentric' child-like subject alerts us to the fact that for Edgerton, perspectival (modern) vision is essentially mechanical and impersonal. Whereas the medieval artist brings his world into being, as it were, as an extension of subjective consciousness, the Renaissance artist—like a living camera obscura—merely receives and records sensory impressions. As Brennan (amongst others) has argued, this passive, supposedly disinterested eye conceals its own embeddedness in a perceiving subject.[46] Perceptual 'evolution' would seem to require the dissemblance of ocular desire.

With the exception of Levin, the commentaries I have mentioned portray medieval vision as a pathological variation of 'normal' sight: Eco because the sensible world is missing from perceptual consciousness, Edgerton because perceptual consciousness is fixated on fragments of the world to the exclusion of the whole. Yet if these accounts play into the mythology of a 'dark age' in which vision was curtailed, if not actually denigrated, the characteristics of neurotic perception have prompted at least one commentator to write of 'an openness to visual sensation that complemented the broader range of medieval sight'.[47]

For Carolly Erickson, 'medieval sight' extends beyond sense-perception to the ways in which individuals perceived (thought about, understood, experienced) their world, both terrestrial and spiritual. So where Eco makes a distinction between what he regards as the restricted visual consciousness of the symbolic outlook and Aristotelian observation, Erickson resists such a split by emphasising the continuity between sense-perception and extrasensory perception, the latter including conceptual or ideological visions of the world.[48] In this 'enchanted world . . . the boundaries of imagination and factuality are constantly shifting'.[49] Because Erickson interprets medieval visual metaphors as an *expansion* of perceptual consciousness and not as a withdrawal from the phenomenal world (Eco) or as the result of a distorting subjectivism (Edgerton), for her the medieval world is 'enchanted' rather than the product of infantile perception.

Notwithstanding Erickson's valorisation of 'enchanted' vision, it should be fairly evident that her formulation is consistent with the primitive—or perhaps more correctly 'mystical'—paradigm. Medieval vision, in short, is still marked by a lack of differentiation between imaginary and sensory perceptions. In this respect, her expanded visual/visionary field comes close to Eco's retreat into the imagination. Absent in all of the accounts of medieval sight I have mentioned so far is the perceptual correlate of an objective world: the objectifying gaze most often associated with modern science. The exclusion is a significant one, not least of all because it ignores medieval developments in optical theory and experimental science.

A number of historians have, in fact, located the beginnings of modern science—and with it a new way of looking—in the later Middle Ages. Of the landmarks in this narrative, the influence of Aristotelian natural philosophy is paramount. For Eco, the universe of symbols eventually yielded under this Aristotelian influence to a 'naturalistic vision' trained upon an intelligible world.[50] Norman Klassen makes a similar point: 'As interest shifts away from ontological realities suggested by symbols, phenomenal details such as the relationship between subject and object begin to attract increasing attention.'[51] Vision itself becomes a focus of scientific curiosity and aesthetic pleasure. Martin Jay links this restoration of sense-based knowledge to the pre-eminence of optics in the thirteenth-century hierarchy of scientific knowledge.[52] The 'secular autonomization of the visual as a realm unto itself' was, in turn, 'crucial in the preparation of the scientific worldview'.[53]

Neurotic or naturalistic? Ocularphobic or visionary? Subjective or proto-empiricist? If there is a common theme in these radically divergent accounts of medieval visuality, it is that the majority describe a moment of transition, transformation or rupture, a paradigm shift in the history of vision. There is little room in this model of historical change for ambivalence or contradiction, for the coexistence of ocularphobia and visual delight, or a synthesis of theology and science. Consequently, what we find in many of these commentaries is a tendency either to elide the significance of medieval optics (Levin, Gombrich, Edgerton, Erickson), or to overlook the religious elements and applications of theoretical optics.

An exception is Klassen's study of the relationship between love, knowledge and sight in Chaucer's poetry, and in fourteenth-century thought more generally. Although his focus is somewhat narrower and slightly later than mine, his central argument is similar: that vision has a parasitic relationship to knowledge and love: a relationship that engenders both hostility and symbiosis.[54] Martin Jay's Middle Ages is also characterised by ambivalence towards vision and the visual. He puts this down to the 'complex intertwining of Hellenic and Hebraic impulses' in Christianity.[55] The Hellenic tradition promotes the nobility of sight, while the Hebraic assertion of God's unrepresentability feeds into medieval ocularphobia. This formulation is not without its critics: Daniel Boyarin, for example, takes issue with Jay's representation of the Judaic tradition as iconoclastic, arguing instead that ocular desire—the desire to see God—is central to Rabbinic Judaism. Boyarin proposes a reversal of the Hellenic–Hebraic model on the grounds that the Hellenised Christian emphasis on allegory is visually repressive, insofar as allegorical interpretation effects a movement beyond visible appearances to invisible truths.[56]

Whichever way the terms are configured, the emphasis on ambivalence —rather than historical rupture and revolution—is, I think, productive. Only by moving away from a dialectical model of historical change is it possible to account for the complexity of medieval visuality: the tensions, competing ideals and desires that give rise to a constellation of metaphors and multiple ways of seeing—not a monolithic 'regime' of vision.

The account of medieval vision offered in this book will not fit easily within the historical narratives I have sketched out in this chapter. It is neither a missing piece in the puzzle, nor an antidote to modern ocular-centrism. The ideas and objects we will be looking at present a highly equivocal picture: encompassing the darkness and opacity of the flesh, as well as the light of reason, and the dazzling night of mystic union. There will be moments of historical prescience, but no sudden 'dawning' of modern sight. By structuring the chapters thematically rather than chrono-logically I have tried to draw out the tensions and continuities between different contexts and conceptions of vision, and to deflect the desire to put *everything* in historical perspective. There is, admittedly, a diachronic element to the work, but this is dispersed across three intersecting fields of vision: carnal, optical and redemptive. In each case one finds an elaboration, reorientation or renegotiation of vision in the period around 1200.

Chapters 1 and 2 focus on the carnal dimension of medieval vision, beginning with the concept of 'flesh'. 'Flesh' and 'body', I argue in Chapter 1, are fluid terms. Through their convergence (the 'fleshly' body, the 'eye of the flesh') they signify humanity's alienation from God; yet the body's delineation from the flesh makes possible a redemptive alignment of body and soul. These shifting configurations of body, flesh and soul—onto which medieval vision is mapped—cannot be resolved within a dualistic conception of medieval Christianity. Chapter 2 extends this definition of flesh to the 'fleshly' eye. Fixated on the sensible world and enmeshed in the Augustinian complex of sexuality, sin and death, carnal vision takes shape not as a faculty of sight so much as a microcosm of the appetites and attributes of the flesh.

In Chapter 3, I discuss how medieval optics shores up the legitimacy and primacy of vision by abstracting it from the unpredictable and opaque matter of the body, and the disruptive desires of the flesh. Sense perception, and knowledge based on it, are conceived as a process of dematerialisation: from the things themselves to mental representations of them. The translation of corporeal bodies—including the eye—into the language of geometry represents a further abstraction from the flesh. In this sense optical theory secures the foundations of modern science in its production of a useful, predictable body: a machine for observation that is itself observable. Chapter 4 complicates the picture by identifying traces of the flesh in Roger Bacon's optics. Bacon's understanding of sight as a physical interaction of viewer and object, his comments on the similarities between sight and touch, and his more guarded acknowledgement of ocular desire all cast doubt upon the universality of an objectifying, dispassionate and distancing Western scientific gaze.

The intersection of vision and redemption forms the third and final strand of the study. Spiritual vision was conceived by medieval theologians both as the opposite and as the analogue of more physical (carnal and bodily) forms of sight. The implications of this paradox are explored in Chapter 5. Where spiritual and bodily modes of perception are polarised, redemption entails the repression or regulation of the latter: the enclosure or 'custody' of the senses. On the other hand, the promise that transcendent spiritual truths might be approached through their visible, material likenesses served to legitimise bodily sight; but only as a necessary means to an immaterial, invisible end. What results is a sublimation of ocular desire: an attempt to use vision to reach beyond one's contingent, bodily existence. Chapter 6 takes as its point of departure the efflorescence of popular piety in the thirteenth century, and associated developments in the visual arts and devotional literature. By reversing the transcendental thrust of sublimation, the devotional image (whether literary, mental or pictorial) anchors redemption in the flesh: in the flesh of an increasingly human, incarnate Christ, and in the flesh of vision itself.

PART I

CARNAL VISION

CHAPTER 1

FLESH

> *Thus man's reason, trodden underfoot by greed, becomes a slave to the flesh and is forced to wait upon it as its handmaiden. Thus the eye of the heart, darkened by the fog of the flesh, grows weak and suffering an eclipse, becomes isolated and inactive. Thus the shadow of the flesh debasingly cloaks the radiance of a human sense and the glory of the mind becomes exceedingly inglorious.*[1]
>
> *Alan of Lille*

As idea and as substance, medieval flesh was by definition elusive. After all, a 'shadow' or 'fog'—to use Alan of Lille's words—could hardly be brought to light for observation, or circumscribed by precise definition. In order to work towards an understanding of the flesh—however partial or contingent that may be—I will use the idea of the body as a kind of foil. By pinpointing instances in which flesh and body do not coincide, where one exceeds or disrupts the other, I hope to elucidate their differences.

The distinction between body and flesh in medieval thought is often a tenuous one, but it is fundamental to the paradoxical status of vision in the Middle Ages, most notably the *embodied* eye's dual relationship to reason and pleasure. There are intimations of this paradox in the opening quote. Aligned with the mind, 'human sense' is radiant. As organs of the flesh, on the other hand, the senses collapse into an obscuring, destructive sensuality. Sight—the sense closest to the 'mind's eye'—is both a tool for the acquisition of *knowledge*, and a locus of carnal *desire*. These permutations of vision are the subject of later chapters, but they would be inexplicable without an awareness of the different resonances of body and flesh.

By way of an introduction to these key terms, 'body' and 'flesh', I will begin with some examples of corporeal disorder from twelfth- and thirteenth-century illustrations of Pliny's monstrous races. The way in which these bodies were read—as not-quite-human—suggests that human corporeality was not homogeneous and stable; that some parts of the body were more 'fleshly' than others. It will become clear in the course of this chapter that flesh and body were imbued with different associations, exhibited distinct characteristics and, by implication, required different kinds of regulation or control. Having prised apart the terms 'flesh' and 'body' I will argue that the presence of the flesh complicates a dualistic model of body and soul, just as the body cannot be contained unproblematically within a dualism of flesh and spirit. Fear of the flesh, in other words, was more complex than notions of medieval dualism would suggest. The remainder of the chapter will trace the permutations of body and flesh through the writings of the Apostle Paul and Saint Augustine, and then through two medieval sources: Bernard of Clairvaux's sermon *On Conversion*, and Robert Grosseteste's *De Dotibus*. The last of these lists the four 'wedding endowments' (*dotes*) bestowed upon the blessed in heaven by their divine Bridegroom. If Pliny's *monstra* represent the human body at its most fleshly, Grosseteste's resurrected bodies find perfection in their abstraction from the flesh.

Disordered bodies

At the edge of a world map in a thirteenth-century English psalter (Fig. 1.1) is an array of minute representatives of Pliny's monstrous races: grotesque creatures 'born outside of nature', and believed to live at the extremities of the earth.[2] If each figure is a variation on human deformation, one is of particular interest here. Said to inhabit the deserts of Libya, the Blemmyae were reputedly a headless race with their eyes, nose and mouth embedded in their bodies (Fig. 1.2). To a medieval viewer like Alan of Lille, the image reproduced here would have been one of contamination: of sensation submerged in the flesh rather than anchored to spirituality or intellection. In this sense Pliny's *monstra* give shape to the fear of fleshly disorder that is so palpable in the opening quote. The debasement of sense and reason from which these creatures suffer is, however, permanent. To quote Thomas of Cantimpré, even if *monstra* appeared, by their actions, to resemble men and women, they 'do not have the physical organization necessary to allow intellectual reason to be informed by sense perception'.[3] Given this deficiency, the monstrous races may be superior to animals, but they could hardly possess human souls.[4]

The Blemmyae's unsettling corporealisation of the senses, and the severing of sense-perception from the mind that this suggests, raises questions about bodily hierarchy and the relationship between human corporeality and animal flesh. As Thomas of Cantimpré's observation indicates, the distinction between humanity and animality did not so much turn on the

Figure 1.1.   World map. Psalter.

possession of a reasoning mind, as the connection between sense and intellect, body and soul. It followed from this that physical deformities were
widely thought to correspond to moral and intellectual degeneracy, and
were seen as the result of 'sin, evil, and heresy'.[5] Leprosy is a case in point.
In advanced stages of the disease sufferers seem to 'speak with their noses',

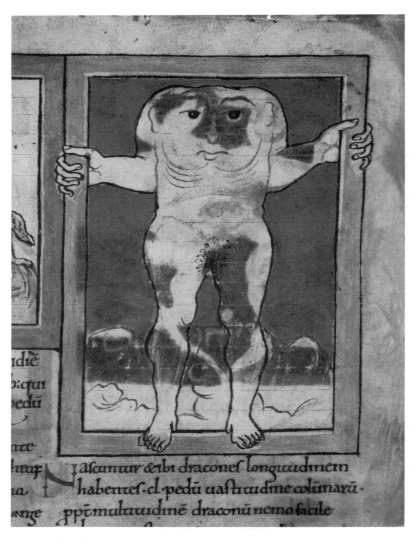

Figure 1.2.   Blemmyae.

said Hugh of St Victor.[6] What was the cause of this visible and devastating disorder of the flesh? The bishop of Arles offered this explanation in a sermon delivered in the first half of the sixth century: 'lepers are generally born not to learned men who preserve their chastity on forbidden days and during festivities but to common peasants who cannot control themselves'.[7] Imagined in this way leprosy is not only a moral disease, the result of fornication or sexual excess. It is a social disorder with political implications. The medieval literate elite, notes Jacques Le Goff, were 'obsessed with the supposed sexual excesses of the illiterate: paupers and peasants . . . Slaves of the flesh more than other men, serfs deserved to be enslaved to their lords.'[8]

In his treatise on 'Moral Philosophy' written in the mid-thirteenth century, Roger Bacon reasoned that 'evil men lose their identity, because the identity of a thing consists in retaining its order and preserving its nature'. Sin, however, 'is contrary to the order of nature . . .' He concludes: 'you cannot regard as a human being the man whom you see transformed by vices'.[9] Viewed in this light, Pliny's races—like lepers—were demonstrations (from the Latin *monstrum*, a portent) of the genetic wages of sin.[10] As signs or portents, figures like the Blemmyae speak not only of what it is to be not-quite-human, but also of the extent to which the human compound of body and soul occupies an unstable position between gross flesh or animality on the one side, and the idealised, fleshless body of the resurrection on the other.

The marginal position and corporeal displacement of the Blemmyae characterise countless other inhabitants of medieval illuminations, and many of these display anatomical and physiological anomalies associated with the organs of sense.[11] In the majority, humanity is compromised by a relocation of 'higher' bodily functions from their exalted position in the head to the 'lower' regions of the body. More than spatial designations, 'higher' and 'lower' represent a hierarchy of functions, as well as a dividing line. The idea was not a new one. Because of the polluting influence of the emotions and appetites, the gods of Plato's *Timaeus* had 'located the mortal element of man in a separate part of the body, and constructed the neck as a kind of isthmus and boundary between head and breast to keep them apart'.[12] The 'mortal element', Plato wrote, is divided in turn by the midriff (or diaphragm), according to its 'better and worse' properties; the emotions being superior to the appetite. To illustrate this idea of the properly ordered and contained body, he used the telling analogy of a house 'divided into men and women's quarters'.[13] This housekeeping arrangement is echoed in Henri de Mondeville's treatise on surgery, written between 1306 and 1320 while Mondeville was surgeon to Philip the Fair. The diaphragm, he says, forms a seal so that the 'malign fumes which rise from the organs of nutrition should not harm the spiritual organs'.[14]

The question of the body's 'ruling' principle—head or heart—was debated during the Middle Ages, but medical authors agreed that the abdomen, or 'inferior ventricle', ranked lowest in the corporeal hierarchy.[15] The organs of the abdominal cavity, along with the vascular system, were responsible for nutrition, growth and reproduction. Blood itself was thought to be crude, dense, coagulated matter, derived from food digested in the stomach and 'cooked' in the liver.[16] As such, the blood conveyed through the veins was differentiated from the refined vital spirit (*spiritus*) produced in the heart and circulated through the arteries. If the arteries, heart and lungs comprised the 'vital' or 'spiritual members' of the body, and the brain, spinal cord and nervous system were commonly associated with the workings of the soul (*anima*), then the belly was the locus of the flesh in a way that the head and the heart were not.[17]

The lower members of the body were also widely associated with the carnal appetites of gluttony and lust. Continuing a tradition established in the early centuries of Christianity, medieval commentators underlined the connection between these two appetites.[18] As Gerald of Wales explained, 'since the stomach and the genitals are so close together, we ought to mortify the one in order that the other may not become wanton'.[19] In the same work, Gerald warns of the consequences of a wanton gaze and un-chaste eyes, in language that reveals the extent to which the eye of the flesh was associated with the carnal appetites.[20] That sight, the noblest of the senses,[21] could become an organ of the flesh was evidence of a misalign-ment of body and soul comparable to the deformities of Pliny's *monstra*. If the human body (or at least the male body) signified order—whether cosmological, social or political—the flesh (often feminised) was equated with transgression or subversion of that order.[22] Hostiensis, a canon-lawyer, cites the following applications of the orderly symbolic body:

All the faithful might be called a single body of which Christ is the head and we the members. A college or a university are said to be a single body of which one calls the head the prelate and the members the college. One calls a body that which gives grace to a soul (*spiritus*) like a tree or a man. Or still that which holds the parts together like a house. Or where the parts are distinct, one from another like a troop or a people or a college. Finally man and woman form but one body.[23]

In its symbolic purity, the body was above all *meaningful*, giving con-ceptual shape to abstract structures and systems, and anthropomorphic proportions to the natural and built environment.[24] In medieval Latin, *corpus* (body) could denote, amongst other things: a group of buildings; the hull of a ship; a corporation or body politic; the nave or congregation of a church; a source of revenue; or a collection of writings.[25] Flesh (*caro* and its cognates) was altogether less useful. From Augustine onwards, the presence of the flesh augured the eclipse of meaning and the suspension of thought. What, then, of the *lived* human body? Defined by original sin, the human condition was one in which the body was shadowed, inflamed and animated by the flesh. Before I elaborate further on these ideas, it is necessary to consider the paradigm most often employed by historians confronted with medieval animosity towards the body or the flesh: dualism.

Medieval dualism and the denigration of the flesh

A well-fed body and delicate complexion
are but a tunic of worms and fire.
The body is vile, stinking, and withered.
The pleasure of the flesh is by nature poisoned and corrupt.[26]

These lines from the late twelfth-century *Verses on Death* make no obvious distinction between body and flesh: the two are rendered virtually synonymous by the corrosive presence of sin. Written by a Cistercian monk, Hélinand of Froimont, the *Verses* are reminiscent in tone and imagery of Bernard of Clairvaux's meditations on sin and mortality. For Bernard, and arguably for Hélinand, his near contemporary and fellow Cistercian, flesh was equivalent to the 'sinful body'.[27] The mortification of the flesh, as the body of sin, is one of the most enduring images of medieval Christianity. Flesh, it is generally agreed, was during this period an expression and externalisation of the debased human condition, bearing the hereditary imprint of sexuality and death. To quote Peter Brown: 'In the Catholic thought of the early Middle Ages, human flesh emerged as a quivering thing. Its vulnerability to temptation, to death, even to delight, was a painfully apposite concretization of the limping will of Adam.'[28] Le Goff notes the perseverance of Platonic metaphors of corporeal imprisonment: 'The body was an *ergastulum*, a slave's prison for the soul. This was not merely a commonplace image but a definition.'[29] Le Goff maintains that body and flesh in the Middle Ages were not only metaphors of fallen human nature; they signified something 'diabolical . . . akin to a place of debauch'.[30]

If flesh enslaves or corrupts, the implication is that there is something there to be enslaved and corrupted: some part of the self that is not flesh. Indeed, medieval hostility towards the fleshly body would be meaningless without an equal and opposite elevation of the mind, soul, spirit or heart: those loci of what St Augustine called the 'inner man'.[31] The Augustinian formula of an 'inner' and 'outer' man was widely used throughout the Middle Ages to evoke a sense of the self, fractured and polarised by sin. The outer and inner man, Augustine said, are like Adam and Christ. Where one signifies corruptible, fallen humanity, the other holds the promise of man's renewal in the 'image and likeness of God'. One is 'the earthly man', living in accordance with a carnal nature; the other is 'the heavenly man'.[32] The former is perishable, the latter immortal. Above all, however, Augustine associated the outer man with the bodily senses, the inner man with mind and intelligence.[33] It is therefore no coincidence that images of the divided self often accompany the desire to escape or transcend corporeality, stained as it is by sin and death. To live according to the inner man does not require the renunciation of the body, or of sensation, but their subjugation—or perhaps sublimation—to intellectual and spiritual goals.

Historians have tended to see these commonly paired terms—body/ soul, flesh/spirit, sensation/reason—as instances of a pervasive Christian dualism, for they almost always imply the denigration of body, flesh and sensuality: if not absolutely and irrevocably, then at least in relation to soul, spirit and reason.[34] At its broadest sweep, this tradition of dualism is said to extend from Plato, through the Pauline writings of the New Testament and the Church Fathers of late antiquity, through twelfth-century Neoplatonism, to Descartes and beyond, under the umbrella of the Western philosophical tradition. Caroline Bynum has described this style of historiography, quite rightly, as a 'vast essentialization',[35] arguing that even in the late Middle Ages one cannot speak of a singular, definitive body; nor, for that matter, a normative physiological, theological or metaphysical body.[36] If bodies are contradictory, polymorphous things, inhabiting a 'cacophony of discourses',[37] they could hardly be adequately represented by such tidy and totalising binary schemata.

Other commentators have emphasised historical changes in attitudes towards embodiment around 1200, confounding any simplistic notion of 'medieval dualism'. In her study of Henri de Mondeville's *Chirurgie*, Marie-Christine Pouchelle makes a speculative connection between developments in surgery and the 'rehabilitation of the flesh which emerges in medieval society from the thirteenth century onwards'.[38] For Pouchelle, it is the surgeon's promotion of 'the solely secular value of the body' that is decisive;[39] but there is evidence that the rehabilitation she speaks of was promoted through religious channels as well.

Drawing on thirteenth-century anthologies of model sermons used by Franciscan preachers, David d'Avray highlights 'a widespread tendency to emphasize the positive significance of the body'.[40] This anti-dualist sentiment took a number of forms: sermons on the goodness of marriage; a devotional focus on the humanity of Christ; the reception (particularly in Franciscan and Dominican circles) of Aristotelian natural philosophy, with its emphasis on the indivisibility of form and matter, soul and body. These trends will be discussed at length in later chapters. What I want to emphasise here is that medieval Christianity was by no means consistently or uniformly dualistic.

Bynum's assault on dualism goes beyond an argument for the discursive variety of medieval bodies. There are, she says, three reasons to reject the notion that '"medieval attitudes" [were] "dualistic" in the sense of "despising" or "recommending flight from" the body . . .'[41] Firstly, medieval theories of perception and knowledge often employed tripartite, not binary, schemata; frequently making 'a sharper distinction between levels of soul than between soul and body'.[42] Secondly, 'the extravagant attention to flesh and decay characteristic of the period was not "flight from" so much as "submersion in" [the flesh]'. Rather than something to be mortified or transcended, the flesh was, for many Christians, 'the instrument of salvation'.[43] And thirdly, Bynum takes issue with scholars who emphasise the alignment of flesh, matter, and body with the feminine.[44] 'Symbolic patterns', she insists, 'do not . . . fit into only a single grid'.[45] The last of these points will be taken up in the section on 'Sexing the flesh' later in this chapter. At this juncture, I would like to say a few words in response to the remaining two observations.

Bynum is right to point out the prevalence of non-binary categories in medieval formulations of perception. However, as I argue more extensively in Chapter 5, tripartite and binary models of sight are not mutually exclusive alternatives. Augustine, for example, uses both binary and trinitarian figures in his writing. In *On the Trinity*, as I noted earlier, Augustine's 'inner' and 'outer' man are coupled with reason and sensation. This basic opposition between interior sense (associated with the mind or soul) and exterior, bodily sense recurs through medieval discussions of perception. The point being made is invariably that in this mortal, sinful, fleshly body we cannot know, or see, the truth with clarity. Polarity thus engenders the desire for mediation or redemption. In the same text, Augustine's equally paradigmatic 'trinity' of sight serves a very different discursive function. Instead of being polarised, corporeal and intellectual vision are now mediated by spiritual vision, enabling reason to 'ascend from the lower to the higher'.[46]

At the bottom of the ladder, *visio corporalis* is restricted to qualities and things that are 'perceived through the body and presented to the senses of the body'.[47] *Visio intellectualis*, at the other end of the continuum, involves the transcendence of both actual sense impressions and mental images. On this 'higher plane' of pure and imageless understanding, 'transparent truth is seen without any bodily likeness'.[48] Occupying 'a kind of middle ground between intellectual and corporeal vision' is *visio spiritualis*.[49] Roughly equivalent to medieval theories of the imagination,[50] spiritual vision was, for Augustine, 'the kind of vision by which we represent in thought the images of bodies even in their absence'.[51] The fact that tripartite and binary conceptions of knowledge can coexist within a single author's *oeuvre*, or even within a single text, suggests that the body was viewed with ambivalence. It was evidence of sin and alienation *and* part of the solution: a source of fear, disgust and hostility, but also pleasure and hope.

This brings me to Bynum's second observation, that the flesh functioned as an 'instrument of salvation', not an obstacle to salvation. Again, this is a subject that will be considered at length in a later chapter; for now, let me merely signal the possibility that the privileged role of the flesh in redemption flowed from its very transgressiveness. In the same way that embodiment engendered a range of contradictory emotions, flesh was a loaded signifier and a volatile condition. In Chapter 5, for example, I will suggest that the sublimation of carnal desire—a movement equivalent to Bynum's 'flight from' embodiment—is reversed at the very apex of the soul's ascent. The mystical sublime, far from being a transcendence of the flesh, is indeed a 'submersion in' the flesh, if the latter is understood as a condition of openness, indeterminacy and suspension of self.

By focusing on the close bond between body and soul, and the participation of bodies in redemption and resurrection, Bynum reveals aspects of embodiment in the Middle Ages that have frequently been ignored. Far more than merely food for worms, the medieval body emerges as variously comical, perverse and sublime. What Bynum does not elucidate is the relationship between body and flesh. If I am right, and these terms do not, or at least not always, coincide, then from the outset we are dealing with something other than a rigidly dualistic framework. As such, the remainder of this chapter could be read as a critique of the dualist paradigm; one that can perhaps better account for the range of responses towards embodiment, and by extension embodied sight.

Body and flesh in the Augustinian tradition

The writings of Saint Augustine are arguably the single most influential source of medieval formulations of the flesh, particularly in its imbrication with sexuality and mortality. Augustine's definition of flesh (*caro*) in *The City of God* can be read as an attempt to distance the matter of the body from its Manichean association with sin and evil.[52] To this end, flesh is insinuated between sin and the body, as the locus of fallen human nature. The result is that two very different bodies emerge from Augustine's account: one, a purely physical organism, is the corporeal home and helpmeet of the soul; the other, marred by original sin, is the seat of rebellious carnality. If the passive body can be likened to the perfect wife, subservient and productive, then the *fleshly* body introduces strife into the marriage of body and soul. Before we look in more detail at these ideas, a brief etymological digression through the Old and New Testaments is warranted. By tracking the meaning of flesh through Hebrew, Greek, and then Augustine's Latin, I want to highlight the provenance of two central characteristics of medieval flesh. The first of these is Paul's figurative expansion of flesh beyond the material body, so that flesh becomes synonymous with sin. The second is Augustine's sexualisation of flesh in the context of the fall.

In the Pauline writings of the New Testament, the Greek term *sarx* (flesh) signifies far more than just the material existence of the body. In its metaphorical scope and complexity, *sarx* can be differentiated from the group of words related to the English term 'flesh', as well as from the equivalent Hebrew word, *bâsâr*. In the Old Testament, *bâsâr* is used predominantly in the sense of corporeal matter, both human and animal. Skin, flesh, bones and sinews make up the body (Job 10.11), and flesh and wine are eschewed while in mourning (Dan. 10.3).[53] The Middle English *flesch*—from the Teutonic word for bacon—shares this emphasis on materiality, although what was originally mere meat has been metaphorically and theologically extended in the intervening centuries. Moving closer to Paul's figurative conception of flesh, *bâsâr* could also serve as a metonym for the body as a whole (1 Kings 21.27), humanity (Job 34.15), or the human and animal world together (Gen. 6.17). Flesh, in such instances, almost always signifies the essential 'transitoriness' of humanity in comparison to God.[54] In the words of Isaiah (40.6–8): 'All flesh is grass, and all its loveliness is like the flower of the field. The grass withers, the flower fades . . .'[55] Nowhere in the Old Testament, however, is it implied that the flesh is a *cause* of sin or corruption.[56] Nor is it possible to transcend one's flesh. To be human, in the Hebrew scriptures, is to be flesh.

Of the 147 references to flesh (*sarx*) in the New Testament, 91 occur in the Pauline writings, in particular the epistles to the Romans, Galatians and Corinthians.[57] Significantly, Paul only once uses *sarx* in the generic sense of human and animal corporeality (1 Cor. 15.39).[58] Sometimes the term refers specifically to the human body; more often it designates man in his entirety. However, having taken up the broader, holistic sense of 'flesh' present in the Old Testament, Paul elaborates it within an economy of sin. This shift can best be discerned in the concept of *kata sarka*, 'according to the flesh' or 'after the flesh' (2 Cor. 10.2–3; Rom. 8.1f.), where *sarx* refers to human (i.e. worldly, secular) concerns, values and attitudes: the sum of which are disparaged as the 'wisdom of this age' (1 Cor. 2.6). The alternative is to live *kata pneuma*, 'according to the spirit' (Rom. 8.4). It is in this sense—and not in the sense of flesh as transient corporeal existence—

that 'those who are in the flesh cannot please God' (Rom. 8.8). Flesh, therefore, becomes a matter of orientation—even a disposition of the mind (Col. 2.18)—rather than the physical condition of being human. *Sarx* also begins to assume an agency or potency entirely foreign to the notion of 'brute matter'. As A. C. Thiselton notes of Romans 8.8, ' "Flesh" here evaluates man as a sinner before God. The outlook of the flesh is *the outlook orientated towards the self, that which pursues its own ends in self-sufficient independence of God.'*[59]

To the extent that *sarx* denotes one's physical existence, flesh and body (*sōma*) are roughly equivalent terms in Paul's writings. However, there is a clear delineation between Paul's understanding of *sōma*, and his concept of a fleshly disposition. Departing from the classical (Orphic and Platonic) notion of the body as a tomb, Paul conceives of the body as 'man in all his potentialities', and in all his limitations.[60] This principle is exemplified in a double metaphor of corporeal order and disorder found in 1 Cor. 6:15. Paul asks: 'Do you not know that your bodies are members of Christ? Shall I then take the members of Christ and make them members of a harlot?' Incorporated into the body of Christ, and subordinated to his will, the human body achieves perfection. Alternatively, appended to vice and given over to carnal pleasure, the body is an instrument of sin. In either case, *sōma* is necessarily in a position of subjection: to Christ or to sin and death.[61] This is the nub of Paul's delineation between the body and the flesh. Whereas the body is typically described as a vessel, a tool or a subordinate member, the flesh emerges as an active power of subjection. 'Like sin', Bornkamm remarks, 'flesh is a power that enslaves.'[62]

For Augustine, writing in Latin, the difference between body (*corpus*) and flesh (*caro*) was equally crucial. It was also complicated, to an extent, by linguistic ambiguity. *Caro* is related to a cluster of terms corresponding to the English word 'carnal'. *Carnalis*, for example, can be used in the sense of bodily or worldly, or it can mean lustful, with the connotation of sexual desire or intercourse.[63] By the early Middle Ages, *caro* could refer to the human body, the physical aspect of a person, the carnal lusts, the human race, the earthly realm, and God incarnate.[64] Two observations can be made on the basis of this list alone. Firstly, in Latin, flesh acquired a sexual dimension that had been absent in Greek and Hebrew. Secondly, one might say that linguistically, the body was well and truly embedded in the flesh. It is hardly surprising that, despite Augustine's efforts to hold these concepts apart, the texts we will be looking at are punctuated by slippages from body into flesh, and flesh into body.[65]

Augustine formulated his definition of the flesh in the context of original sin. It is here that he makes the connection between carnality, concupiscence and death, through an intertwining of corporeal, spiritual and intellectual components of the first human beings; elements that, in turn, will dominate the language of carnal vision. For Augustine, as for the medieval heirs to the Pauline–Augustinian tradition, 'flesh' and 'spirit' are opposing principles.[66] Those who live 'by the rule of the flesh' do so with their minds as well as their bodies.[67] The path of the spirit, on the other hand, leads to redemption and reconciliation. As a result of Adam and Eve's fatal act, 'man who would have become spiritual even in his flesh, by observing the command, became carnal even in his mind'.[68]

It is evident from Augustine's terminology that flesh refers to a condition of the mind or soul, as well as to a type of corporeal motivation or appetite. Perverted by sin, the fleshly body and soul agitate against a spirit that is apparently incorruptible, for to live by the spirit is to inhabit the city of God. Not quite so apparent, however, is the *body's* relationship to the flesh on one side, and the spirit on the other. For an answer to this question we must turn to Augustine's interpretation of Genesis Chapter 3, and the events surrounding the fall.

Augustine's desire to shift the burden of sin away from the body can be taken as a logical, if not chronological, beginning. In order to maintain the inherent goodness of the human body as one of God's creations, he contends that the body is ravaged by unruly desires and by mortality as a *result* of original sin. Once perfect, the body now bears the inscription of God's punishment in its subjection to passion, pain and finally death. In his words: 'the corruption of the body, which weighs down the soul, is not the cause of the first sin, but its punishment'.[69]

The question remains as to how and where sin enters the picture in the first place, and how it impairs the relationship between body and soul thereafter. Augustine's answer hinges on the orientation of the will, itself a component of the soul. The fall, he maintains, is essentially a movement of the will away from God: a 'defection' from God. What results is a 'deficiency' or privation of humanity in relation to Supreme Being.[70] This account of original sin would seem at face value to have no direct bearing on the body or the flesh. Yet in his subsequent elaboration of this principle, Augustine translates the first twinges of disobedience in the will into the stirrings of concupiscence (*concupiscentia carnis*) in the flesh. Original sin thus serves as the prototype for all sins of the flesh, of which sexual lust is paramount. At stake in all this is the relationship between body and soul; specifically the disintegration of their original, harmonious bond.[71]

The moment seized upon by Augustine as most fully signifying the tragic consequences of the fall is Adam and Eve's awareness of their nakedness: an awareness centred on their 'organs of shame' (*pudenda*). He recounts: 'These organs were the same as they were before, but previously there was no shame attaching to them. Thus they felt a novel disturbance in their disobedient flesh, as a punishment which answered to their own disobedience.'[72] In Genesis, shame is the first symptom of disobedience: the fruit is eaten, the eyes are 'opened', innocence is lost. There is no mention in the Biblical account of sexual desire, or anything that would equate with Augustine's suggestive 'disturbance' in the flesh. Furthermore, in the text of Genesis Adam and Eve's 'awakening' (and its accompanying sensation of shame) occurs prior to God's spoken judgement, and seemingly in the absence of any divine intervention. The experience of nakedness or bodily shame, in other words, is not amongst the punishments enumerated in Genesis 3.16–19.[73] Why, then, should this moment of *sexual* self-consciousness be so crucial for Augustine? Why does he insert that movement of the flesh into Adam and Eve's shame? The most likely reason seems to be that for Augustine, concupiscence, specifically in its sexual form, is the primary manifestation of the body's dislocation from the soul: a fault line rendered visible in his writing by repeated use of the term 'flesh' to denote the bodily manifestations of an incorporeal event. In that instant of self-reflection (Adam and Eve's awareness of their visibility to, and hence separation from, their creator) *body is transformed into flesh.*[74]

The reasoning behind Augustine's analysis is that man's wilful turning-away from his divine Master precipitates a symmetrical punishment: the soul's loss of dominion over the body.[75] The hierarchy of God–soul–body is wrenched out of alignment, and the resulting dislocation alienates humanity from God, and body from soul. Augustine is clearly reading Genesis causally rather than strictly chronologically. Just as a movement of the will away from God precedes the forbidden act itself, so too an invisible stirring of concupiscence prefigures the agony of death.

Although Augustine uses *concupiscentia carnis* (lust) as 'the general name for desire of every kind', the sexual appetite or *libido* is prototypical.[76] There are, he explains:

> lusts for many things, and yet when lust is mentioned without the specification of its object the only thing that normally occurs to the mind is the lust that excites the indecent parts of the body. This lust assumes power not only over the whole body, and not only from the outside, but also internally; it disturbs the whole man, when the mental emotion combines and mingles with the physical craving, resulting in a pleasure surpassing all physical delights. So intense is the pleasure that when it reaches its climax there is an almost total extinction of mental alertness . . .[77]

At the climax of sensual pleasure the original 'integrity' of the body dissolves into an undifferentiated ocean of flesh. Sensation—in a perfect inversion of the well-ordered body—overwhelms and subjugates the mind.[78]

Foreshadowing the ultimate disintegration of the bond between body and soul at the moment of death, orgasm is truly *le petit mort*.[79]

St Augustine's wives: body, flesh and the feminine

In the passage quoted above the dangerous pleasures of the flesh are un-ambiguously sexualised; but Augustine's flesh is also gendered. Quite apart from the longstanding association of woman with corporeal matter (of which more will be said shortly), flesh is feminised as a wilful, insubordi-nate wife. 'Your flesh is like your wife', Augustine tells the husband-soul. 'It rebels against you, just as your wife does. Love it, rebuke it, until it is made into one harmony, one bond [of body and soul].'[80] Medieval writers often used gendered language when discussing the relationship between body and soul. In *The Plaint of Nature*, for example, the 'entire material body, adorned with the noble purple vestments of nature' is united in an 'acceptable union with spirit as a husband . . .'[81] Richard of St Victor similarly invokes the harmonious and fruitful bond between interior and exterior sense, 'for who does not know that Adam received his Eve for assistance?'[82] Behind this allegory of harmonious union, however, is the Eve who offered the forbidden fruit; the archetype of seductive and disobedient femininity. Thus we find Bacchilatria, one of the daughters of Idolatry in *The Plaint of Nature*, 'robbing her lover of his little spark of reason, [and] expos[ing] him to the darkness of brutish sensuality . . .'[83]

Augustine's image of lovingly 'breaking-in' the flesh so as to restore marital harmony between body and soul suggests a reversal of the fall. Commenting on this passage, Karma Lochrie argues that 'Augustine places the wife not at the site of the body but at the fissure of the flesh where concupiscence forever agitates against the will, the gap through which the self fell from God and from itself.'[84] Arguably, however, the text encourages a more equivocal interpretation of the allegorical alliances between woman and body/flesh.

Recent feminist scholarship has drawn attention to the recurrence of gendered metaphors in philosophical and religious texts.[85] At its most sim-plistic, this method has been dedicated to exposing the sub-structure of binary oppositions that supposedly underpins Western thought and culture. In the list of 'inferior' terms 'woman' is joined with (amongst others): body, matter, lust, disorder, irrationality, immanence, sensation, emotion and passivity. The paired 'dominant' terms might include: man, mind or soul, spirit, self-control, order, rationality, transcendence, intellect, activity and reason. Eleanor Commo McLaughlin, for example, claims that 'fear and denigration of women' can be attributed to a Platonic and Augustinian 'dualism that identified *vir*, the male, with spirit, and the female polarity with the earthward drag of the body'.[86]

The generalising sweep of McLaughlin's argument brings to mind Bynum's 'single [symbolic] grid'. It should be evident by now that in Augustine's thought at least, the battle lines are not so clearly drawn. Not only is the dualism of which McLaughlin speaks confounded by the presence of the flesh; there is no monolithic 'female polarity'. Rather, Augustine has recourse to two allegorical 'wives', and each performs a very different symbolic function by virtue of their identification with the body and the flesh. One, passive and productive, is brought to perfection in a 'marvellous mating' of body and soul.[87] The other, responsible for the sensuous desires and appetites that contaminate and inflame the body, is the embodiment of wilful, disruptive and insubordinate femininity.

Identifying gendered metaphors is one thing; determining their significance—both within and outside a given text—is more complicated. Pointing to the 'polymorphous . . . uses of gender categories and images' in the Middle Ages, Bynum insists that 'it is inaccurate to see medieval notions of *corpus, caro, materia* [matter], *mundus* [world], *tellus* [earth], *limus* [primordial clay, mud, slime], or *stercus* [waste, excrement] as gendered feminine'.[88] Feminists who argue otherwise are, in her view, guilty of 'deliberate misreading', however politically motivated that misreading may be.[89] From this perspective, Augustine's two 'wives' merely signify the benefits of bodily control, and the consequences of unbridled sensuality. I want to suggest on the contrary that the sexing of body and flesh underwrites this text: not as a rigid 'grid' generating consistent discursive effects, but as a range of imaginative possibilities. In the interest of clarity, I will treat the feminine associations of corporeal matter and flesh separately, beginning with the conceptual identification of woman and *body*.

Augustine's union of body/flesh and soul is consistent with a theory of embryology that would continue to exert its authority on medical and theological discourse well beyond the Middle Ages. According to Aristotle, the material substance of a foetus derived from the mother, while its vital spirit and form was contributed by the male seed.[90] In the simplest terms, 'the female always provides the material, the male that which fashions it. . . . While the body is from the female, it is the soul that is from the male.'[91] The raw matter of the maternal body was also characterised by its receptiveness, requiring—indeed desiring—the spark of life contained in the male seed for its actualisation.[92] In Latin these associations have a further resonance: 'woman' (*mulier*, related to 'softness', *mollities*) suggests yielding, receptive corporeality, while 'man' (*vir*) derives his name from the force of life (*vis*).[93] For Augustine, the harmonious union of husband and wife suggested the integration of complementary parts into a perfect whole. This is not to say that soul and body were 'gendered' in any essential or even consistent sense; rather, their hierarchical organisation in a specific context determines the attribution of gender. Gendered metaphors, in other words, reflect and are contingent upon power relations. For this reason, in relation to God the soul may be envisaged as a child or a bride—dependent, humble, adoring; but the soul's sovereignty over its 'own' body renders that body passive, receptive, material and feminine.[94]

The Aristotelian theory of sexual reproduction almost certainly helped to bind the idea of 'woman' to latent and passive physicality. But this does not account for the special relationship between femininity and *flesh* in Augustine's writing, where 'flesh' connotes disruptive sensuality and an appetite for sin. Woman was dangerous because she *exceeded* her nurturing, reproductive capacity. She embodied (literally and conceptually) the forces opposed to reason. In 'her mind and her rational intelligence' she might lay claim to 'a nature the equal of man's'. But in sex, wrote Augustine, 'she is physically subject to him in the same way as our natural impulses need to be subjected to the reasoning power of the mind . . .'[95] Women, in other words, are like men in their potential for rational thought, and feminine in their carnality.[96]

The physiological and imaginative intertwining of femininity and flesh was further cemented, in the Middle Ages, by the widespread and medically corroborated opinion that women were sexually voracious. The influential encyclopaedist Isidore of Seville (d. 636) declared in no uncertain terms that 'Females are much more sensual (*libidinosiores*) in human beings just as in animals.'[97] In a twelfth-century source, the uterus is compared to an iron vessel: if a man's desire, like straw, is rapidly ignited and as quickly spent, a woman 'warms more slowly but holds heat longer'.[98] The analogy itself betrays the coexistence of competing medical theories. In the Galenic system, where the womb is understood as the interior equivalent of a penis, it becomes an active sexual organ. As Joan Cadden explains, 'it draws to itself the male seed or the combined seed of the male and female', inevitably recalling more colloquial (and theological) stereotypes of woman as 'all appetite' in the sense of craving 'all the pleasures of the flesh'.[99] Yet the uterus was regarded by many embryologists as an empty, passive container, and the word *vas*—meaning 'vessel' or 'jar'—appears in medieval texts as a synonym for woman.[100] Despite the apparent incompatibility of these reproductive models, Cadden notes that they share the 'underlying suggestion that women are empty, void, lacking—that by not having the male principle they both lack masculine activity and need (and therefore desire) men's active principle, semen'.[101]

In summary, woman as *body* signifies receptive matter (either passive or desiring), but also the potential for completion and perfection within a well-ordered whole. Augustine's corporeal wife enables thought to be embodied—and fulfilled—in action. As *flesh*, on the other hand, woman is aligned with the disruptive forces of sensuality and appetite. The broad Biblical and Augustinian contours of medieval flesh are now in place. In the next section these themes will be extended and recast by St Bernard, abbot (from 1115) of the newly founded Cistercian monastery of Clairvaux. Bernard of Clairvaux's flesh is unmistakably Augustinian in its symbolic breadth as well as its theological framework.[102] Like Augustine, Bernard attempts to dissociate the productive body from destructive flesh, while accounting for their convergence in the 'sinful body' of our earthly existence.

The shadow of carnality: Bernard of Clairvaux's allegories of the flesh

In his sermon *On Conversion*, presented to an audience of students and scholars in Paris in 1140, Bernard constructs in meticulous allegorical detail a portrait of fleshly humanity.[103] Many of the familiar Pauline and Augustinian features make an appearance, including the battle between flesh and spirit for control of the body. In its role as a passive subject, the body 'finds itself located between the spirit it must serve, and the desires of the flesh or the powers of darkness, which wage war on the soul . . .'[104] Blameless in itself, the body is at once a constant reminder of humanity's vulnerability to sin and death, and the instrument of the soul's rehabilitation.[105] In Bernard's words: 'while we are in this body we are in exile from the Lord. That is not the body's fault, except that it is yet mortal; rather *it is the flesh which is a sinful body*, the flesh in which is no good thing but rather the law of sin reigns' (emphasis added).[106] Thus the passive body of our 'exile' is overlaid with another body: the 'sinful body' of the flesh. Despite repeated assertions of the body's innocence, subordination and passivity, its mortal life at least is lived in the shadow of sinful carnality.

In addition to the body's animation by fleshly desires, the convergence of body and flesh lends the flesh a certain density as well as a physiognomy. That is, the body is made carnal, but at the same time the flesh is corporealised. Predictably, flesh again takes shape in a female body, in accordance with the Augustinian prototype of the corporeal or fleshly wife. Bernard's feminine personification of the will, however, is both bleaker and more detailed than Augustine's rebellious but ultimately malleable spouse. 'Mistress Will' is the epitome of a non-productive body. Portrayed as a grotesque old woman, she makes her appearance with 'hair standing on end, her clothes torn, her breast bared, scratching at her ulcers, grinding her teeth, dry-mouthed, infecting the air with her foul breath'.[107] Together with the memory, Mistress Will and her unfortunate mate, Master Reason, comprise the three faculties of the human soul. Yet this is no simple tripartite cate-gorisation of the soul. By 'fleshing out' the sinful will with images of bodily dysfunction and decay, Bernard provides a commentary not only on an aspect of the soul, but on the relationship between sin and the body.

Metaphors of internal contamination begin Bernard's discourse on the flesh. The memory is described as a cesspit or stomach, the senses as gate-ways through which filth enters the soul. Moving to the exterior of this allegorical organism, the sermon builds to the crowning image of Mistress Will's monstrous body: a body in which the organs and members cata-logued by the author are inflamed and distended by the appetites of the flesh. Berating Reason for his conjugal shortcomings, the Will declares:

> I am voluptuous. I am curious. I am ambitious. There is no part of me which is free from this threefold ulcer, from the soles of my feet to the top of my head. My gullet and the shameful parts of my body are given up to pleasure; we must name them afresh, one by one. The wandering foot and the undisciplined eye are slaves to curiosity. Ear and tongue serve vanity . . . [W]ould that sometimes the body were all eye or the members all turned into a gullet to eat with.[108]

This catalogue of corporealised vices would not appear out of place in a moralising account of the Plinian races. More importantly, though, the image of this 'little old woman' incessantly picking at her ulcerated flesh speaks of the passive body's transmutation in response to the appetites of the flesh. The more the Will scratches her 'itch', the more it itches and sup-purates, until her body is entirely transformed into a porous and libidinous surface. Her fervent desire is to be 'all eye' or all mouth: a body both con-suming and consumed by desire, penetrated and penetrating. In the next chapter, the figure of the fleshly eye will be crucial, both in the role of vulnerable orifice—through which sense impressions flood the soul—and as an extension of the flesh beyond the body; a desiring gaze capable of caressing, grasping and penetrating its objects.

Karma Lochrie's definition of flesh as 'excess, permeability, disruption' is a fair assessment of the dilated and volatile carnality embodied by Mistress Will, albeit without the potential for ocular extension that exists in Bernard's sermon.[109] Imagined as a voracious porosity of the body and soul, flesh is not body-*matter* so much as the passions that inflame and traverse it: passions in the sense of suffering and illness as well as desire or appetite. In fact 'passion' (*passio*) was understood principally in the sense of undergoing, enduring or experiencing something, whether a violent emotion or a violent death.[110] As such, passion—like ageing, sickness and decay—was essentially *change*. This brings me to a second feature of the fleshly body in Bernard's sermon. Not only is it a body transformed by desire; it is subject to disease and putrefaction: symptoms of mortality so unflinchingly expressed by Mistress Will. Inasmuch as flesh is a sinful body, it is also a body that ages and dies.[111] Conversely, as Bynum observes: 'Glory means the absence of pain, want, putrefaction—that is, the absence of change.' The body 'taken up again at the Last Judgment . . . is in fact the same thing as the earthly body; but in its reassemblage it is purified, etherealized, beautified, and hardened into immutability'.[112]

There is yet another sense in which flesh is a sinful body for Bernard, and for many of his contemporaries. The impenetrable opacity of bodily existence was a feature of carnality. Alan of Lille was referring to this peculiar attribute of the flesh in the opening quote when he described it as a 'fog' darkening the 'eye of the heart', and a 'shadow' that 'debasingly cloaks the radiance of the human sense . . .' The image of a veil of carnality obscuring the radiance of the intellect is echoed in Bernard's assertion that 'it is sin alone which dulls and confuses the vision; nothing else seems to stand between the eye and the light, between God and man'.[113] Insofar as sinful flesh stands in opposition to the 'light' of God or Reason, carnality has an optical dimension. It is a privation of intellectual sight; an occlusion of the inner eye.[114] In Chapter 5, I will return to the complexities of this polarisation of sight, whereby carnal vision enshrouds or darkens the inner eye. At this point, it is notable that this characteristic of the flesh has its roots in Augustine's equivocal understanding of bodily sensation. Sensation, for Augustine, is at once a faculty of the passive body, and a disruptive power of the flesh. One might say that sensation is the point at which corporeality yields to the desires of the flesh; where legible sensory 'impressions' degenerate into pleasurable, but meaningless, sensations. The process by which sin insinuates itself into the body/flesh via the senses is described as follows:

> This evil thing creeps stealthily through all the entrances of sense: it gives itself over to forms, it adapts itself to colors, it sticks to sounds, it lurks hidden in anger and in the deception of speech, it appends itself to odors, it infuses tastes, by the turbulent overflow of passion it darkens the senses with darksome affections, it fills with certain obscuring mists the paths of the understanding, through all of which the mind's ray normally diffuses the light of reason.[115]

If the fleshly body is defined by the turbulence of its passions, its mutability and its epistemological limitations, the *resurrected* body is a body denuded of flesh and united harmoniously with the soul. The final section of this chapter considers corporeal perfection. By focusing on this ideal it will be possible to consolidate our definition of the flesh, this time through its exclusion, and set in place the fantasy of a pure, unchanging body abstracted from the flux of desire and mortality.

Blessed bodies

In a short treatise probably written between 1225 and 1230 Robert Grosseteste (a prominent Franciscan scholar and, at the time, chancellor of Oxford University) lists the wedding gifts promised to the blessed by Christ, the heavenly Bridegroom.[116] Of these endowments, four relate to the perfection of the body: impassibility (*impassibilitas*), clarity (*claritas*), agility (*agilitas*) and subtlety or elusiveness (*subtilitas*).[117] By comparing these attributes with their opposites—passibility, darkness or obscurity, slowness and gross materiality—Grosseteste constructs an image of the fleshly body as a counterpoint to the spiritual body.

Subtilitas, to begin with the last of the body's gifts, literally means 'thin' or 'subtle'. It refers to 'a disposition of matter' as far removed as possible from gross physicality, implying a decorporealisation of the earthly body.[118] For medieval Christians intent on approximating the heavenly ideal of corporeal 'subtlety' in this life, the wasting of the body through fasting was as close as one could get. 'Fast', wrote Alan of Lille, 'macerates the flesh, elevates the soul, restrains the spark of concupiscence, and excites reason'.[119] This understanding of flesh as something that exceeds (and can be subtracted from) the ideal limits of the body/self is related to the idea of flesh as generic—therefore surplus—matter. In the *Ancrene Wisse* (*Guide for Anchoresses*), a devotional handbook written at roughly the same time as Grosseteste's treatise, the weight of the flesh—like a 'heavy clod of earth [tied] to the soul'—is contrasted to the dowered body of the resurrection. If in this life 'the heavy flesh . . . pulls the soul down', in the next 'the body shall . . . become very light, lighter than the wind and brighter than the sun . . .'[120] The idea of flesh as raw corporeal matter can be traced back to the soft 'padding' of flesh in the *Timaeus* that protects the skeletal structure and internal organs, but in so doing retards mental functioning.[121] For this reason, Plato explained, the skull has the barest covering of flesh, while those parts of the body 'devoid of intelligence . . . are well covered with flesh'.[122]

The 'subtle' body is also agile, for it is not weighed down—mentally or physically—by excess corporeal baggage. In the *Ancrene Wisse*, for example, 'swiftness' is glossed as the body's ability to 'be wherever the soul desires, in an instant'.[123] Clarity intersects with Grosseteste's philosophy of light, and is rather more complicated.[124] The treatise *On Light*, which influenced a generation of scholars interested in optics, will be discussed in Chapter 3. For our current purposes, it is significant that light, for Grosseteste, is 'the swiftest, most transparent, most luminous form of matter'.[125] So to say that bodies are possessed of *claritas* is to claim that they are luminous, transparent, composed of a substance so rarefied that it approximates pure ideas.[126] In English, 'clarity' is most often applied figuratively to cognition: one has lucidity or clarity of thought. Grosseteste's use of the term also has epistemological significance: light is necessary for sight, and sight—as the noblest of the senses—is both metaphorically and causally related to knowledge. If *claritas* is absent, darkness and obscurity reign. And with *tenebrae* and *obscuritas* we return to the fleshly condition described by Alan of Lille as a 'shadow' or 'fog'.

Impassibility is the most precious of the body's gifts, the essence of its perfection (that which concerns being, *esse*). If 'passibility' denotes the corruptibility of the earthly body—the inevitable process of ageing, death and putrefaction—heavenly bodies by comparison are 'cleansed of all corruption' and thereby liberated from the vagaries of a fleshly, human existence.[127] More generally, *impassibilitas* can be defined as the 'state of him who is not subject to passions'—a state of eternal stasis.[128] We can conclude from this inventory that the glorified, resurrected body is incorruptible, translucent, agile and thin to the point of weightlessness. It is, paradoxically, a body characterised by its *in*corporeality, freed from biological determinants, and transfigured into light. The flesh that is absent from this perfected body is not only an immaterial force of sin or evil. It is the body as it is *lived*, and as it dies: mortal, vulnerable to sickness and ageing, often tired, weak or clumsy, rarely dazzling, and certainly not transparent.

One final point should be made about this renovated body. Alain Boureau has described flesh, in medieval theology, as 'either lacking or in excess' in relation to 'the abstract precision of the body'.[129] Ontologically, he says, the body is aligned with the soul, although it is only in the eucharistic body and the resurrected body—from which all traces of the flesh are excised—that this perfect union is realised. Extending this line of argument, one could say that the fleshless body does not just perfectly match its spiritual spouse, it is a fluent expression of the soul, both a vehicle of meaning and a subordinate member unimpaired by passion. Having opened this chapter with Alan of Lille's carnal eclipse of the mind and the disorderly bodies of Pliny's monstrous races, it seems appropriate to conclude with an image of the orderly and fluent body of the resurrection.

Closely following his Augustinian source, Peter Lombard writes that
the living 'body is such a burden because its governance is difficult and
serious', but:

> when it receives not an animal but a spiritual body [1 Cor. 15.44], equal
> to the angels, it will have the perfect expression [*modum*] of its nature,
> obedient and ruling, vivified and vivifying, with such ineffable ease that
> what was to it a prison will be to it a glory.[130]

CHAPTER 2

THE EYE OF THE FLESH

> . . . she seduced me, because she found me dwelling externally in the eye of
> my flesh, chewing over, within myself, such things as I had taken in through
> it.[1]
>
> *St Augustine*

> If only we lacked sight . . .[2]
>
> *Pseudo-Dionysius*

In the last chapter I began to map the elusive contours of medieval flesh
in contrast to the ideal of an orderly, passive and useful body. My argument here is that carnal vision extends the appetite and attributes of the
flesh beyond the boundaries of individual bodies. Sight lends the flesh an
intersubjective dimension; it literally carries carnality outside the viewer's
corporeal envelope and into the world: even into other bodies. As evidence for this claim I will consider the discursive relationship between the
flesh and the eye of the flesh, beginning with the increasingly prominent
role of sight in medieval commentaries on the temptation and fall. The
second half of the chapter will focus on the sexualised nature of carnal vision in moral theology and amatory literature. In both discourses of desire
the eye is eroticised as an organ of penetration and a penetrated orifice,
closely resembling the flesh in its permeability and libidinal activity. For
anyone familiar with psychoanalytic theory, these figures of sight will seem
familiar. Yet carnal vision cannot adequately be explained by current notions of the gaze. In the sources discussed here there is no paradigmatic
masculine gaze which might be denied to, or appropriated by female
viewers.[3] Rather, *looking with the flesh* is a means of sensory and sensual
intercorporation: erotic, but also potentially threatening; and if anything,
feminised by virtue of its grounding in carnality.

Original sin and the fall of vision

And the serpent said to the woman . . . 'God knows that in the day you eat of [that tree] your eyes will be opened, and you will be like God, knowing good and evil.'

So when the woman saw that the tree was good for food, that it was pleasant to the eyes, and a tree desirable to make one wise, she took of its fruit and ate. She also gave to her husband with her, and he ate.

Then the eyes of both of them were opened, and they knew that they were naked; and they sewed fig leaves together and made themselves coverings.[4]

It would be very difficult indeed to relate the events of the fall without referring to sight. Eve is seduced by the pleasant looking fruit, and tempted by the serpent's promise of omniscience. Knowledge is itself coded by the tempter as a God's-eye view of good and evil. A desiring gaze foreshadows the original sin. And finally, Adam and Eve's awareness of their own visibility is the immediate consequence of that sin. During the twelfth and thirteenth centuries—a period in which vision held a growing fascination for preachers, scholars, poets and ordinary Christians—the visual subtext of the fall came into focus. Elaborating on the Augustinian account of original sin, Peter the Chanter likened the 'opening' of Adam and Eve's eyes, and their consequent shame, to the opening of a child's eyes to concupiscence at puberty.[5] Prior to puberty (and by extension, prior to the fall), he explained, children's eyes are 'closed to lust . . . but afterward these channels are open admitting the natural forces of concupiscence to flood through the members and to produce sensations of craving'.[6] I will say more about the mechanics of ocular desire later. The point I want to emphasise here is that both Augustine and Peter describe this carnal awakening as a *consequence* of sin. In *The City of God* the 'movement of disobedience in [the] flesh' is a symmetrical punishment for the will's disobedience—not its cause.[7]

In fact, most medieval commentaries on the fall—whether iconographic or textual—highlighted an earlier visual moment: Eve's desiring, indeed 'devouring' gaze at the fruit. 'Eve would not have touched the tree', writes Gerald of Wales in his thirteenth-century guide for the clergy, 'unless she had first gazed upon it heedlessly'.[8] A more detailed account of Eve's sin is given in the *Ancrene Wisse*, written for three female recluses.[9] In illustration of the more prosaic dangers, for his readers, of watching the bustling world outside the anchorhold windows, the author of this handbook writes:

Of Eve, our first mother, it is recorded that at the very beginning of her sin its entry was through her eyes . . . This apple, my dear sister, symbolizes all

those things towards which desire and sinful delight turn. When you look
upon a man . . . you are looking on the apple.[10]

Eating the fruit becomes merely the outward sign of Eve's disobedience:
her fate—the fate of humanity—is sealed with a look. More than a predic-
tion of the fatal act, Eve's gaze is invested with intent. In a culture for which
sight was a physical act—involving the extension of one's soul to the object
seen, and a reciprocal impression of that object on one's body and soul—the
idea of sinning with one's eyes was more than a metaphor. Where Eve's eyes
went, so went Eve.[11] This may be why medieval depictions of the temptation rarely show her actually eating the fruit. Instead, the emphasis is on the
visual interactions that both anticipate and enact the serpent's seduction of
Eve, her ocular consumption of the fruit, and Adam's acquiescence.

    In a late thirteenth-century miniature of the temptation of Adam and
Eve from St John's College, Cambridge, an anthropomorphic serpent in-
clines her sinuous limbs and maidenly face towards Eve (Fig. 2.1). Taking
the fruit with her left hand, Eve extends her right hand to her spouse in a
gesture of invitation. Adam accepts the fruit, which he raises to his mouth.
As he does so, his right forefinger brushes his eye in a mirror image of Eve's
fateful desiring glance. The gestures of the three protagonists—an unholy
trinity haloed by the branches of the tree—compress the chain of events
in the garden into a single composition; but their exchange of gazes lends
psychological depth to the drama. Nor is the external viewer of this image
(which prefaced an English psalter) entirely excluded. We are implicated
by virtue of genealogy with the first parents and their sin, but we also re-
enact it in the very act of looking: at the beguiling serpent, at the fruit as
it circles the tree, and at the no longer innocent bodies of Adam and Eve.
That this is not a closed circuit of events, finished once and for all, is
further indicated by the toes peeping over the lower border, as if at any
moment Adam or Eve might step out of the garden, into the viewer's
space and time.

    There is one final point to be made about this version of the fall, and
it concerns Eve's visible affinity with the serpent. The serpent with a
maiden's-head seems to be a thirteenth-century pictorial innovation.[12] It
is consistent, of course, with the idea of woman as a duplicitous seductress;
but the feminine serpent's seduction of Eve—rather than Adam—provides
a twist to this well-worn misogynist theme. Peter Comestor's interpretation was that God 'chose a certain kind of serpent, as Bede says, which had
the countenance of a virgin, because like favours like . . .'[13] The serpent,
then, mirrors Eve: she is seduced by her own image.

    Both Eve and the serpent serve, on occasion, as signifiers for the
sensual side of human nature. I mentioned in Chapter 1 that the bond

Figure 2.1.   The Temptation of Adam and Eve.

between body and soul, and between the bodily senses and the mind, was often likened to a troubled marriage. More optimistically, but in the same vein, Richard of St Victor noted that the interior sense is aided by its bodily 'wife' just as Adam was given Eve for assistance.[14] Eve, the archetypal wife, personifies the useful body spoken of by Richard, as well as the sensuous, rebellious flesh. And as the embodiment of the flesh, Eve was united in nature and purpose with the serpent.

Sensuality, wrote Thomas Aquinas with a nod to Augustine, 'is symbolized by the serpent'.[15] Not just because we are tempted by sensual pleasures as Eve was tempted by the serpent, but because sensuality is a movement. Like the rippling muscular contractions of a snake, sensuality 'creeps' (*serpit*) through one's flesh, soliciting the soul's affections.[16] The analogy suggests a kind of furtive, spreading arousal, reminiscent of that unbidden movement in the flesh which for Augustine was the first symptom of Adam and Eve's disobedience.[17] In fact, in *The Trinity* the serpent provides Augustine with an image of the fall: 'the slippery movement of falling away [from the good] takes possession of the careless little by little . . .'[18] Aquinas's diagnosis of the movement of sensuality is rather less poetic: it results from 'a bent [*inclinatio*] attached to physical sensation, being a desire for what we know by our body-senses'.[19] In other words, because bodily sensations are (for the most part) pleasurable, the sensitive soul is drawn towards the source of those sensations. Indeed, the French term *sens* (from which the English 'sense' is derived) retains something of this motility and 'sense' of direction.[20]

Unlike Augustine, Aquinas makes a clear distinction between sense knowledge (what we would call perception) and sensuality. Sensuality, as an appetite, is 'fulfilled when the lover is drawn by what is loved'. When we derive knowledge of the world through the senses, however, 'the things apprehended are in the knower'. [21] For Aquinas, perception is something that takes place within one's sense organs; it does not involve a power of extension, or a movement of desire towards an object. Take Eve for example: Aquinas's bifurcation of sense and sensuality would mean that Eve's sight (i.e., sensory apprehension) of the apple was in itself passive, and quite unrelated to any desire to see, or will to disobey God's commandment. Having seen, however, her sensual appetite was aroused. From that moment, Eve was borne by her desire towards that apple. However, for most of Aquinas's contemporaries, educated and uneducated alike, sensation was not a passive, internal event; and the dividing line between sensation and sensuality—like that between body and flesh—was very faint indeed. Looking, as the most spatialised of the senses, was generally believed to be indivisible from the libidinal excursions of sensuality.

So far I have talked about the role of sight in the Fall, but there is a sense in which vision itself 'falls' away from God. Medieval vision, as I noted in Chapter 1, is often plotted on to a perceptual hierarchy. At the apex of this 'ladder' the pure gaze of the spirit or soul soars above the sensible world. Conversely, the body's senses draw the soul earthward in their sensual pursuit of transient things. The twelfth-century monk Bernard of Cluny evoked this tension between spiritual ascent and the gravitational pull of the flesh when he wrote that the 'eye within, the keen vision of the mind, beholds thee . . . Because I cannot with the body, I often make way to thee in spirit; but flesh is earth, and earth is flesh, and now I fall back.'[22] In this sense, the 'fall' of vision describes the slippery—one might say serpentine—descent of the body and soul, from their original condition of complementarity to their present state of fleshly discord. The fleshly eye, then, is the eye held in thrall by earthly delights, and moved by sensual desires.

Ocular erotica: commentaries on the sexuality of sight

In its visual re-telling, the story of the temptation and fall offered both a prototype and paradigm for the convergence of sight, desire and sin in carnal vision. The moral consequences of that convergence, however, were most fully worked out in relation to a passage on adultery in the Gospel of Matthew (5.28–9). Commenting on the seventh commandment (Exod. 20.14) Matthew wrote:

> . . . I say to you that whoever looks at a woman to lust for her has already committed adultery with her in his heart.
> And if your right eye causes you to sin, pluck it out and cast it from you; for it is more profitable for you that one of your members perish, than for your whole body to be cast into hell.

These verses, or at least their underlying sentiment, were the subject of scholarly discourse from the early Christian period right through to the later Middle Ages. One finds the same equation of looking and lusting in the writings of Origen, Lactantius, St Ambrose, St Jerome, St Augustine, Isidore of Seville, Peter Abelard, St Bernard of Clairvaux, Hugh of St Victor, Peter the Chanter and Gerald of Wales: a sample large enough to indicate a continuous and not insignificant awareness of the carnality of vision.[23] But exactly what did it mean for a look to be adulterous? Is it the look itself that is sinful, or the intention behind that look? How does the concept of ocular adultery shift when sight is understood as a physical encounter? And to what extent is the recipient of the lustful gaze implicated in the viewer's sin?

Peter Abelard (1079–1142) throws some light on first of these questions by locating sin in the mind's assent to temptation; not in the sensual appetite of the flesh, or in the bodily enactment of sin. It is 'not a sin to desire a woman', he insisted, 'but rather to consent to the desire'.[24] Behind Abelard's formulation of sin is the Stoic ideal of the virtuous man; one who, through the exercise of reason, maintains a detachment from 'physical impulses'.[25] Desire or appetite are like the serpent, he implies: Eve could have said no, despite her appetite for the apple and all it represented. By highlighting consent—and bracketing desire and action—Abelard departs from the Gospel's moral equation of lust and adultery (or desire and the act itself). Significantly, however, when he visualises adultery in more personal terms, the role of the mind to grant or withhold consent pales into insignificance. Just 'suppose', he says, 'that someone sees a woman, and falls into lust, and his mind is affected by delight of the flesh: he is inflamed for the filth of sexual intercourse'.[26] Abelard's use of the verb 'fall' brings to mind the downward slide of sensuality; but it also implies that the action is involuntary: a sensual reflex rendering the mind impotent to intervene on reason's behalf.

It would seem that the (male) mind is apt to lose its grip when it comes into contact with the slippery temptations of feminine flesh; and for most commentators on carnal vision, the passage from sight to sin is ineluctable. Perhaps the most exhaustive (if not the most persuasive or eloquent) treatment of this theme is in Gerald of Wales's *Gemma Ecclesiastica*. Unlike Abelard, Gerald was not concerned with the finer points of theological argument: his advice was intended for the edification and instruction of the clergy. So although the text resembles a pastiche on the dire consequences of ocular promiscuity, it does indicate the range of metaphors and examples that would have been disseminated to the lay population via sermons. The chapter 'On not staring at women' opens as follows:

Just as one should avoid the company of women, so too should one avoid staring at them or being stared at by them. Jeremiah writes: 'Death climbs in through the windows [of our eyes] and enters our home.' And Job says: 'I made a covenant with my eyes that I would not so much as think of a virgin.' Jerome warns: 'A harlot's eyes are a snare for the sinner.' And Augustine: 'Even if your eyes should fall upon a woman, you must never fix your gaze.' And elsewhere: 'The desire for women searches through our sight and is sought by the affections.' Jerome says: 'Our lewd and curious gaze wanders about [seeking] a woman's figure; in such a man the mind also is unchaste.'

Pope Gregory comments on Genesis: 'We should not gaze at what we may not desire lest we get involved in dangerous thoughts. In order that the mind may be kept free of lustful desires, the eyes must be checked and restrained as if they were guilty robbers. Eve would not have touched the tree [of forbidden fruit] unless she had first gazed upon it heedlessly. We who live mortal lives must consider, therefore, how much we ought to guard our sight against illicit objects. For if our first parents, who were created with a kind of immortality, brought death upon themselves through the eyes (by desiring visible things they lost invisible virtues and through their bodily eyes the heart's treasure was carried away), we must then discipline our external senses in order that we may preserve cleanliness of heart. As the prophet says: "My sight has ravaged my soul." ' And Augustine: 'Those who have unchaste eyes will strive in vain to lead pure lives.' And Jerome: 'An unchaste eye is the sign of an impure mind.'[27]

The eyes enumerated by Gerald seem in many ways to conform to current notions of a possessive, violating male gaze. They participate actively in the mortal sin of adultery. The 'lewd and curious gaze' untiringly pursues its prey. Unrestrained eyes are even likened to 'guilty robbers', evoking an image of visual kleptomania in which, presumably, the stolen goods consist of snatched impressions of the female form. One's bodily eyes are, moreover, liable to 'ravage' one's own soul, pollute the mind and excite the appetites of the flesh. Interspersed with these images of visual rapine, however, are references to ocular vulnerability. The eyes are the windows through which death enters; one's sight must be protected against 'illicit objects' and the 'heart's treasure' is carried off through the eyes.

From a twentieth-century perspective, the fleshly eye seems paradoxical, if not contradictory. It is penetrating, but apt to be penetrated in turn. It consumes its objects, but might also consume its own soul in an act of self-cannibalisation. In order to tease out the implications of this paradox for a visual relationship between gendered participants, it will be necessary first to disentangle these two attributes of the fleshly eye. To this end, I will start with the gaze that wounds or penetrates, then consider ocular vulnerability. The chapter will conclude by assessing the relevance of current theories of the gaze to the penetrating orifice of carnal vision.

The wounding gaze

In the twelfth-century French romance *Eneas* the heroine Lavine is wounded by Love's arrow while she feasts her virginal eyes on the handsome Eneas. This is love at first sight in the tradition of Ovid,[28] with the exception of one important detail. Lavine, reflecting upon the turn of events that have so overcome her, remarks that it was Love's *eye* that caused her wound: 'He has wounded me with a glance. He has struck me in the eye with his dart, with the gold one which causes love: he has struck me to the heart.'[29] As Ruth Cline has argued, the eye that casts a dart, dagger or arrow into the eye of its victim is not Ovidian. On the contrary, in classical Latin literature the eye is primarily a passive, receptive organ—not an agent of love.[30] Cupid's exploits are accomplished with conventional weapons, and his victims are wounded in the heart, not shot through the eye.[31]

The wound inflicted upon Lavine by Love's glance prefigures her ultimate ocular deflowering. Gazing down at Eneas from the window of her chamber, she is 'seized' by Love as he penetrates her eye and inflames her body.[32] Thus transfixed, Lavine secures the door of her chamber, and, returning to her position at the window, surrenders to her passion: 'She began to perspire, then to shiver and to tremble. Often she swooned and quaked. She sobbed and quivered; her heart failed; she heaved and gasped and gaped . . . She cried and wept and sighed and moaned.'[33] Lavine's transport as she gazes upon Eneas eclipses the sexual act itself.[34] This is a love for which literal consummation by a human lover can be little more than a pale reproduction of Cupid's dart. Subsequent discoursing on the nature of 'true love' leaves the reader in no doubt as to the significance of Lavine's transformation: her heart now resides with Eneas, and she can share herself with no other.[35] Love's glance, described in terms that suggest sexual penetration, has seemingly taken the place of coitus.

There is corroborating evidence that the desiring gaze carried a phallic connotation in late medieval French literature. Jacqueline Cerquiglini points out that the term *borgne* ('one-eyed') often signified impotence, just as *essorber* ('to blind') could mean *rendre impuissant*, 'to make impotent'.[36] She concludes: 'The loss of an eye is interpreted in the Middle Ages as a sign of impotence, as the symbolic transposition of another deficiency: the eye is a metaphor for the sexual organ.'[37] If blindness was equated with impotence in the French vernacular, a further link between sight and sexual performance existed in Latin sources. Albert the Great relates a story about a monk whose eyes and brain were destroyed as a result of having ' "desired" a beautiful lady seventy times before matins was rung'. The autopsy revealed a brain reduced to 'the size of a pomegranate', which Albert interpreted as a 'sign that coitus drains, above all, the brain'.[38] Albert is not explicit about the actual connection between coitus and blindness; it seems to be self-evident to him, and to numerous other 'authorities'.[39] The scientific explanation—if one were needed—would almost certainly have been that both semen and the refined *pneuma* (Latin *spiritus*) required for sight derived from the brain. Emission of visual rays or *spiritus* was thus physiologically equivalent to seminal ejaculation.

In the collection of medical and scientific writings known as the *Prose Salernitan Questions* (compiled around the turn of the twelfth century) the pleasure accompanying love is attributed to this ocular emission. *Delectatio* (sexual pleasure):

operates thanks to the appropriate instruments and by means of certain parts
of the body, namely the eyes. The spirit transmitted by the optic nerve is
emitted outwards to apprehend the things outside; having grasped those
things, it embraces them and represents them to the superior part of the
soul.[40]

Ruth Cline has traced the lineage of the erotically aggressive eye from its
origins in pre-Christian Greek literature and philosophy (from Hesiod onwards), through Arabic erotic literature, and into Western Europe through
the twelfth-century Provençal troubadours.[41] It is surely no coincidence
that Greek optical theories follow an almost identical trajectory, entering
Western scholarship at the same time, through Latin translations of Arabic
texts. Indeed, if one compares Plato's efflux (or emanation) theory of
vision with his highly erotic account of the mutual gaze of lovers in the
Phaedrus, Lavine's wound can be seen in a broader context.
    In the chapter of the *Timaeus* devoted to the eyes and vision, Plato
writes of the 'pure fire within us' that flows 'through the eyes' forming a
'visual stream'. This stream, upon leaving the body:

> falls on its like and coalesces with it, forming a single uniform body in the
> line of sight, along which the stream from within strikes the external object.
> Because the stream and daylight are similar, the whole so formed is homo-
> geneous, and the motions caused by the stream coming into contact with an
> object or an object coming into contact with the stream penetrate right
> through the body and produce in the soul the sensation which we call
> sight.[42]

When Plato turns his attention to eros, it becomes clear that this
'sensation which we call sight' is remarkably similar to the symptoms of
love. If a man finds himself in the presence of 'a god-like face or a physical form which truly reflects ideal beauty', he:

> first of all shivers and experiences something of the dread which the vision
> itself inspired; next he gazes upon it and worships it as if it were a god . . .
> Then, as you would expect after a cold fit, his condition changes and he falls
> into an unaccustomed sweat; he receives through his eyes the emanation of
> beauty, by which the soul's plumage is fostered, and grows hot, and this heat
> is accompanied by a softening of the passages from which the feathers grow
> . . . As the nourishing moisture falls upon it the stump of each feather under
> the whole surface of the soul swells and strives to grow from its root . . . So
> now it is all in a state of ferment and throbbing . . .[43]

Flooded with desire, the lover returns this 'stream of longing' to its source,
whereupon it 'enters in at [the beloved's] eyes, the natural channel of com-

munication with the soul . . . and in its turn the soul of the beloved is filled with love'.[44] As Lance Donaldson-Evans has remarked, the existence of a scientific explanation for the eyes' active participation in love means that we are dealing with more than a literary topos.[45] The libidinous, penetrating and penetrated eye of the flesh exceeds the realm of metaphor and becomes 'real' in its convergence with the eye of science.

Platonic love allowed for—indeed required—the mutual (ocular/affective) penetration of lover and beloved. The equality and reciprocity of gazes is not, however, usual in amatory literature, whether Greek, Arabic, Latin or French.[46] Love between men and women is rather more violent, it seems, than Plato's vision of exalted love between men. In pre-Christian Greek literature the beloved's eye casts poisoned darts, arrows, flames and thunderbolts; eyes become snares, trappers or hunting hounds. They even magically enchant their victims, bringing the erotic eye within the orbit of the evil eye.[47] One finds almost identical imagery in Arabic literature, both amatory and mystical. Donaldson-Evans dates the motif of the piercing eye as early as the sixth century AD, in the *Mu'allaqa of Imr Al-Qais*, where the poet says to his beloved: 'Your eyes only shed those tears so as to strike and pierce with those two shafts of theirs the fragments of a ruined heart.'[48] These are eyes that slay with flashing blades and blazing arrows. The *Arabian Nights* is particularly rich in such ocular imagery.[49] Carnage is wrought again and again by the heavily armed eyes in the *Nights*, and at one point, in the '49th Night', the narrator exclaims: 'those eyne! What streams of blood they shed! How many an arrowy glance those lids of thine have sped.'[50]

The eye that bewitches its victim is commonplace in Greek and Arabic sources, and often appears as a variation on the aggressive eye motif.[51] But if the wounding eye is the property of both men and women, the evil eye is characteristically female. In a late thirteenth-century anthology for preachers entitled *De Oculo Morali* (*On the Moral Eye*) the Franciscan scholar Peter of Limoges explains the phenomenon of the evil eye in light of contemporary optical theory.[52] Under the heading: 'How eyes of women have much unchasteness by which many are wounded', Peter invokes the figure of the mythical basilisk, the 'king of the serpents', which was believed to kill by sight, but adds the gloss: 'It is by means of the visual rays issuing from its eyes', that this remarkable feat is performed.[53] Advancing his argument by analogy, he then remarks: 'No one, without being out of his mind would look at a basilisk whose sight kills, therefore no one should look at a woman whose sight destroys and kills.' Why is the female gaze so lethal? Here is Peter's explanation:

> It seems probable that similar kinds of poisonous rays (*radii venenosi*) are given off when a woman looks at a man lustfully, for then a libidinous vapor

arises from the heart of the woman up to her eyes; henceforth the vapor infects her visual rays, which, so infected as they are emitted, come to the eyes of men and infect them, whence the infection enters the heart of man.[54]

This particular formulation of the evil eye, in which the 'disease' of lust is ascribed a physiological and optical aetiology, is found in the writing of Plutarch and Heliodorus,[55] although belief in some form of destructive gaze appears to be fairly universal. Certainly, the evil eye is a recurrent motif in the Old Testament,[56] yet in none of these sources do we find the gynophobia of Peter of Limoges.[57] How is he able to maintain that the *female* heart and eye are especially pernicious to men, without the reverse also being true? For an answer to this question we must turn to the synthesis of medieval folklore with Galenic and Aristotelian theories of vision that linked the polluting, venomous female gaze with menstruation. The same conjunction of science and superstition was responsible for the seminal associations of the male gaze.[58] Ocular 'ejaculation', however, is represented as a closed system: looking was a source of sexual pleasure for the viewer (in the *Salernitan Questions*); and one's own eyes were rendered impotent—literally desiccated—by sexual excess. In contrast, the 'menstrual' eye is a source of infection; a symptom of the inherently unstable, leaky, and therefore dangerous female body.

The concept of ocular menstruation seems to have been in fairly wide circulation by the end of the thirteenth century, based on the principle that the eyes, as especially porous organs, receive any overflow of accumulated menses.[59] Post-menopausal women, and those with irregular periods, were considered particularly prone to the retention of this excess matter because of their inability to efficiently evacuate or metabolise it. Even in healthy women, however, menstrual blood was thought to contain evil humours which could be emitted, with the visual rays, as a kind of poisonous vapour, infecting or 'impregnating' adjacent objects through the medium of the air. It was said (by way of proof) that if an infectious woman looked in a mirror or other reflective surface she would leave a red stain on the surface of the mirror.[60] An analogy was drawn between this characteristic of the poisonous female gaze and the basilisk, which could be destroyed only if its lethal gaze was turned back upon it with the aid of a reflective object.[61]

For the authors of the troubadour lyrics and courtly romances the wounding gaze represented the violent *passio* of sexual love. In the context of moral theology, however, the erotic eye was inseparable from the eye that infects and kills. How can we account for these differing interpretations? In the first place, the weight given to the destructive aspect of desire by medieval theologians and preachers conforms to the convergence, in Augustine's account of the fall, of concupiscence, sin and mortality. Secondly, for celibate preachers and theologians sexual desire was potentially a source of both fear and frustration. One way of alleviating the burden of guilt was to ascribe at least part of the blame for one's own carnal appetites to external forces: most notably the seductive power of the female form.[62] Alternatively, one could point the finger at the fleshly woman *within* the man of reason, for if femininity was an external threat, it was also internalised as the sensual component of the soul. We 'cannot be tempted by the devil', wrote Aquinas (quoting Augustine), 'except through that psychic part of us which bears or reflects a feminine image'.[63]

When male theologians like Gerald of Wales and Peter of Limoges contemplate the dangers of carnal vision, it is predictably a woman whose gaze poisons, penetrates, entraps, seduces or otherwise harms the implicitly male beholder. If the male gaze is ascribed an active role in sin, it is because the chastity of his eyes—the gateway to his soul, heart or mind—is not guarded. In the next section I will argue that chastity, like sensuality, assumes 'the likeness of a woman'.[64] More specifically, a series of analogies in medieval literature link the eye with architectural apertures—windows, doors, gateways—and with the vagina, that most closely guarded of corporeal 'gateways'.

Ocular chastity and the vulnerable eye

Courtly love, enacted as an exchange of gazes, relies on the receptiveness of the beholder's eye to Love's (or the beloved's) wounding glances. To expose oneself—especially one's eyes—to another's gaze is thus an open invitation to ocular penetration. In a scene in *Eneas* following Lavine's encounter with Love, her confidante castigates her for compromising her eyes, and by extension her chastity. 'Foolish Lavine', she remarks. 'You have protected yourself very poorly . . . It was in no way wise that you came here to look at [Eneas].'[65] Lavine, it is clear, has not behaved with the modesty that becomes a lady. And although her retort is witty—'I would be in very bad straits indeed if I could not look at a man without having to love him'[66]—it carries little conviction in light of her love-stricken condition. She has courted Love, and will pay the consequences with her 'mortal pangs'.[67]

Not surprisingly, the theme of ocular chastity is most fully developed in the context of sin, where the vulnerable, often eroticised and implicitly feminine eye becomes the devil's gateway.[68] Just as Eve was seduced by the serpent, so the fleshly, sensual, *feminine* component of the soul would always be the loose chink in man's spiritual armour. In discussions of carnal vision, these associations tended to be overlaid with a metaphor borrowed from Jeremiah 9.21: 'For death has come through our windows, has entered our palaces . . .' Where the senses, in Classical philosophy, were conceptualised as windows upon the soul,[69] the Church Fathers used Jeremiah 9.21 as an adjunct to the proscription against looking at women found in Matt. 5.28.[70] Certainly by the thirteenth century, when Gerald was compiling his *Gemma Ecclesiastica*, sin was not only *enacted* by a look, it could *enter in* through one's eyes. To look at a desirable woman was to throw open one's windows to sin and death.

Bernard of Clairvaux's depiction of the senses as apertures in man's corporeal abode is particularly vivid. As a consequence of leaving one's windows unguarded, the memory becomes an 'overflowing sewer', a reservoir of polluting sense-impressions that have flooded in from the external world to contaminate 'the whole house with intolerable filth'.[71] This is the fleshly body defined by its permeability; an organism in which 'every single member is a window . . .'[72] It is also, however, a body whose orifices are *actively* receptive. Bernard's sensory 'entrances' are not just holes. The 'roving eyes, the itching ears, the pleasures of smelling, tasting, and touching' combine appetite with openness.[73] They are apertures that crave penetration, and the influx of the world coincides with an efflux of the soul. This two-way traffic ceases only after death, when 'all the gates of the body by which the soul has been used to wandering off to busy itself in useless pursuits and to go out to seek the passing things of this world will be shut . . .'[74]

Sermons and *exempla* literature show that the theme of the five gates or windows corresponding to the five senses was, by the thirteenth century, both formulaic and widespread, and that the senses were often associated with specific sins.[75] Sin, it is implied, enters one's corporeal home through the openings of sense (and particularly vision, the sense most like a window). Conversely, the five senses are the first line of defence against incursion by the world, the devil, or the flesh. Thus, in *The Plaint of Nature*, Alan of Lille writes that the senses protect the material body 'like sentries', ensuring that the soul, as husband, 'might not be disgusted by the baseness of his partner'.[76] He also describes Chastity as a lady whose eyes, 'guarded by simple modesty, did not wanton in any impudent forays'.[77] Whether the senses are conceived as guardians or as points of entry, the ideal behind these metaphors of enclosure and its transgression is the same: namely, the contained and impregnable body imagined as a chaste, submissive corporeal bride.

There is an obvious link to be made between the topos of the five windows or gateways and late twelfth- and thirteenth-century allegories of the body as a castle, anchorhold or church.[78] The well-defended castle is exemplified by Robert Grosseteste's *Chateau d'amour*, written some time before his death in 1253.[79] This 'castle of love' is the virginal body of

Mary, into which Christ descends in order to fulfil his redemptive role. In this instance the castle is guarded by the seven virtues: humility, charity, abstinence, chastity, largesse, patience and spiritual joy. These weapons of good are deployed against the seven vices that assail the castle from without. The latter originate in the world (envy and avarice); the devil (pride, anger and sloth); and the flesh (lechery and gluttony).[80]

The castle of love in the thirteenth-century *Romance of the Rose* could almost be a parody of Grosseteste's chaste *Chateau d'amour*.[81] Where Grosseteste had emphasised the Virgin's impregnability to sin and vice, Jean de Meun transforms the attack into an extended allegory of the art of love. Venus assists the lover in his pursuit of the desired 'rose'; a pilgrimage that moves inexorably towards its climax as Venus penetrates the tower in which the prize is held. Foreshadowing the lover's ultimate victory,[82] the goddess of love 'took aim at a little loophole that she saw hidden in the tower. It was at the front rather than the side of the tower, and Nature had set it very skilfully between two little pillars.'[83] If the written text leaves the significance of this little hole to the reader's imagination, the same cannot be said of an early fifteenth-century illuminated manuscript in which the aperture is located between the architectural 'legs' of a life-size female statue.[84]

Venus's performance brings to mind that of Love in *Eneas*, for Lavine had been wounded while standing at the window of her tower, and her ocular penetration, though more thickly veiled in euphemism, was equally erotic. In her analysis of the 'metonymy between architectural space and bodily privacy' in Chaucer's *Troilus and Criseyde*, Sarah Stanbury makes the observation—equally applicable to *Eneas* and the *Rose*—that the male lover's visual and spatial entrance into successive architectural interiors, often through private or secret openings, evokes (and indeed effects) his movement towards the beloved's bedchamber and, ultimately, the act of love itself.[85] As with *Eneas*, in *Troilus* the spatialised drama of courtly love is enacted through 'lines of sight' which transect the boundaries between public and private, exterior and interior space.[86] If this ocular component of the game of love is overshadowed in the *Rose* by the author's virtuoso display of sexual innuendo, it is nonetheless present. Not only is the lover struck in the eye by Love's arrows when he first glimpses the rose-bud,[87] but the consummation of his desire is prefigured by a scene of fervent contemplation of the shapely reliquary figure:

> I found more pleasure in gazing at this than at any place I had ever seen; indeed, I would have fallen on my knees and adored it, together with the reliquary and the aperture. No archer with her bow and brand could have made me abandon my contemplation of it or my desire to enter freely . . .[88]

Grosseteste's *Chateau d'amour*, the castle in the *Rose*, the architectural staging of Lavine's encounter with love—and we could add the Virgin Mary's identification with Ecclesia: all of these symbolic alignments boil down to a basic homology between the vulnerable corporeal edifice (punctuated by openings) and the female body. Even in its generic form—when 'man' is conceived as a castle, for instance—the concept of enclosure and its transgression depends on a cultural understanding of embodied femininity as both bounded and permeable.[89]

One further variation on the theme of the feminised architectural corpus should be noted: the cloistered body. In the *Ancrene Wisse* the recluse's body is likened to a castle whose 'battlements are the windows of her house'.[90] Drawing on the familiar eye–window homology, the author of the *Wisse* cautions: 'Let her not lean out from [the windows] lest the devil's bolts strike her between the eyes when she least expects it.'[91] The anchoress's body with its sensory apertures is also mirrored by the architecture of the anchorhold. Spatially, the anchoress occupies a marginal position between the church and the world (her cell, bolted on the outside, adjoins the outer wall of the church). Of the three windows in her cell, one looks into the church so that she can participate visually in the mass; one opens into a parlour, and one onto the street.[92] And herein lies the paradox: although urging his readers to 'be truly enclosed' and 'blind to the outside world', the author's attention (and, one assumes, that of the women concerned) lingers on those three windows:[93] windows that, as Linda Georgianna observes, 'serve to *connect* the solitary with the world'.[94]

While invoking the sealed chastity of anchorhold and castle, the author of the *Wisse* is cognisant of sensation's peculiar ability to extend the reach of the body and the affections (indeed the heart itself) outwards through corporeal and architectural 'windows'. This could be said of all the senses to some extent; but sight is the sense most able to penetrate space, to reach out, grasp or caress the myriad objects in the visual field. Like Eve, who 'leaped after her eyes had leapt',[95] for the anchoress vision is a means of motility; dangerous because it transforms the anchorhold into an 'unwalled city'.[96] The solution to the influx and efflux of sensation is not denial or retreat into a realm of pure interiority; nor is it mystical transcendence of the body and its carnal nature. Instead, the anchoress is advised to direct her desire and imagination—sensory and sensual—towards a very human Christ.[97] Significantly, in the final chapter of the *Wisse* Christ is the courtly lover who approaches the lady-anchoress in her castle. The danger, to quote Georgianna, is that 'Having shut out the world, she has also shut out Christ . . .'[98]

Clearly the eye-as-orifice was as metaphorically loaded as the penetrating eye. If one moves freely across the nominal discursive borders signified by the terms 'religious' and 'secular'—as Jean de Meun and the author of the *Ancrene Wisse* do—it becomes possible to read the theologians' concern with the eye's vulnerability to sin as a response to the ocular erotica of courtly romance. I have described the fleshly eye in terms of penetration and permeability, but the question remains as to what extent this modality of medieval vision can legitimately be compared to twentieth-century conceptions of the sexualised and eroticised gaze. Because the intersection of vision and sexuality is a vast topic, I will confine my comments to the proposition that the active, sexually aggressive gaze is paradigmatically masculine.

Theorising the medieval gaze

In her study of *Troilus and Criseyde*, Sarah Stanbury agrees with E. Ann Kaplan that the 'gaze is not necessarily male (literally), but to own and activate the gaze, given our language and the structure of the unconscious, is to be in the masculine position'.[99] Stanbury's argument is about power rather than sexuality or desire *per se*: the power to look and possess on the one hand, and the absence of that power on the other. However, because the primary signifier of power (in this psychoanalytic model) is the phallus, the masculine gaze is imagined as a phallic gaze: penetrating, possessive, and sexually potent.[100] Medieval texts, Stanbury maintains, construct gender through ocular narratives in which the 'predatory male eye' is met by its 'gestural reflex, the cloistered and restricted female gaze . . .'[101] Women, or at least ladies, did not (and do not) look back: their sanctioned role is as passive, chaste objects of the male gaze. If a woman looks, it is not from a position of 'mastery', but rather one of 'reflexivity'.[102]

When Criseyde returns her lover's gaze, the narrator describes the scene according to the conventions of ocular erotica. '. . . Love hadde his dwellynge', we are told, 'Withinne the subtile stremes of hir yen [eyes]'.[103] For Stanbury, the lady's returned gaze reflects her lover's desire. Like a gilded mirror, Criseyde is both an object and a signifier of male fantasy. It would seem in this instance that the erotic encounter has nothing to do with female desire; and everything to do with masculine myths and patriarchal ideology. Yet Stanbury writes elsewhere of a 'cupidinous, seductive, aggressive [and] thoroughly transgressive' female gaze.[104] How might a woman look *as a woman*, rather than masquerading as a man? In her essay on the Virgin's gaze in fourteenth- and fifteenth-century Passion lyrics, Stanbury offers a compelling possibility.[105] Mary's gaze, she argues, 'takes its power—transformative, fusive, and ultimately transgressive—from the drama of first love', the love of mother and child.[106]

When Mary beholds Christ's naked and bleeding body, he is indeed 'held' or embraced by a gaze that negates corporeal and emotional boundaries, collapses the space of detached observation, and effects a mingling of self and other. Seen in this light, the female gaze is both potent and dangerous because it threatens to dissolve male autonomy, subjectivity and authority: to re-absorb the masculine subject into maternal flesh. But is this gaze specifically or originally *maternal*? Might one not read the devouring or wounding gaze as fusive also? And the penetrated eye and soul as infused with its object? In short, if one interprets carnal vision as an extension of the flesh, and if flesh is understood as a condition of libidinal permeability, then the Virgin's maternal gaze is not so easy to distinguish from the ocular interpenetrations of the flesh.

I do not want to suggest that vision was not a gendered practice in the Middle Ages, or that medieval visuality is entirely discontinuous with modern ways of looking. However, the gazes surveyed in this chapter cannot easily be classified according to gender. As we have seen, the male gaze is by no means always phallic; and ladies' eyes are not always chaste, reflective orbs or instruments of maternal love. The ocular attributes that, for a modern reader, are so sexually resonant—the 'penetrating' gaze, the 'wounded' eye and all its attendant symptoms—seem repeatedly to be assigned to the wrong sex. Both men and woman are capable of inflicting wounds of love with a glance, and men as well as women receive those wounds in their eyes and hearts. A woman's eye may entrap or seduce, but men too can have 'whoring' eyes. The female recluses addressed in the *Ancrene Wisse* are admonished to take custody of their senses, and in particular to guard the chastity of their eyes; but the chastity of men's eyes requires equal vigilance. The one characteristic that is not shared between the sexes is the menstruating eye, and even then there is less scope for sexual differentiation than one might expect. As we have seen, the ocular overflow of female blood is physiologically equivalent to the 'seminal' efflux of the male gaze. In any case, this variant of the evil eye is feminine neither by virtue of chastity nor maternity: it impregnates its objects with maleficent humours.

Ultimately, the (hetero)sexual morphology of Stanbury's psychoanalytic model confuses rather than elucidates the medieval gaze. Nor is she well served by her faith in a continuous 'cultural unconscious', or indeed a continuous history of vision.[107] Certainly, carnal vision was a locus of heterosexual fantasy; of course, ideologies of proper and improper conduct are embedded in the discourse of ocular desire; but in addition, the fleshly eye takes shape within a symbolic economy of the flesh.

As organs of the flesh, eyes are both physiologically and metaphorically related to the 'lower' appetites and functions of the body; hence their connection with virility, impotence and menstruation. The fleshly eye, as I have said before, is not an instrument of observation. It is a vehicle of desire: a means of grasping, devouring, adhering to the objects of one's sensual appetites; and a spontaneous dilation of one's own senses in anticipation of the world's influx. Furthermore, carnal vision, like the flesh, has a special relationship with the feminine, so that *man's* nature (as well as woman's) is split between fleshly appetite and the supposedly masculine faculty of reason. One might say that when a man looked with desire in the Middle Ages, he looked as a woman.

PART II

PERSPECTIVA

CHAPTER 3

SCIENTIFIC VISIONS

sight . . . most of all the senses, makes us know[1]

Aristotle

Roger Bacon, in what was to become one of the most influential works on optics in the Western Middle Ages,[2] reflected that the superiority of sight over the other senses was manifest in two ways: in visual pleasure, and in the necessity of sight for knowledge of the natural universe. We 'take especial delight in vision', he wrote in his introduction:

> and light and color have an especial beauty beyond the other things that are brought to our senses, and not only does beauty shine forth, but advantage and a greater necessity appear. For . . . vision alone reveals the differences of things; since by means of it we search out experimental knowledge of all things that are in the heavens and in the earth.[3]

The commitment to empirical or experimental knowledge so evident in Bacon's writings is often seen as heralding the nascence of modern science, and the renaissance of pictorial naturalism. And for historians of vision, the optical foundation of thirteenth-century science has been taken as evidence of a restoration of the classical (specifically Aristotelian) primacy of sight.[4]

Yet if Bacon's words on the value of sight suggest a new awareness of the scientific possibilities of observation, they give equal weight to the affective component of vision as the sense in which 'we take especial delight'. It is my contention that this visual 'delight' is symptomatic of an awareness that sight exceeded its role as an instrument for acquiring knowledge. This chapter and the next will elucidate these two basic—and some would say contradictory—aspects of thirteenth-century optics. I will argue here that the optical gaze legitimates bodily sight and opens up a space for observation *by abstracting vision from the flesh*. In this respect medieval optics could indeed be said to lay the foundation for early modern science and Renaissance naturalism. At the same time, however, a continuing emphasis *within optical theory* on the corporeal and affective phenomena of sight mitigates against the disembodied and distancing gaze that is so often associated with Western science and philosophy. These residues of the flesh in Bacon's optics will form the basis of Chapter 4.

If the fleshly eye served sensuality to the detriment of mind or reason, we have to ask how it was that vision became the primary means for acquiring scientific knowledge of the natural world. Part of the answer is that during the twelfth and thirteenth centuries—coinciding with the reception of Aristotelianism in the West—there was a realignment of sensation. The bodily senses, freed (at least in this context) from their Augustinian association with fleshly sensuality, were able to be aligned with experimental knowledge. Having outlined this transition, I will examine the specific connection between the goals of medieval science and the sense of sight in the work of Robert Grosseteste, whose philosophy of light made optics fundamental to later medieval science.

The second half of the chapter will focus on Grosseteste's younger contemporary and fellow Franciscan, Roger Bacon. By the time Bacon was writing his treatise on optics in the 1260s he was able to claim with authority that 'no other science has so much sweetness and beauty of utility. Therefore it is the flower of the whole of philosophy and through it, and not without it, can the other sciences be known.'[5] The certitude afforded by scientific vision relied on two basic premises: that mathematical models are equivalent to the reality they describe; and that sense perceptions and mental concepts are visual simulacra of a visible world. If sight, to quote Aristotle, 'makes us know', it is because reality is a picture and the mind an eye to view it with.

Scientific curiosity and the legitimacy of experimental knowledge

Thirteenth-century scholasticism is often seen as a confrontation between two ultimately irreconcilable world-views: one naturalistic—represented by Aristotle—the other theological in outlook, and identified with Augustine.[6] Hans Blumenberg makes the more specific claim that in their efforts to synthesise these 'two great authorities', thirteenth-century scholars like Albert the Great and Thomas Aquinas simultaneously paved the way for modern science, and resisted its implications.[7] For Blumenberg the transition from early to high scholasticism turned on the legitimacy of experimental knowledge, and it was in relation to this question that the tension between Augustine and Aristotle was most apparent.

Augustine regarded the desire for worldly experience and knowledge, indeed scientific inquiry in general, as a feature of our fleshly nature. In the *Confessions*, he writes of a 'vain and curious desire':

> cloaked under the name of knowledge and science—not for fleshly enjoy-
> ment, but for gaining personal experience through the flesh. Because
> this consists in the craving to know, and the eyes are the chief agents for
> knowing among the senses, it has been called *concupiscence of the eyes* in
> holy scripture [emphasis added].[8]

There is little possibility here for the kind of detached or dispassionate observation we have come to associate with scientific objectivity; instead, as Augustine claimed elsewhere, 'the reason of science has [sensual] appetite very near to it . . .'[9] Beginning in the twelfth century, however, and gathering momentum in the thirteenth century, the Augustinian prohibition against scientific curiosity yielded ground to a potent practical and philosophical interest (indeed curiosity) in the physical world.[10] Central to this shift was the translation and dissemination of Aristotle's writings; and along with them, the principle that 'all knowledge is good' (*Omnis scientia bona est*).[11]

Whereas for Augustine human knowledge realises its potential only by *transcending* the phenomenal world,[12] for Aristotle knowledge is not only grounded in our experience of the world,[13] but *completed* in the natural world.[14] I will be using Grosseteste's commentary on Aristotle to illustrate, and complicate, Blumenberg's argument.[15] This will have the twofold advantage of elucidating the Aristotelian basis of medieval science (along with its Augustinian tensions), and providing a broader context for Grosseteste's contribution to medieval optics.

Robert Grosseteste (c. 1170–1253) has been described as a 'transitional figure'.[16] Although essentially a Platonist, he paved the way for the thirteenth-century assimilation of Greek and Arabic learning; in the process drawing together the divergent traditions of practical and theoretical science. If the 'twelfth century was an age of reason, rather than of experimentation'—to quote Charles Burnett—then Grosseteste was instrumental to their union.[17] In the process he drew heavily on Aristotle's *Posterior Analytics*. This complex work on the principles of scientific knowledge had been available in Latin from the latter half of the twelfth century through its translation by James of Venice (who died after 1147),[18] but was largely neglected until Grosseteste's commentary on the text, probably completed around 1225.[19] The significance of the *Posterior*

Analytics for the development of Western science is a topic in itself. Of importance here is Grosseteste's response to the Aristotelian doctrine that sensation is a precondition of scientific knowledge.[20]

Grosseteste's equivocation on this issue highlights the difficulty of reconciling the transcendental thrust of his theology—the gaze *beyond* the sensible world—with the project of natural science. The existence of a divine intelligence negates the necessity of sensation in any absolute sense. '. . . I say that it is possible to have some knowledge without the help of the senses', Grosseteste insists in his commentary. 'For in the Divine Mind all knowledge exists from eternity, and not only is there in it certain knowledge of universals but also of singulars.'[21] He goes on to argue that true and complete knowledge will be available to the intellect only 'when the soul is drawn forth from the body'.[22]

In its earthly, post-lapsarian incarnation, however, human intelligence must proceed from particulars to universals through the medium of sensation. Aristotle's method of inductive reasoning is thereby recast within a theological framework. Retarded by the flesh, the human capacity for reason is dependent upon the bodily senses. Grosseteste's explanation of this process brings to mind Augustine's distinction between the sensual paralysis of the flesh, and the helpful corporeal wife. In this fleshly existence, Grosseteste writes, 'the powers of [the] rational soul born in man are laid hold of by the mass of the body and cannot act and so in a way are asleep'. Through the 'many interactions of sense with sensible things', however:

> the reasoning is awakened mixed with these very sensible things and is borne along in the senses to the sensible things as in a ship . . . This, therefore, is the way by which the abstracted universal is reached from singulars through the help of the senses; clearly the experimental (*experimentale*) universal is acquired by us, whose mind's eye is not purely spiritual, only through the help of the senses.[23]

In this life at least, then, reason requires the stimulation and assistance of the senses.

One further point should be highlighted here, and that is Grosseteste's fondness for ocular metaphors. Although he is writing about the utility of the bodily senses in general, the paradigmatic relationship is that between the 'mind's eye' and corporeal sight (configured in this instance as scientific observation). There is, of course, nothing new in this: most Indo-European terms for mental activity derive from words for vision or the visible.[24] Aside from securing the primacy of sight in relation to theoretical knowledge, the equation of seeing and knowing privileges a mimetic logic.[25]

Ideas (from the Greek *idein*, 'to see') are imagined (Latin *imaginare*, 'to picture to oneself') as visual representations set before the mind's eye.

Grosseteste made optics fundamental to any scientific inquiry by arguing that light is the agent behind all physical causation;[26] but he also extended to natural science a widespread, colloquial equation of looking and knowing. In the following discussion of Grosseteste's 'optical abstractions' I will focus on these interconnected themes of geometrical optics (as a general explanatory model) and sight (as a privileged instrument of knowledge). With regard to geometrical optics, it is significant that the object of scientific knowledge is lifted out of the flux of its natural existence by the same method of mathematical abstraction that transforms the eye into an instrument of knowledge. Stripped back to their geometrical essence, observer and observed participate in a single, theoretically transparent universe. So sight occupies a privileged place in Grosseteste's system because vision lends itself—in a way the other senses do not—to precise geometrical definition. Abstracted from the flesh, the bodily eyes are thus recuperated as the conduits linking a knowable world to a reasoning mind.[27]

The optical abstractions of Robert Grosseteste

In the Middle Ages the flesh signified humanity's inherence in the material world and alienation from God; but as we saw in Chapter 1, it was possible for the body to be purified of flesh. It is no coincidence that Grosseteste wrote admiringly of heavenly bodies so lucid, swift and subtle that they resembled light itself. In the absence of the flesh—ponderous, permeable, concupiscent and corruptible—the body was decidedly incorporeal. Turning to the question of Grosseteste's optics, we find that sight is abstracted and rarefied in much the same way that the bodies of the blessed were to be denuded of flesh. While *carnal* vision was conceived by many of Grosseteste's contemporaries as a condition of opacity or darkness, Grosseteste defines *corporeal* vision as light.[28]

Grosseteste's brief but influential treatise *On Light* was probably written around 1235–40, shortly after he had become bishop of Lincoln.[29] In it he describes light (*lux*) as 'the first corporeal form'.[30] Creation takes place through the union of this originative form—the first light of Genesis—with primordial matter (*materia prima*). Light, in this Neoplatonic cosmogony, has two basic functions. As it diffuses outward in every direction light extends matter, giving rise to spatial dimension (magnitude). It is also 'the original physical cause of all natural movement or change'.[31] But Grosseteste's philosophy goes beyond theories of creation and causation:

radiant light provides a model for the acquisition of knowledge and, ulti-mately, the expression of divine and moral truths.[32] In terms of the history of optics, the crucial part of Grosseteste's argument concerns the relation between originative light (*lux*) and its secondary, visible manifestation.[33] By studying visible light (*lumen*), he says, we can observe the fundamental and universal principles of all creation.

Visible light could be described or represented in a number of ways, but for Grosseteste the language most appropriate to the study of light was geometry. It is worth noting at this juncture that medieval optics, or *perspectiva* as it was then known, was from a modern point of view a very eclectic discipline. In addition to the mathematics and physics of light and vision, the 'perspectivists'—among them Roger Bacon (c. 1214–92), John Pecham (c. 1235–92) and the Polish scholar Witelo (c. 1235–c. 1275?)—studied the anatomy and physiology of sight as well as the relation between vision and cognition.[34] They were also well versed in the theological sig-nificance of optical science: the concluding chapters of Bacon's *Perspectiva* are devoted to spiritual and practical applications (the latter mostly con-cerned with the use of mirrors in battle). Nevertheless, it was the mathe-matical strand of medieval optics—specifically the application of ray geometry to the eye and vision—that had the most enduring influence, culminating in the seventeenth century with Johannes Kepler's theory of the retinal image.[35]

It would not be an exaggeration to say that geometrical 'perspective' —from *perspicere*, to survey or scrutinise, to investigate thoroughly, to 'see through'—became the metadiscourse of the later Middle Ages. As David Lindberg observes, because 'optics could reveal the essential nature of material reality, of cognition, and indeed of God himself, its pursuit became not only legitimate, but obligatory'.[36] More than just an *object* of study, *perspectiva* was a way of seeing—and knowing—with certainty (*perspicue* means 'with clarity of perception'). In Grosseteste's *De lineis, angulis, et figuris*, geometry is the key with which the scientist will unlock the natural world:

> The usefulness of considering lines, angles and figures is the greatest, because it is impossible to understand natural philosophy without these. They are ef-ficacious throughout the universe as a whole and in its parts, and in related properties, as in rectilinear and circular motion. They are efficacious also in cause and effect (*in actione et passione*), and this whether in matter or in the senses . . .[37]

Applied to perceiving subjects and the sensible world, the laws of mathe-matical physics promised a universal, objective scientific language. What

Grosseteste accepted without question was that a mathematical model could adequately express the world it described.[38]

Grosseteste's geometrically articulated universe addresses the fundamental requirements of classical science articulated by Patrick Heelan: that the physical world consists of standardised, mathematically defined units; that space has an objective, geometrical structure; that theoretical explanations are universally applicable; and that 'scientific laws are indifferent to human perceivers, to what they do and to where they are located . . .'[39] Together these principles of atomism, geometry, universality and objectivity produce what Roland Barthes (in a different context) called a 'reality effect'.[40] In this case, the 'language' of mathematics is taken to be a direct and unmediated representation of a prior, indeed 'primordial' reality.[41]

With the advent of scientific relativism and the current theoretical interest in 'subjectivities' the totalising project of classical science has come under fire. Once we begin to see medieval science not as a sudden 'awakening' to the natural universe, but instead as a cultural production (not reality, but a reality *effect*), we can ask more productive questions. Such as: what is the common ground between science and theology? I opened this chapter with Blumenberg's analysis of the tensions between experimental science and transcendental theology; but it would be a mistake to regard medieval Christianity and thirteenth-century science as entirely oppositional impulses—the one religious and transcendental, the other grounded in a new experience of nature. In the first place, Grosseteste and his followers regarded theology and science as indivisible parts of a single system; or rather, science could be accommodated by theology as the means to an end.[42] In the second place, as Steven Goldman argues, modern science shares with medieval Christian thought a certain symbolic or 'iconic' tendency.[43]

Instead of rejecting the symbolising sensibility of Augustine and his medieval followers, geometrical optics could be said to have extended that mentality into the equally symbolic language of mathematics. Well tutored in reading nature as 'a book whose author was God',[44] Grosseteste and his successors (including Roger Bacon) were fluent when it came to the elaboration of physical or geometrical 'allegories'. In this light, scientific naturalism—like its pictorial equivalent—must be regarded not as natural, inevitable and universal, but as cultural and contingent.[45]

Grosseteste's appeal to optics as a foundational science does not, as one might expect, correspond to a particular interest in vision. One possible reason for this is that his knowledge of Greek and Arabic sources was still fairly limited. He had read Latin translations of Euclid's *De speculis*, Avicenna's *Liber canonis*, Aristotle's *Meteorologica* and al-Kindi's *De aspectibus*. But, as Lindberg points out, 'he did not have access to the most important optical works of the past': Ptolemy's *Optica* or Alhazen's *De aspectibus*.[46] Sight, for Grosseteste, is but one manifestation of a philosophy of nature and cognition that is elaborated through more general optical principles. Nevertheless, his geometrical conception of sight seems in many ways to predict the objective, empiricist gaze of modern science, and the perspectival vision associated with pictorial naturalism. For this reason, I will first consider the operation of sensation in general, then show that sight in particular is both paradigmatic and privileged in relation to knowledge.

Following the passage in *De lineis, angulis, et figuris* quoted earlier, Grosseteste explains that:

> a natural agent propagates its power (*virtutem*) from itself to the recipient (*patiens*), whether it acts on the senses or on matter. This power is sometimes called species, sometimes a similitude, and is the same whatever it may be called; and it will send the same power into the senses and into matter, or into its contrary, as heat sends the same thing into the sense of touch and into a cold body. *For it does not act by deliberation and choice, and therefore it acts in one way, whatever may meet it, whether something with sense perception or something without it, whether something animate or inanimate.* But the effects are diversified according to the diversity of the recipient. For when received by the senses this power produces an operation in some way more spiritual and more noble; on the other hand when received by matter, it produces a material operation . . . [emphasis added][47]

Defined according to quantifiable—and verifiable—mathematical principles, sensation is divested of subjective variables ('deliberation' and 'choice') and transformed into a purely objective process. Highlighting the significance of this mathematical turn, A. C. Crombie notes that this 'is the principle that, in order to be described in the language of science, "subjective" sensations should be replaced by concepts amenable to mathematical treatment'.[48] Distanced from the unpredictable and indeterminate conditions of fleshly embodiment, sensation assumes a certain 'nobility'. But of all the senses the greatest degree of certainty and nobility was invariably ascribed to sight.[49] As Augustine himself put it: 'Let us, therefore, rely principally on the testimony of the eyes, for this sense of the body far excels the rest, and comes closer to spiritual vision . . .'[50] In order to account for vision's superiority, we will need to look more closely at the connection between light and sight.

Grosseteste's Neoplatonism embraces degrees of perfection within a continuum of being. Light is the subtlest, most refined material entity; so refined in fact that it has more in common with pure, incorporeal forms (the 'intelligences') than with corporeal bodies.[51] At the other end of the spectrum is dense, inert matter. The earthly sphere, Grosseteste says, possesses this 'denseness of matter which is the principle of resistance and stubbornness'.[52] Composed of heavy, compacted corporeal matter and an incorporeal soul, each individual is a microcosm of this cosmic hierarchy. And in the same way that *lux* united primordial matter with spiritual forms, it mediates between body and soul, and between the human intellect and sensible objects. Light itself can be distinguished both from corporeal bodies and immaterial spirit. As one commentator notes, 'Being an intermediary, [*lux*] possesses neither the special attributes of thinking and willing peculiar to spiritual beings nor the grossness of body.'[53] It is because of this mediating effect of light that sensation can function as a vehicle for intelligence: the 'ship' bearing reason to its sensible objects.[54]

In fact Grosseteste conflates the optical (mathematical and physical) attributes of light with the ocular mechanism of sight. In *De iride* he insists that the emission of rays from the eyes should not to be thought of as 'imagined and without reality . . .' Rather, 'it should be understood that the visual species [issuing from the eye] is a substance, shining and radiating like the sun, the radiation of which, when coupled with radiation from the exterior shining body, entirely completes vision.'[55] The act of sight (conceived here according to the Platonic theory of visual fire) approximates the radiation of light from a luminous body. Sight, in other words, cannot be fully accounted for by Aristotle's theory of intromission, according to which an external agent 'operates' on a passive organ of sense.[56] For Grosseteste, as for Bacon, sight is both passive and active: the eye is altered by its objects (intromission), but it is also the channel for a radiant power of vision (extramission).

It is arguable that this convergence of vision and light has played a role in delimiting what counts as scientific knowledge. As I mentioned earlier, Grosseteste's philosophy of light had an epistemological dimension in addition to its theological, physical and cosmogonical applications. Because cognition was modelled on the physical and geometrical properties of light, knowing, reasoning, understanding and remembering were thought of as ways of seeing. In his commentary on the *Posterior Analytics* Grosseteste describes the intellectual acumen of the philosopher in optical terms:

Sollertia[57] is the penetrating power in virtue of which the mind's eye does not rest on the outer surface of an object, but penetrates to something below the visual image. For instance, when the mind's eye falls on a coloured surface, it does not rest there, but descends to the physical structure of which the colour is an effect. It then penetrates this structure until it detects the elemental qualities of which the structure is itself an effect.[58]

Sight—as a clear and incisive 'perspective' on the world—opens in-eluctably into knowledge because the eyes of the mind and the body are perfectly calibrated. If bodily sight is a power of physical extension (again, the model is extramissionist), 'insight' or understanding pursue the same radiant course. As John Wyclif wrote more than a century later, 'corporeal vision is the means to imaginative and intellectual vision and also more subtle than the other senses and nearer to the intellect . . .'[59]

Grosseteste's account of observation is reminiscent of the ocular pene-trations of courtly romance. But while the acts of observing and desiring are equally invasive, their effects are rather different. The image of rays of light penetrating to the 'deep' structure of an object and illuminating its 'elemental qualities' brings to mind the disembodied and disembodying 'sight' of an x-ray. This is not vision as an expression of desire or envy; it is vision as technology.

The ancient and medieval 'art of memory' follows a similar abstractive and ocularcentric logic (though memory, like vision, is also conceived as a physical impression). As Mary Carruthers explains, the ancients 'persis-tently thought of *memoria* as a kind of eye-dependent reading, a visual process'.[60] And although medieval texts encourage synaesthetic memory images—they speak and sing, 'they play music, they lament, they groan in pain', they smell sweet or foul—the visual image served as a kind of schematic map and anchor.[61] Remembering, like understanding, was a way of seeing. Here is Thomas Bradwardine's advice in 'De Memoria Artificiali', written around 1325–35:

> For trained memory, two things are necessary, that is, firm locations and also images for the material; for the locations are like tablets on which we write, the images like the letters written on them . . . Each location should be of moderate size, as much as one's visual power can comprehend in a single look . . . Indeed memory is most powerfully affected by sensory impression, most strongly by vision; wherefore something occurs in memory as it cus-tomarily occurs in seeing.[62]

In Grosseteste's writings the abstractive and mechanistic attributes of sight are left implicit. Bacon, however, is more expansive on the workings of the 'veridical eye'. He recognised that the validity of experimental knowledge depended on the nature of the relationship between the ob-server and object; between the content of the mind and extramental real-ity.[63] In the absence of a reliable bridge between things and our knowledge of them, how could one be sure that the senses accurately represented ex-ternal reality, or indeed that mental concepts were truthful? For Bacon, this doubt could be dispelled if the relationship between objects and concepts was physical and causal. By placing extramental and mental phenomena on a continuum of progressive abstraction; by making sensible forms or 'species' responsible for all action within that continuum, he believed he could provide perceptual certitude.

Roger Bacon's veridical eye

Roger Bacon is generally credited with extending the programme of experimental science begun by Grosseteste.[64] There is no evidence that the two English scholars knew each other personally, but Grosseteste's writings would almost certainly have been available at Oxford, where Bacon, like his predecessor, joined the Franciscan order and began his major works.[65] By this time (the 1260s), Bacon also had access to translations of a wealth of Arabic material on optics that had not been available to Grosseteste, and it is the synthesis of Greek and Arabic learning for which he is most famous.[66]

One of Bacon's key sources was the Arab mathematician and philosopher Ibn al-Haytham (c. 965–c. 1039), or Alhazen as he was known in the Latin West.[67] Alhazen's theory of intromission was novel in that it fulfilled mathematical as well as physical and psychological criteria. As such, it represented a significant advance on earlier intromissionist models of vision; most notably the atomistic account associated with Epicurus (341–270 BCE), and Aristotle's theory of perception. Epicurus had proposed that particles were 'continually streaming off from the surface of bodies'. These 'films' of atoms retained the colour and shape of their agents, and the 'position and arrangement which their atoms had when they formed part of the solid bodies'.[68] Aristotle's explanation seemed more plausible: sensible objects cause a change in the surrounding medium, which in turn affects the humours of the observer's eye. So the eye 'does not *receive* the visible object, as in the atomistic theory, but *becomes* the visible object'.[69] The problem was that although Aristotle could account for the transmission of colour, he had failed to explain how we perceive shapes or space.[70] He addressed physical, but not mathematical criteria. By synthesising Alhazen's optics, Grosseteste's Neoplatonic account of species, and Aristotle's model of physical causation,[71] Bacon sought to provide a firm and complete foundation for knowledge.

The rest of this chapter will look at Bacon's response to Aristotle's assertion that 'there is no knowledge outside perceiving'.[72] In order to uphold this basic Aristotelian tenet, Bacon had to explain *how* and *what* we perceive; not only in relation to the bodily organs of sensation (external and internal), but in relation to an immaterial intellect. I will treat these interconnected concerns in two parts, beginning with Bacon's geometrical articulation of species and the eye, and concluding with the internal operations of the perceptual continuum.

Picturing vision: Bacon's theory of species

The linchpin of Bacon's project is the role of 'species' as the basic principle of causation and the *modus operandi* of sensation, cognition and intellection. Derived from the Indo-European *spek* ('to see'), the term itself is etymologically rooted in the order of the visible. In this archaic sense, species simply means 'aspect, form, or exterior appearance'.[73] Augustine, for example, described sense perception as the continuity of 'species' from the object, through the bodily senses to the 'gaze of thought'.[74] It is no coincidence that he also regarded all five bodily senses as kinds of sight, of which 'ocular vision is the most perfect'.[75] Bacon's account of species retains this original idea of visual—one might say pictorial—representation; but it also draws on Grosseteste's use of the term to explain the operation of light. Radiating 'from everything in the world to produce effects', species are responsible not only for sensation or thought, but physical causation generally.[76]

I suggested earlier that Grosseteste's philosophy of light made *perspectiva* the basis of natural science, and sight paradigmatic of sensation and knowledge. To these characteristics of 'scientific vision' we can now add the pictorial inflection of species and its synonyms. The latter, listed by Bacon, include: 'similitude', 'image', 'idol' (from the Greek *eidolon*, meaning image or replica), 'simulacrum', 'phantasm', 'form' and 'impression'.[77] In this respect, reality is both geometrically defined and infinitely reproducible; and the eye—as sense organ and as mind—is an organ of pictorial reproduction.[78]

This understanding of species is quite distinct from Platonic, Galenic or Atomistic theories of material emanation, according to which light or particles of matter flow between the object and the eye. Bacon points out that any *transmission* of matter would involve the decomposition or depletion of the agent (an object or its species). Nor is it possible for species to have corporeal being and dimension, for 'the medium and [such a] species could not coexist [in the same place] at the same time'.[79] It is from Aristotle and his Arabic commentators that Bacon derives the principle of *transformation* through a medium, whereby the form or species of an object is reproduced in the air or other transparent medium and subsequently effects a change in the humours of the observer's eye.[80] A species, then, is 'a corporeal form, without, however, dimensions *per se*, but it is produced subject to the dimensions of the air; and it is not produced by a flow from a luminous body, but by a renewing from the potency of the matter of the air . . .'[81]

I will return to the 'potency' of matter in the next chapter; for now, I want to emphasise the paradoxical fact that although species are not objects in any real sense, they do have material existence.

Bodied forth in the matter of air, light, water or the transparent humours of the eye, species have corporeal being. At the same time, they are extended through these material substances by a process of continual regeneration or 'multiplication'. One could say that species colonise matter: the corporeal nature of a species is identical to that of its recipient because the latter is merely a 'host', transformed into the likeness of its coloniser. Or, to use an analogy more in keeping with Bacon's visual orientation, the agent (species) 'impresses' its form on the recipient. Not, strictly speaking, as a seal is reproduced in wax, but in the sense of a deep impression capable of effecting a transformation 'in the interior of the recipient' and not just 'in a surface'.[82]

Bacon's theory of the multiplication of species through a corporeal medium ensures perceptual certitude because the external object, its species, and the mental representation of the object are ontologically continuous. Species not only convey the pictorial 'form' of an object; they are vehicles of meaning. In *De signis* Bacon explains that species are *natural* signs of their objects, because they communicate the nature and essence of those objects to the recipient. Natural signs—those that signify unintentionally by their essence—are differentiated from intentional signs such as discourse and argument, which rely on 'the deliberation of reason and choice of the will . . .'[83] Both sensory 'effect' and natural sign involve a re-presentation of the object independent of any act of the human will, reason or intellect; and as Katherine Tachau notes, 'This relation of natural sign to the object that it "signifies" is the nexus of knowing and meaning (*significatio*).'[84]

We have come some of the way towards accounting for the truth value of knowledge derived from the senses. Bacon's concern with the principles of physical causation, however, is matched, if not surpassed, by his interest in geometry. If the causal theory of species addresses the physical and psychological aspects of sensation and cognition, geometry translates the sensible world into intelligible, reproducible forms: the basic, geometrical components of a 'world picture'. The action of species explains *how* sensation occurs (through predictable causes and effects); geometry describes *what* we see. It should be noted that while both theories are premised on a dichotomy of form and matter, sensible species—unlike geometrical forms—reproduce themselves *in matter* (Bacon runs into trouble when he attempts to explain how species pass between an enmattered mind and an incorporeal intellect). Geometry, on the other hand, enabled forms to be isolated or *abstracted from matter*.

This reductive impulse was already present in Grosseteste's vision of a universe comprised of 'lines, angles and figures', a universe mirrored in the microcosm of the human mind. Also present was the primacy of mathematics as the scientist's means of isolating quantities (magnitude and multitude) from the confusion of material existence. Both Domingo Gundisalvo and Hugh of St Victor, writing around the middle of the twelfth century, define mathematics as a method of separating forms (or abstract quantities) from matter.[85] Gundisalvo goes so far as to use the term 'abstractive' as a synonym for 'mathematical', noting that *mathesis* is interpreted as abstraction'.[86] He also identifies four successive levels of mathematical abstraction, beginning with bodily sight (there is no suggestion that the other senses might have an abstractive function). Because sight 'apprehends [the form of a thing] only in the presence of matter', it effects a partial abstraction. Further abstraction takes place in the internal senses of imagination and estimation (or judgement). The intellect, however, 'apprehends forms with perfect abstraction', entirely 'stripped of matter'.[87] Bacon's application of mathematics (specifically geometry) to the visible world, to the perception of that world, and to the anatomy of the eye, should be seen against the background of this abstractive logic.

Like Grosseteste, Bacon's optical theory is based on the equivalence of species (as a general force) and light. Visible light is used as the model for all species because 'the multiplication of light is more apparent to us than the multiplication of other things, and therefore we transfer the [terminology of the] multiplication of light to the others'.[88] Species behave like radiant light in their conformity to geometrical principles. As a consequence, 'the lines along which multiplication [of species] occurs must be straight, in so far as the nature of multiplication determines, until they meet impediments that cause reflection and refraction or are altered for the sake of the soul's needs . . .'[89] Here, in a sentence, is the backbone of geometrical optics. We now need to consider how this perspectival science shores up the veracity of sensory and mental 'representations'.

Bacon accepted the basic proposition that the visible world interacts with us through an infinite number of rays of light, radiating outward from every point on the surface of objects to the entire surface of a beholder's eye.[90] The problem was: if the eye received light indiscriminately from all points in the visual field, the result would be confusion. Drawing on Euclidean geometry, Alhazen had proposed a mathematical theory of vision in order to explain how objects were reproduced in the eye if their forms were not transmitted as coherent entities. The crux of this theory, which Bacon adopted in turn, was that only those rays that penetrate the eye at an angle *perpendicular* to its convex surface are strong enough to form a distinct impression. Other rays, falling obliquely on the lens, are refracted and therefore weakened.[91] A visual pyramid or cone is formed by the perpendicular rays, with its base coinciding with the surface of the object and its apex in the centre of the eye. Although a potentially infinite number of these pyramids will encounter the convex surface of the cornea, Bacon insists that:

> the chief requirement is that vision should perceive distinctly the object itself both with certainty and sufficiency, and this can be done by means of one pyramid in which there are as many lines as there are parts or points in the body seen. Along these lines the separate impressions come from the individual parts to the anterior glacialis [lens], in which is the visual force. And those lines will terminate at the individual parts of the glacialis, so that the impressions of the parts of the thing seen are arranged on the surface of the perceiving member just as the parts are arranged in the thing itself . . . Those lines, moreover, are perpendicular to the eye, in order that stronger impressions may come, so that it may be possible to see with perfect vision and judge concerning the thing as it really is.[92]

Bacon employs this figure of the 'radiant pyramid' in order to account for the perception of size, shape and distance with mathematical precision;[93] and his distinction between 'strong' perpendicular and 'weak' refracted rays is an attempt to explain the eye's ability to focus on one or more objects, or part of an object, with everything falling outside this range remaining indistinct. Bacon suggests that there are in fact two pyramids: the 'visual' or 'radiant' pyramid described above, the rays of which penetrate the eye perpendicularly effecting a sharp image; and a 'greater pyramid', inclusive of but exceeding the perimeters of the principal pyramid. Rays of light from the periphery of the visual field (Bacon's greater pyramid) strike the pupil obliquely and, 'since the species falling perpendicularly is the strong one, therefore the perpendicular species conceals all the oblique ones'. This is not to say that the objects in our peripheral vision are occluded; but rather that they are seen 'imperfectly'.[94]

The visual pyramid also circumscribes the eye's visual power. Citing Augustine, Bacon asserts that the soul produces its own species, which are extended from the eye, through the medium, to the object of sight. These animate species (of the soul, *anima*) are required to 'ennoble' the inanimate species propagated by the object, thereby rendering the latter 'analogous to vision'.[95] More will be said of this process in the next chapter. Of relevance here is Bacon's claim that 'the species of the eye . . . travels in the locality of the visual pyramid',[96] and moreover, that these species, like any other, obey the laws of ray geometry. Just as the *intromitted* rays of a visible object form their apex in the eye, so too the species *emitted* by the eye form vertices on every point of the object. Thus:

> from the surface of the glacialis [lens] there are pyramids in an infinite number, all of which have one base, and the vertices of these pyramids fall upon the separate points of the thing seen, so that . . . all parts of the visible object are seen with such intensity as is possible.[97]

Predictably, this convergence of animate and inanimate species within the visual pyramid is at its greatest intensity along the axis of the pyramid, perpendicular to its base, and 'passing through the center of all parts of the eye . . .'[98]

Bacon's insistence on a demonstrable point-by-point correspondence between objects in the world and their species received in the eye relates directly to the statement that sight, more than the other senses, is the basis of knowledge. We have seen that the relation of physical causation between objects in the world, sense data and mental concepts privileges sight by analogy (that is, by describing tactile or auditory sensations as simulacra). In addition, the treatment of all species as variants of light effectively subsumes all sensation within the optical paradigm of ray geometry. Yet geometrical optics is of limited use as an explanatory model for hearing, taste, touch and smell: a criticism raised in the fourteenth century by William of Ockham.

Ockham argued that the perspectivist theory of species—and its corollary, the idea of sensation as representation—is based on the erroneous assumption that vision is the 'prototypical sense'.[99] Dispensing with species altogether, he maintained that perception and cognition occur through intuition and abstraction, at a distance, and without the mediation of species. Effectively dismantling the causal and mathematical logic of perspectivism that had guaranteed the primacy of sight in relation to knowledge, Ockham states unequivocally that 'there is intuitive cognition in every sense, interior as well as exterior . . . granted, this is not ocular intuitive cognition. And in this, many are deceived: for they believe that there is no intuitive cognition unless it is ocular, which is false.'[100]

Ockham's radical departure from the perspectivist programme was, significantly, rejected by the majority of his contemporaries.[101] The reason for this, as Tachau explains, was that the *species in medio* had seemed necessary to most late thirteenth- and early fourteenth-century thinkers, who understood cognition to involve a process of abstraction from sense experience'.[102] To this enduring conception of species as a mode of action amenable to progressive abstraction from material objects to mental concepts might be added the appeal of mathematics as an abstractive science; and also a pervasive tendency to think of sensation in terms of representation. For Bacon, these ideas are inseparable from the conviction that sight has a special relationship to science. Although he extends the action of species to sensation in general, only in sight do we find an attempt to apply geometry to the organ of sense itself.

While species propagated through touch, for instance, must follow the 'twisting threads of the nerves from the skin of the body through winding paths to the instrument of touch',[103] the acuity of sight is ensured by the underlying geometrical principles not only of the external world or the light that illuminates it; but also by the geometrical structure of the eye. For Bacon, the eye was made up of three membranes and three humours. These are shown here in an illustration from the *Opus majus* (Fig. 3.1).

Moving inwards from the outer skin of the eye, the first membrane is the consolidativa or conjunctiva. The second membrane, the uvea, includes the cornea—so called because of its resemblance to 'transparent horn'— which allows light to pass through the pupil. Finally, the retina forms the 'interior coat of the [optic] nerve, which comes from the pia mater'.[104] The sacs formed by these membranes contain three humours: the humour albugineus, the glacial humour (the anterior part of which forms the lens, or anterior glacialis), and the vitreous humour.[105] I will return to the physiology of eye in Chapter 4. What is of interest here is that Bacon makes much of the eye's sphericity, and the geometrical relation of its parts. 'The whole eye', he writes in the *Opus majus*, 'approaches the form of a sphere, and the coats likewise and the humors owing to the admirable qualities of the spherical form, because it is less subject to obstacles than a figure with angles, and is simpler than other figures . . .'[106]

When he considers the relationship of the coats and humours, however, Bacon is forced to concede that they do not form concentric spheres. The eye, in other words, does not have one centre, but many. What seems at first to be a deviation from mathematical principles turns out to be further evidence of the eye's precise geometrical calibration. As Bacon goes on to say:

> although the centers are different in the parts of the eye, yet all are in the same line, which is perpendicular to the whole eye and to all its parts . . . This line is the axis of the eye, by which the eye sees with certainty and by which it passes over the separate points of a visible object, so that it may make certain of each in succession . . . *This arrangement is a necessary one, in order that the eye may grasp most strongly and with utmost certainty what it should* [emphasis added].[107]

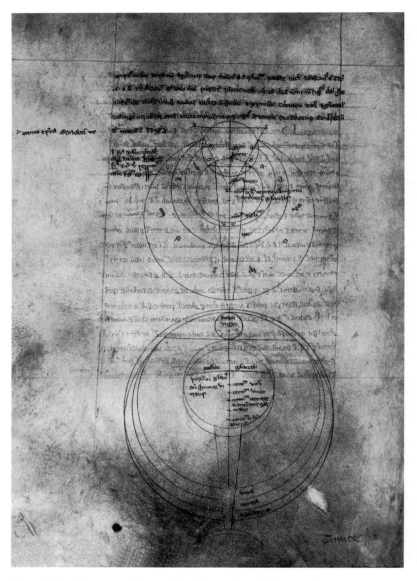

Figure 3.1.   Diagram of the eye from Roger Bacon's *Opus majus*.

Why should the soul prefer perpendicular lines, when Bacon has argued elsewhere that sensible species can be diverted by the sensitive soul along 'twisting paths'? The answer is surely that geometry signifies certainty and intelligibility. Furthermore, by imposing a geometrical structure upon the eye it is transformed from an opaque bodily organ into an object and instrument of knowledge. In *De multiplicatione specierum* Bacon makes the point that 'in a medium animated by the power of the soul'[108] a species is not bound by the laws of rectilinear multiplication. Species propagated through an inanimate medium, on the other hand, are confined entirely to 'straight lines'.[109] While Bacon by no means envisaged the eye as inanimate, it nonetheless begins to resemble a tool for 'taking pictures'. Certainly it is no longer a libidinous organ of the flesh.

The perceptual continuum

I have been concentrating on the physical and geometrical relationship between objects and the eye, but Bacon's commitment to intromission demanded that he negotiate a path through the otherwise discontinuous realms of matter and intellect. It bears repeating that the polarisation of sight into outer (carnal or corporeal) and inner (spiritual or intellectual) operations saw the bodily senses relegated to the domain of the flesh, foreclosing on sensation as a valid source of knowledge. To evaluate Bacon's attempt at bridging this polarity we will need to follow the trajectory of his sensible species beyond the material plenum of the sensible world,[110] and the geometrical mechanism of the eye, through the internal senses and finally within the realm of pure intellection. Here too we shall find Bacon using the theory of species (not entirely successfully) to locate extramental objects on a continuum: not only with embodied mental concepts, but with an incorporeal intellect.

Comprising five internal senses—the common sense, imagination, estimation, memory and cogitation—the sensitive soul consisted of the 'marrow-like substance of the brain' joined with the immaterial powers of the soul.[111] As bodily organs housed in three chambers within the cranial cavity, the internal senses provided the latent matter necessary for the actualisation of sensible and intelligible species; and as cognitive powers they organised and evaluated sensory information.[112] I will outline Bacon's account of each of these faculties, before turning to the problem of an immaterial and active intellect.

At the front of the anterior chamber is the common sense which, as its name suggests, receives the species from the individual sense organs. In addition to this aggregation of the object, however, the common sense also 'judges concerning each particular sensation', so that the whiteness of milk, for example, is differentiated from its sweetness.[113] The common sense is coupled with the imagination, located directly behind it in the same chamber. While the 'excessive slipperiness' of the common sense makes it unsuitable for the retention of species, the imagination is physiologically disposed, 'owing to its tempered moistness and dryness', to retain the impression of species conducted through the common sense.[114] As such, the imagination serves as the 'coffer and repository of the common sense'.[115]

Together, the organs of the anterior chamber apprehend twenty-nine sensible properties. In addition to the 'special properties' associated with sight (light and colour), touch (heat and cold, moistness and dryness), smell (odours) and taste (flavours), there are some less predictable inclusions such as writing and painting as well as 'eagerness, laughter, and sadness' which, Bacon explains, are 'apprehended from the figure and form of the face'.[116] Clearly, then, we are not dealing with 'raw' sense impressions, or with the intellectual interpretation of sense data. Meaning already inheres in the object and its sensory simulacrum.

The chamber at the back of the skull houses the estimative and memorative faculties whose receptive and retentive functions parallel those of the common sense and imagination, but are attuned to the 'insensible' nature of sensible objects. By 'insensible' Bacon means innate qualities that are not reducible to the sensory contents of sight, hearing, touch, taste or smell, and are therefore not apprehended by the common sense and imagination. These 'complexions' or complex forms trigger instinctual behaviour in animals, as well as the emotive content of the sensitive soul. Just as proper sensibles inform the common sense and imagination, so too certain objects 'produce strong impressions, which change greatly the sensitive soul, so that it is moved to states of fear, horror, flight, or the opposites'.[117] In his lectures on Aristotle's De anima, Aquinas explained the workings of memory in similar terms. Memory images, he said, 'dwell within' us as 'traces of actual sensations . . . just as sensations arouse appetitive impulses [emotions] whilst the sensed objects are present, so do images when these are absent'.[118] Psychological states, then, are not subjective responses to a thing or a situation, but originate in the objects themselves.

Cogitation, located in the middle cell, is described by Bacon as 'the mistress of the sensitive faculties'.[119] Though it is not identical with reason (and so is found in animals as well as in the human soul), the cogitative sense in man is united to the rational soul 'primarily and immediately'.[120] In the hierarchy of the human soul, cogitation has a direct instrumental relationship to intellection or rational thought, just as it in turn subordinates the four 'lower' internal senses to its requirements.[121] The sensitive soul, thus conceived, is both body and mind. As Tachau points out, this complicates any notion of a mind–body dualism. Because the human mind and soul (both designated by the term *anima*) are embodied, the issue for Bacon and his contemporaries was not how the mind interacts with the body, but 'how an immaterial intellect grasps material entities'.[122]

So far I have described the transmission of species from objects to the eye, and the internal operations of the sensitive soul: those faculties (common to humans and animals) that link sense impressions received in the external sense organs to the content of the mind. We have seen, too, that continuity between objects and concepts is provided for by a physiological account of perception in which sensation and cognition are modelled on physical causation, and that this theory enables Bacon to regard mental concepts and affective states as the natural and necessary effects of extramental objects. The real gulf, then, is not between objects and their cognitive representation within a receptive, incarnate mind. Objects and mind (or at least the sensitive faculties of the mind) already exist on a material continuum. Rather, to reiterate Tachau's point, Bacon's dilemma is how a definitively immaterial and separable agent intellect can interact with this passive, embodied mind.

In the *Opus majus* Bacon follows Aristotle and Avicenna in differentiating between an active (or agent) intellect and a possible (or potential) intellect.[123] The latter, wedded to the body, is roughly approximate to the rational soul, which derives its content from species impressed in the sensitive soul. It is 'potential' in the same way that the eye and the internal senses are actualised by species originating in the sensible world; and this is why Bacon can claim that species act on the intellect in the same way that they act on matter and on sense.[124] The multiplication of species thus represents a chain of causation extending from 'agents' in the material world to the potential intellect, *but only insofar as this intellect is embodied.* This 'real' connection between sense and intellect (or matter and spirit) underpinned the Aristotelian principle that sense perception is a precondition of knowledge. The problem with the idea of a purely *receptive* intellect, however, is that it excludes human agency, including the existence of free will.[125]

The problem of free will must have contributed to Bacon's equivocation on the existence and role of the active intellect. It certainly makes sense of his determined (if ultimately unsuccessful) efforts to graft an Augustinian account of active intellection on to the basic Aristotelian model of a sense-based epistemology (that 'perceptual continuum' stretching from objects to their mental likenesses).[126] Unlike the potential intellect, the active intellect is 'not attached to an organ like other parts of the soul'.[127] It is a definitively spiritual substance: incorruptible, immaterial and separable; and it functions both as a repository of universal truths and as a source of divine illumination.[128] Just as natural vision requires the presence of natural (corporeal) light, so the intellect requires spiritual illumination in order to 'see'—and therefore know—its objects.[129]

It would seem that a true continuum of sensation and intellection can be achieved only at the expense of an agent intellect; and that conversely, a separable, disembodied intellect replete with innate knowledge would have little need for sense perception. Bacon is clearly caught between the two conflicting imperatives of his generation. As a scientist he is attentive to the world of sensible forms; as a Christian he cannot dispense with a realm of pre-existent, universal and immutable truths. But while Bacon's synthesis exemplifies the difficulty of reconciling science and theology, I have suggested that it also illuminates their points of convergence. Both science and theology are motivated by a desire for epistemological certainty: either through the abstraction of concepts from sensations, or by virtue of a transcendental, illuminating intellect. And as Steven Goldman argued, both exhibit an iconic tendency. In this respect, the symbolising mentality associated with medieval Christianity is continuous with the mathematical 'allegories' of medieval science. The next chapter will further complicate the idea of a Western scientific perspective by elucidating aspects of Bacon's optics in which sight is treated not as a geometrical abstraction, but as a dynamic and transformative bodily phenomenon.

CHAPTER 4

THE OPTICAL BODY

We are what we desire and what we look at.[1]

Plotinus

W e saw in the last chapter that sight could provide a secure foundation for scientific knowledge by virtue of its privileged relation to
the mind and its conformity to mathematical principles. As such, medieval
optics played an important part in the rationalisation and disembodiment
of vision; distancing the eye from the inchoate and obscuring matter of the
flesh. This chapter will approach the optical gaze from a different direction. Instead of asking how Bacon's optics anticipates modern science, I
will consider its residual affinity with carnal vision. Indicative of this affinity between thirteenth-century science and other medieval discourses of
vision is the reciprocity implicit in Bacon's synthesis of intromission
and extramission optics; his emphasis on physical contact so that looking
becomes analogous to touching; the idea that we are altered in every act
of perception; and finally the inescapable presence of ocular desire. In light
of these more foreign aspects of the optical gaze, we can begin to rethink
the relationship between the subject and object of vision, and between science and sight.

Roger Bacon's commitment to a mathematical and causal theory of
intromission was largely motivated by a desire to guarantee perceptual certitude and, by extension, the legitimacy of experimental knowledge: if
things external to us are able to reproduce their essential qualities in
our senses and minds then the content of the mind is assuredly objective.[2]
According to this model of causality, the agency of sight resides in sensible
objects, the impressions of which are merely received and retained by
sentient beings. Certain difficulties arise, however, from an exclusively
intromissionist account of perception. As we have seen, the theory sits

uneasily alongside the doctrines of free will and intellectual agency. Furthermore, Bacon himself points out that the eye is not only the organ we see with: it is also a visible object and must therefore propagate its own species. How else, he asks, would it be possible to see one's own eyes in a mirror?[3]

That the eye is more than a receptive instrument is, as far as Bacon is concerned, beyond dispute. The question is whether these emitted species constitute a 'force of vision'.[4] Do the eyes merely radiate sensible species like any other material object? Or do they actively 'see' by conducting the sensitive soul into the sensible world? Bacon's conclusion can accommodate both propositions. Vision, he says, is both 'active and passive' because 'it receives the species of the thing seen, and exerts its own force in the medium as far as the visible object'.[5] In one respect, the eye behaves like any other body in its active propagation of species. We might call this the weak version of extramission. More significant is Bacon's acceptance of the Platonic idea that the soul sees (and is seen in turn) through the bodily eyes. This 'strong' account of extramission treats the visual 'force' as a literal—not poetic or metaphorical—extension of the embodied soul.

Bacon's account of visual species represents an effort to retain a robust theory of intromission while reserving an active role for the observer that answers to theological and psychological requirements. While it would be possible to catalogue the inconsistencies arising from the resulting synthesis, this would be to overlook Bacon's motives. The appeal of intromission as an objective, causal account of perception was discussed in the last chapter. What I want to emphasise here is that the *synthesis* of extramission and intromission gives rise to a perceptual *relationship*, as distinct from a unidirectional act of perception. As such, Bacon's account differs from modern theories of perception, which as Merleau-Ponty points out, typically fall into one of two camps: idealism or empiricism.[6]

Exemplified by the Cartesian *cogito*, the idealist or intellectualist model makes the world a product of our thoughts (or those of a divine Creator). Consciousness is thus prior to, and constitutive of reality. Empiricist accounts of sense-perception work in the opposite direction, so that our perceptions and knowledge become products or reflections of a pre-existing world. Ultimately, empiricism brackets out our *encounter* with the world, treating our bodies, perceptions, even thoughts as 'parts or moments of the Great Object'.[7] For Merleau-Ponty, this 'absolute object'—no less than the 'divine subject' of idealism—denies the lived experience of perception.[8] Our experience of perception is inherently contradictory: on the one hand, the act of seeing seems to take us outside our bodies, into the world; yet on the other hand what we see is inside us, somewhere 'behind' our eyes. To quote Merleau-Ponty, 'my vision is at the thing itself', but it is also 'my own or "in me"'.[9]

Bacon's synthesis could be read as an attempt to embrace (rather than resolve) these contradictory propositions of what Merleau-Ponty calls the 'perceptual faith': the conviction that sight is both inside *and* exterior to us.[10] What Bacon offers, in the final analysis, is an objective, extramental world that reproduces itself in the mind; and an equally real sphere of human agency, consciousness and curiosity.

Reciprocal vision

Bacon cites Plato, Ptolemy, Tideus, Euclid, Augustine and Alkindi on the existence of visual rays or species; rays that are emitted from the eye and extend to the object seen.[11] Careful to distance himself from Plato's assertion that this action of one's own visual power is sufficient in itself, he argues instead that emitted species are necessary to *complete* vision.[12] Specifically, sight occurs when the species emitted by objects are '*aided and excited* by the species of the eye' (emphasis added).[13] The nature of this change is only hinted at, and relies on a distinction between 'animate' and 'inanimate' species. Thus, the species emitted by the observer's eye 'prepares the passage of the species itself of the visible object, and, moreover, ennobles it, so that it is quite similar and analogous to the nobility of the animate body, which is the eye'.[14] Evidently for Bacon, the eye is not simply an object like any other: it is only as an organ of the sensitive soul ('animate') that it has the power to 'ennoble' and assimilate the sensible species of inanimate objects. But, as we shall shortly see, this assimilation of the object's inanimate species to the animate eye of the observer also occurs in reverse. Bacon, following Aristotle, regards perception as a bodily alteration in the perceiving subject, a 'transmutation' effected by the object and its species. What results is a *mutual* assimilation of subject and object.

The philosophical implications of the type of visual interaction described by Bacon have not gone unremarked. Martin Jay has commented that medieval theories of vision seem to emphasise intimacy and reciprocity rather than separation and, in so doing, cast doubt on the notion of a detached observer. Following Hans-Georg Gadamer and others, Jay extrapolates from this mode of looking an epistemological attitude based not on objectivity, but on participation. Intellectual vision (of which knowledge is a product) could, like physical sight, be imagined as an 'intertwining of viewer and viewed'.[15]

From a twentieth-century perspective, the idea of visual reciprocity is untenable for at least two reasons. First, it implies that in some way—like Lacan's glinting sardine can—the world *looks back* even if we are not 'seen' by it in any anthropomorphic sense.[16] I will return to this point later in the chapter. Second, although we think of vision as an active force, a 'gaze' that extends into the world, this aspect of sight is not ascribed physical existence. The gaze, notes Teresa Brennan, is 'immaterial, symbolic indeed, "metaphorical"'.[17] She suggests, plausibly, that the theory of extramission was finally rejected not because it was incompatible with scientific advances in optical theory, but rather because the idea of an active eye and its physical gaze was at odds with a model of physical sight that stressed passivity in order to ensure the veracity of its internal 'representations'.[18] Increasingly envisaged as a camera obscura, the eye merely registered sense impressions: it did not seek out, probe or penetrate its objects.

Given the modern 'split' in vision between '[active] psychical and [passive] physical effects',[19] it is not surprising that historians have sometimes interpreted the theory of extramission as a psychological account of perception. It has been suggested, for example, that Bacon (and Grosseteste before him) conceived of extramission as 'a psychological act of vision' quite distinct from 'the physical light which went from the visible object to the eye'.[20] Seen in this way, extramission becomes a cognitive disposition rather than a physical engagement. And intromission, isolated from subjective psychological factors, can be treated as a more or less coherent, optical and physiological account of sensation. However, I find no evidence in Bacon's optical writings of such a separation of the psychical and physical aspects of sight. The very fact that the mind is understood as an organ composed of body and soul suggests that we are dealing here with a psychosomatic unity and not isolated functions.[21]

If Bacon regards species as having *corporeal* existence when joined with the material substance of the air, water or sense organs, then the intertwining of subject and object in carnal, spiritual and intellectual vision exercised more than the medieval imagination. There is, however, another important reason why extramitted as well as intromitted species were assumed to have real existence in the thirteenth century: the veracity of knowledge derived from the senses was premised not on psychological or even physical *disengagement*, but on chains of cause and effect. And as we have seen, these causal relationships depended on the proximity and interaction between agent and recipient.

Vision and distance

Much has been made by contemporary theorists of the 'fact' that vision, more than any other sense, requires and/or interposes a certain distance between subject and object and further, that this physical distance corresponds to the emotional distance of detached intellectual scrutiny.[22] Pointing to the preponderance of this equation in French psychoanalytic theory, Elizabeth Grosz explains that:

> Of all the senses, vision remains the one which most readily confirms the
> separation of subject from object. Vision performs a distancing function,
> leaving the looker unimplicated in or uncontaminated by its object. With all
> of the other senses, there is a contiguity between subject and object, if not
> an internalization and incorporation of the object by the subject.[23]

Common to this line of argument is a tendency to conflate 'vision'—
both physical and epistemological—with geometrical optics. In fact the
visual pyramid described by Bacon has taken its place as one of, if not *the*
dominant metaphor of Western ocularcentrism.[24] More than this, geometrically defined 'perspectival' vision is often installed as the *natural ground*
of objective science and other manifestly ocularcentric discourses.[25] It is
because sight is inherently, 'naturally' distancing that ocular metaphors lend
themselves so readily to discourses of domination, observation, objectification; or so the reasoning goes. If this were correct, one would expect it to
be corroborated by medieval optics—assuming of course that the nature
and culture of ocularcentrism spring from the one perspectival source.

In several respects this expectation is satisfied. Physical sight provides
the prototype for the inner sight of the mind in medieval no less than in
modern thought; and there are unmistakable parallels between the scientific vision described in the last chapter and the kind of vision Grosz writes
about. Yet when we turn to thirteenth-century optics for confirmation of
those supposedly definitive characteristics of perspectivism—detachment,
immobility, disembodiment and mastery—we find a far more ambiguous
picture. For all his apparent efforts to abstract the essence of the optical
gaze from its material existence, Bacon does not assume a disembodied or
distancing gaze. His scientific vision is not even dispassionate. Indicative of
this complexity is his equivocation on the subject of perceptual distance.

At first glance, Bacon appears simply to confirm that distance between
the eye and the object is a requirement for vision. His claim that 'the act
of seeing is the perception of a visible object at a distance' strikes us as self-
evident, and entirely consistent with Grosz's assessment.[26] Yet paradoxically,
the theory of sensible species collapses this distance because it works on a
principle of contact: the species of an object reproduces itself *as a corporeal
entity* between the object and the eye and, from there, through the internal senses. So if the object does not itself come into direct contact with
the eye, its species not only touches the sense organ, but materially alters
it. Bacon's visual pyramid simultaneously creates distance between agent
and recipient by imposing a geometrical framework on vision—and circumscribes a visual field that is, if not quite an extension of the human
body, then akin to the libidinal extrusions of the flesh. If the mathematical
dimension of vision made it uniquely suited to the requirements of

experimental science, the physical operation of sight was analogous to that of the other senses.

A close reading of Bacon does indeed reveal a similarity between the senses, but rather an unexpected one. Far from being a unique feature of vision, distance is regarded as a basic requirement for any sensation, because touch no less than vision or the other extrinsic senses (hearing and smell) requires the existence of a corporeal medium. This might be a 'body' of air, water, glass or crystal, or it might be part of an animate body. For Bacon, 'every sense acts by external transmission, that is, by emitting from itself its own force into the medium, so that the sensible species is returned more fitted to the sense . . .'[27] It is this understanding of perceptual distance—as a *mediating body* and not as empty space—that enables Bacon to state that 'flesh perceives in touch, just as the eye in vision'.[28] Flesh is the medium of touch, of which the 'sensitive force' is located in the nerves beneath the skin. And the eye itself, no less than any external medium, is the medium of sight.

The ease with which Bacon moves between vision and touch must surely lead us to question the notion that vision is *inherently* distancing, let alone antithetical to touch.[29] As a medium and mediator *between* the sensitive soul and the sensible world, the eye, like the skin, is both part of us and external to us. Moreover, by virtue of the passage of species across and through it, the flesh of the skin and eyes constitutes a permeable membrane and not—or not only—the body's border.

The skin's indeterminacy has been fairly widely remarked upon.[30] For Georges Didi-Huberman, the epidermis is 'a complex structure, reticular, defying geometric thinking, separating and non-separated, intervening yet indistinct'.[31] It is at once a protective covering, and an organ of sense; differentiated from the underlying body and its sensory apparatus, but at the same time integral to the body as a locus of sensation. It is difficult to think of the eye and sight in terms of these paradoxes, but if looking and being looked at are analogous to touching and being touched, how is it possible to describe sight in terms of mastery or objectification? Where is the physical and psychical distance—that sense of 'standing back' from one's objects—demanded by the reifying gaze of scientific observation?

A further complication arises from Bacon's understanding of perceptual distance as the existence of an extrinsic medium (air, water or any transparent substance) *or* an intrinsic medium like the skin or humours of the eye. We think of touch and taste as particularly intimate senses, based, as Grosz noted, on 'contiguity' rather than on distance and separation. But as we have seen, for Bacon touch no less than sight requires the distance afforded by an intervening body: a body that separates as well as mediates.

The skin, for example, is said to perceive because 'the sensitive force which is in the nerve scatters its force in the medium of touch . . .'[32] This raises the interesting possibility that *any* medium animated by a 'sensitive force' is in some way sentient—an extension of the perceiving subject. 'Ennobled' by the species of vision, air or water are not so dissimilar to the skin or the jelly-like substance of the eye. In fact Aristotle uses this very analogy. Likening the function of the skin in touch to that of the air in vision, hearing and smell, he writes:

> the flesh plays in touch very much the same part as would be played by an *air-envelope growing round our body*; had we such an envelope we should have supposed that it was by a single organ that we perceived sounds, colours, and smells . . . [emphasis added][33]

Aristotle was not referring to the active power of sight to reach into the visible world. In an extramissionist context, however, his image of atmospheric grafting implies an extension of the sentient body. Indeed Galen had described the action of outgoing visual rays in similar terms. Sight takes place, he said, when, in the presence of light, the air between the eye and its object is infused with pneuma. The intervening medium—air—has the same relation to the eye that the optic nerve, or the nerves near the surface of the skin, have to the brain.[34] Air can be 'sensitive' in the same way that the eye, skin or underlying nerves are loci of sensation. Either way—from the position of Aristotelian intromission *or* Galenic/Platonic extramission—sight is not something that takes place solely in the eye or mind. When Bacon claims that 'vision perceives what is visible by its own force multiplied to the object', it is as if the act of seeing formed an invisible connective tissue between the observer's body and that of the object.[35] Invisible but not immaterial, because species—whether entering or radiating forth from the eye—take on the corporeality of their medium. Understood in this way, vision—like the flesh—exceeds the boundaries of the body.

If sight, as Bacon describes it, is difficult to place because it exceeds the sentient body, so too is the eye. As a *medium* it passively 'receives the impressions of sensible things, so that there may be an act of sensation'.[36] In this respect the eye is no different from the skin or the material substance of the air. Yet as an *organ* of sight the eye '*passes over* the separate points of a visible object', 'grasp[s] its surface and contain[s] its extremities'.[37] More than a receptive medium then, the eye embodies the active faculties of the soul.[38] It is both a fixed, dehumanised point (as the apex of the visual pyramid produced by the object); and an animate power of projection (describing its own pyramid of radiation); at once 'here' on the dilating and contracting surface of the body, and 'there' reaching forward like a hand to grasp or feel its objects. Vision, as Bacon defines it, cannot be pinned down to the absolutes of proximity and distance: to see is to be in at least two places at once.

The disembodied eye

The claim that sight is naturally distancing (or culturally constructed as such) is often coupled with the observation that vision—unlike the other senses—is somehow disembodied. In contrast to touch, taste, hearing and smell, it is proposed that sight is not really a *sensation*, not *felt* or experienced in the way the other senses are. So not only does sight objectify —and thus disembody—its objects; it has the same effect on the viewer. Before I offer a counter-argument based on Bacon's theory of perception as corporeal change or affect, I will outline two versions of visual disembodiment by way of comparison. The first, proposed by Evelyn Keller and Christine Grontkowski, turns on the equation of sight and light, and the privileged relationship between the eye and the intellect. The second, drawn from Lacanian psychoanalysis, aligns sight with the specular self or externalised mirror-image, while touch, taste, smell and hearing are taken to constitute the 'felt' self.

In their survey of the visual metaphors that have informed Western epistemology, Keller and Grontkowski contend that vision 'connects us to the truth as it distances us from the corporeal'.[39] Their argument has two prongs, which correspond loosely to my own division of the optical gaze into carnal and mathematical elements. Sight, they argue, *either* serves as a model of communion and communication—this is the 'erotic' pole of visual experience and knowledge—*or* it functions as a means and metaphor of objectification. Although 'originally intertwined' (the origin, somewhat predictably, being Plato), these metaphoric functions have, 'through history . . . become quite distinct', leaving us with two eyes: the eye of the mind, and the eye of the body.[40]

Setting aside the 'relegated' tradition of visual communion for a moment,[41] it is notable that the objective gaze is distanced from corporeality by virtue of its assimilation to light. Because their argument is grounded in Plato, Keller and Grontkowski discuss metaphorical and functional relationships—eye, sun, light, intellect—that were, in turn, central to medieval theories of vision.[42] They also point to certain implications of these alignments that are consistent with my own discussion of Grosseteste and Bacon. Most importantly, conceived as a kind of pure, radiant light, vision has nothing of the density and opacity, the gross materiality that we asso-ciate with bodies.[43] Abstracted from the bodily eye, sight becomes the privileged instrument for the 'dematerialization of knowledge'.[44]

Towards the end of their essay, Keller and Grontkowski speculate about the reason for this disembodiment of sight in Western science and episte-mology. It ensures, they contend, that 'knowledge is safeguarded from desire'.[45] Why is desire so undesirable? Because it is 'intimately associated with the female', or more exactly, with the implicitly disruptive forces of feminine eroticism.[46] Thus, motive and method are laid at the door of 'patriarchal culture'.[47]

While I agree that the 'man' of reason is typically hostile to his fleshly 'wife', the bond—as Augustine realised—is perhaps more intimate than Keller and Grontkowski suggest. Desire, eroticism, human bodily exis-tence: all these are wedded to the abstractive and objectifying aspects of Bacon's optics. I would therefore be more inclined to see femininity and flesh as inter-implicated in the masculinist mythologies of science, at least in the later Middle Ages. Bacon *needs* the body just as he cannot dispense with desire. If one wants to highlight the sexualised poetic economy in which these terms circulated (as I have in previous chapters, though Bacon does not do so explicitly) then femininity is the not entirely trustworthy handmaiden of experimental science.

There is a more serious problem with Keller and Grontkowski's argu-ment for a progressive disembodiment of vision. Quite simply, there is no *embodied* gaze in their account to begin with. Visual communion as described by Plato is 'intangible', transcendent: in a word, 'incorporeal'.[48] His idea of ocular eroticism is (they argue) a 'meeting of soul with soul'.[49] Indeed, one senses that on some (unargued) level the authors regard vision as 'naturally' disembodied. Why else would they conclude with the obser-vation that 'Sight does not require our being part of the material world in the way in which feeling by touching does?'[50] Had they paused over Aristotle or Roger Bacon on their way from Plato to Descartes, a differ-ent picture would surely have emerged.[51]

Where Keller and Grontkowski attempt to make sense of the way we 'view' our world by tracing its historical antecedents, the psychoanalytic model of visual disembodiment is ontogenetic. Lacan's famous account of the 'mirror stage' details the role of sight in the formation of the indi-vidual, the 'I'.[52] The mirror stage is associated with the inception of the child's ego: its sense of an autonomous, coherent and bounded self.[53] By placing Bacon's understanding of vision side-by-side with Lacan's, I want to foreground the *strangeness* of Bacon's ideas from a twentieth-century perspective, while at the same time illuminating points of consonance between the two.

Lacan begins by noting that from around six to eighteen months the human infant displays less 'instrumental intelligence' or motor coordination than a chimpanzee, yet is able to 'recognize as such his own image in a mirror'.[54] As a result of this paradox, the reflected image is both *accurate*— it matches the child's movements and gestures—and *delusory*, for it is not (or not yet) the body of the child's fragmentary, incoherent experience. Accordingly, the reflection in the mirror is a source of both alienation and narcissistic delight: while it jubilantly takes in the image of itself as a stable, unified identity, the child also experiences frustration and anger because its *felt* body falls short of that unity and stability. For Lacan, these two experiences of the self—one felt, the other seen—are never fully reconciled: one cannot ever attain the completeness, the unified and stable presence of one's specular double. The resulting vacillation between identity and difference, self-recognition and alienation, is the origin of a fundamental ambivalence that characterises the subject's relationship with itself and others.[55]

What interests me in this account—and particularly in Grosz's reading of Lacan—is that the split in the subject corresponds to a split between vision and sensation or 'looking' and 'feeling'.[56] The infant's 'sensory' or 'kinaesthetic' experiences (Grosz's terms) coincide with the *lived* body, the body 'it claims as its own'.[57] It is important to remember that at this stage these experiences—smells, tastes, and sounds, the feel of things on the skin, the sense of one's own muscular exertions—are not integrated. The specular body, on the other hand, is an integrated totality: 'an other [the child] strives to be like'.[58] In the mirror the child sees itself from *outside*, from a position of exteriority. It becomes an object (for itself and for others) *as well as* a subject.

The question is, what is vision if not sensation? We already have part of the answer: for Grosz, vision is something that distances. Because of this effect, the 'look is the domain of domination and mastery; it provides access to its object without necessarily being in contact with it'.[59] The delineation of sight from sensation and motility (Grosz's 'sensory' and 'kinaesthetic' experiences) is understandable only if vision is interpreted as a psychical—not bodily—phenomenon. Here is what Lacan says about our specular other/selves:

> this [visual] *Gestalt* . . . symbolizes the mental permanence of the *I*, at the same time as it prefigures its alienating destination; it is still pregnant with the correspondences that unite the *I* with the statue in which man projects himself, with the phantoms that dominate him, or with the automaton in which, in an ambiguous relation, the world of his own making tends to find completion.[60]

Statues, phantoms, automata: Lacan's choice of terms for the visual and visible 'I' are as far removed from *bodily* existence as Robert Grosseteste's luminous, weightless 'bodies' of the resurrection (which in their own way were haunted by an alienating, 'felt' experience of the flesh). My point is that both Lacan and Grosseteste align sight with mind or psyche (for Grosseteste it would be the rational soul), rather than body (for Grosseteste, the *fleshly* body). And both emphasise the relationship between vision and geometrically defined light.[61]

There are evident similarities, then, between the child's induction into the specular economy in the mirror stage, and the abstractive and decorporealised model of sight that I elaborated in the last chapter. Conceived as hostile to the biological rhythms and inscrutable interiority of the body, vision lends itself to the abstractive endeavours of objective science. As I have been arguing in this chapter, however, there is another dimension to medieval vision, one that is definitively a bodily process. In fact, Bacon both exploits and resists the dichotomising structures of inside and outside, thinking and feeling. We have seen that the reciprocity and proximity in Bacon's theory of vision confound the notion that sight is inherently distancing or objectifying. In the next section I will extend this line of argument. As an account of embodied vision, my reading of Bacon will address the historical and theoretical gap in Keller and Grontkowski's analysis. More specifically, it will show that sight *can* be understood as a physical affect, a 'feeling' on or in the body; and as a form of motility—both voluntary (as one moves through the visible world), and in the sense that we are 'moved' by objects.

Seeing and feeling

In the fourteenth century William of Ockham claimed that the intellect was capable of grasping its objects intuitively, at a distance. By dispensing with the theory of species, and the Aristotelian principle of physical causation, he effectively 'denied the need for sensation'.[62] I begin with Ockham's intervention because it foregrounds the ambiguous status of sight, in the Middle Ages as well as today. His theory of intuition (by this Ockham meant an act of the mind, independent of the body) also provides a more immediate counterpoint to Bacon's emphasis on the *physical interaction* between object and sense organ. Fundamentally, for Bacon, sight is a change in the sensitive humours and membranes of the eye; and as such, it is accompanied by a certain amount of pain. Here is his description of the effect of intromitted species on the lens:

[The anterior glacialis] must be somewhat thick, in order that it may experience a feeling from the impressions [species] that is a kind of pain. For we observe that strong lights and colour narrow vision and injure it, and inflict pain . . . Therefore vision always experiences a feeling that is a kind of pain . . .[63]

This image of responsive, mutable biological matter is a long way from Bacon's geometrical articulation of the eye as an instrument for seeing. Indeed, it is closer to the contemporary literary tropes of ocular penetration or wounding. Central to both discourses of vision—amatory and scientific—is the idea that we are altered by the things we look at; that the objects of our gaze 'move' us physically and emotionally. It is significant—and further evidence of the complex relationship between carnal vision and the optical gaze—that this movement or alteration is denoted by the term 'passion' (*passio*).

In Chapter 1 we saw that passion—defined as any violent physical or emotional change—was a characteristic of the fleshly body. A 'passion' was something one underwent or endured; a process of transformation. As such, the action of species 'is called "passion" because the medium and sense, in receiving species, undergo a transmutation in their substance . . .'[64] Moreover, just as 'passion' in current English usage suggests a state in which the line between pain and pleasure is indistinct, so too sensation is for Bacon a source of pleasure or delight as well as a kind of suffering. He notes that 'although in sense there is some suffering and injury . . . nevertheless there is simultaneously a pleasure that prevails over the suffering and injury . . .'[65]

The potential of sight to cause physiological change is a recurring motif in medieval theology as well as folklore, the obvious example being the evil eye. So far my examples have been confined to the ocular intercourse between human agents and recipients, but for Bacon the sight of any object, living or inanimate, would precipitate a 'transmutation' in the viewer. There was nothing novel in this: Augustine had cited a number of phenomena illustrating our extraordinary responsiveness to the visible world. These range from the predictable—the chameleon's ability to assume the colours of its surroundings—to the bizarre. For instance, he reports that the tender and malleable flesh of foetuses will 'follow the inclination of their mothers' soul, and the phantasy which arose in it [the soul] through the body upon which it looked with passion'.[66] Bacon's more prosaic explanation is that:

before the action, the recipient [medium or sense organ] is of itself dissimilar to the agent, and through the action it becomes similar . . . and when the

agent acts on the recipient, it at once assimilates the latter to itself and makes
the recipient to be such as the agent is in actuality . . .[67]

This is not an account of a mental event. Following Aristotle, Bacon insists that sensation occurs in the bodily organs of sense: the eyes, the nerves
of the skin and surrounding flesh, the internal organs of the brain. It bears
repeating that we are not, therefore, dealing with a duality of mind and
body; nor a mind–body 'problem'. The images of the visible world reproduced in the eyes and brain are, for Bacon as for Aristotle, *material* images.
The separable intellect may be able to grasp pure abstractions, but the
sensitive soul is embodied; its perceptions and emotions enmattered.[68]

Grosz's polarisation of seeing and feeling does not work in an
Aristotelian or Baconian context. Seeing *is* feeling in every sense: a physical 'touch', a sensation of pleasure and pain, an emotion 'expressed in
matter'.[69] It is also a movement. I have argued already that sight, for Bacon
and his contemporaries, involved an extension of the sensitive soul (or, in
a different context, the flesh) beyond the body's visible limits. According
to this interpretation of extramission, sight is not only the most spatialised
of the senses; it is a form of motility. If we read descriptions of the roaming, grasping, probing or penetrating eye as literal rather than metaphorical, then medieval vision had a kinaesthetic dimension. It involved a
sensation of movement (from the Greek *kineo*, 'move' and *aisthesis*, 'sensation'). Once again, the existence of a mobile, palpating gaze disrupts
Lacan's concept of a static visual *gestalt*.

The theory of extramission is implicit in the idea that sight is a way of
moving around in the world. But intromission was also understood as a
kind of movement or alteration of the viewer: Bacon's word was 'transmutation'. When we talk of being 'moved' by something, we are using a
figure of speech that derives ultimately from the Aristotelian precept that
sensation is a 'qualitative alteration (*alloiosis*)'.[70] To perceive or sense (there
is no distinction between sensation and perception for Aristotle or Bacon)
is to be materially altered.[71] An alteration is not, of course, a movement
(*kinesis*) from one place to another. Instead, the term refers to the actualisation of a potential in matter. It is a precondition of sensation that the
sentient soul is 'potentially like what the perceived object is actually . . .'[72]
Even when dormant our bodily senses must have the capacity and
proclivity for sensation, in the same way that fuel is combustible but 'never
ignites itself spontaneously'.[73]

Potentiality is an actively receptive state of being: visible species are
reproduced through transparent substances and through the sense organs
because they are 'brought forth out of the *active potency* of matter' (emphasis added).[74] While the agent 'informs' or impresses itself upon latent

matter, the potentiality of that matter actively draws forth the species from an adjacent medium. So the receptive humours of the eye elicit species from the surrounding air; the organ of the imagination draws forms from the common sense, and so on throughout the perceptual continuum. As Aristotle put it, matter desires form as the female desires the male.[75] I will say more about this sexualisation of perception later. What is important here is that the idea that we are 'moved', altered or affected by things in our sensory world presupposes a capacity and desire to be moved or affected.

As a condition of latent matter, potentiality is for Bacon a pre-requisite for any perceptual or cognitive act. But there was another, quite different sense in which potential was realised in perception. Plotinus had written of 'percipients and things perceived' as 'members of one living being'.[76] From a Neoplatonic point of view, perception depended not on the active potency of matter—or indeed on any causal relationship between agents and recipients—but on a psychological disposition of the subject: a sympathy with one's objects (the term Plotinus uses is *sympatheia*).[77] The source of this inborn affinity, and a precondition of perception, is the original creative principle in which all things participate: the 'One', the 'Intellect' or 'Soul'. Every act of sense-perception, every thought was thus a recognition or remembrance of a pre-existing, inborn reality. Each sensation carried an intimation of this 'organic unity' of being; a sense that 'our eyes are parts of the same organism as the objects of vision'.[78]

I have attempted to elucidate medieval vision through comparison and contrast with two versions of Western ocularcentrism: one historical, the other psychoanalytic. While the abstractive, geometrical tradition embraced by Bacon and his contemporaries could be accommodated within both of these accounts, other aspects of medieval vision are undeniably foreign to them. Here it seems we are dealing with two divergent visual worlds: one characterised by the sharp delineation and separation of seer and seen; the other by bodily interaction and affinity.

Returning to Lacan's mirror stage, this contrast can be encapsulated in a specific symbolic detail. Lacan notes that 'the formation of the *I*' in the mirror stage is often represented in dreams as a fortress.[79] A comparison of his edifice with the same topos in medieval literature reveals a telling discrepancy. I argued in Chapter 2 that the allegory of the castle is used in amatory and devotional literature—for example the *Romance of the Rose* and the *Ancrene Wisse*—to signify the permeability of the body/self.[80] Time and again the reader's attention is directed to windows, doors, gateways: architectural openings representing the five bodily senses. Sight in particular was the 'window' through which the world flowed in, and the soul slipped out. In these medieval texts, the allegory of the castle or fortress serves—however paradoxically—to dramatise and amplify the interpenetration of self and world; a meeting that is often erotically charged.

Lacan's imaginary edifice, on the other hand, is isolated and impregnable. His castle stands alone, 'lofty, remote;' and the dream-subject 'flounders' in the surrounding wasteland of 'marshes and rubbish-tips'.[81] If we read these renditions of the same trope as commentaries on the visually mediated relationship between self and world, they do indeed suggest different experiences, and divergent symbolic economies. For Lacan, the mirror locks the child within its binary logic: the world and others are reduced to a version of the self through absolute identification or alienation.[82] The 'spell' is not broken until the resolution of the Oedipus complex. Only then, through the interpolation of the father's authority and language into the dyadic bond of self and (m)other, does the child make a more or less successful transition from the visual domain of the Imaginary to the Symbolic order structured like a language.[83]

Stripped to its structural bones, the narrative of the Mirror Stage and Oedipus complex configures human subjectivity in terms of a scopic dualism on the one hand, and on the other, linguistic mediation provided by the word of a third party: the father. Yet when we turn to medieval theories of sight we find mediation internal to visual relationships.[84] For Bacon, sight constitutes a fluid and ambiguous zone; an intermediary between the external world and the internal faculties of the sensitive soul. And instead of an agonistic oscillation between difference and sameness, vision entailed an assimilation of the viewer to his or her object.

To understand the lived experience and symbolic range of medieval vision, we clearly need to rethink the relationship between viewing subjects and visible objects. What exactly does Bacon mean when he says we are 'actualised' or transformed by our objects? How can we conceptualise that relationship of partial identity or assimilation? I will try to answer these questions with the help of a familiar metaphor. The 'pregnant' idea 'conceived' in the imagination attests to a more ancient equivalence between mental acts and sexual reproduction. If we reinvest this long dead metaphor with something of its original, quite literal meaning, it offers a very different slant on the relationship between objects in the world and their sensory or cognitive 'reproduction'.

Perceptual conception

Peter of John Olivi, another Franciscan theologian, observed that the internal senses 'conceive' sensible species 'within the capacious and material sinew' of the internal sense.[85] The same conditions governed memory, the difference being that for Olivi, the 'memorative' species are produced not by the object, but by the agent intellect, 'in the material womb of the intellect itself'.[86] Olivi's account of perception differs in a number of significant respects from Bacon's—most importantly, he replaced Bacon's passive theory of mind with a model of active cognitive attention—but on this issue they stand on common cultural ground.[87] Although Bacon does not himself use the metaphor of perceptual conception, his understanding of sense-perception as a causal, physical event supports the analogy between seeing (or thinking) and sexual reproduction. In order to elucidate this association, it will be helpful to reiterate a basic tenet of Aristotelian natural philosophy: the relationship between form and matter. For it is this principle that underpins Aristotle's explanation of animal reproduction, as well as his theory of perception.

It has been suggested that Aristotle was concerned, above all else, with two interrelated problems: firstly, how can we account for the changes we see all around us in the natural world? And secondly, what is the essence of things; what persists through those changes that would enable us to speak of a continuous identity?[88] His answer, according to Hilary Putnam and Martha Nussbaum, is that 'the nature of things [is] to be forms embodied in ever-changing matter'.[89] Thus, the soul is the form or organising principle of the body; the body the matter in which the soul is realised. In the context of embryology the male seed informs female matter. Although that embryonic matter subsequently absorbs more matter—from the maternal body, then from other nutritive sources—grows, and eventually ages and dies, the identity of the individual remains constant.

Form—this 'essence or very nature of the thing'[90]—is also the continuous element in perception (and remember that for Bacon, 'form' is synonymous with 'species'). When it encounters the receptive, latent matter of the eye and brain, the form or species of an object actualises that potential, producing a sensory image. It is this process of alteration that is felt as a pleasurable pain. The crucial point in all this is that for Aristotle and Bacon, when we perceive something, that thing in a very real way becomes *part* of us: the essence of the thing is drawn forth from the object (or adjacent medium), and impregnates the receptive matter of our sense organs and mind. So our perceptions are neither entirely our own, nor independent of, or indifferent to us. They are born of the intercourse between self and world.

For Olivi, the brain was a womb-like chamber in which sensory representations germinate, and memories are born. In his discussion of the physiology of the eye, Bacon gives the organs of sight a similar function. While he delineates the anatomy of the eye according to geometrical principles—thereby ensuring the optimum passage of radiant species to the optic nerve—it is as a bodily organ, and not a mathematical model, that the eye fulfils its 'reproductive' function.

This organ consists of 'three coats or membranes, and three humors, and a web like that of a spider'.[91] In keeping with the ancient and medieval penchant for etymology, the terms for many of these components derive from familiar substances or objects. The *uvea* (or vascular tunic), for instance, looks rather like a grape (*uva*) with the stalk removed; the *cornea* resembles 'transparent horn;' the *glacialis* is 'like ice and hail and crystal;' and the *humour albugineus* 'like the white of egg'.[92] Most of these analogies are unremarkable, although they do fill out the abstract geometry of the eye, imbuing it with a palpable, organic materiality. The most interesting etymology from our perspective relates to the inner layer of the eyeball—the *uvea*—made up of the choroid (at the back) and ciliary body (at the front). Bacon notes that the network of 'veins, nerves, and arteries' comprising the posterior section of the *uvea* is known as the *secundina*, 'because it is similar to the after-birth [*secundinae*]'.[93]

A physiological similarity between the eye and the womb is further suggested by Bacon's description of the eye's nutritive humours. The 'well-digested' blood flowing through the vessels of the *secundina* forms and nourishes the *vitreous humour*, located inside the nerve at the back of the eye. This humour, in turn, nourishes the even more refined *glacialis* or 'crystalline humour', which is 'quite white and clear'. And finally, the *humour albugineus* receives 'the overflow of the crystalline humor'.[94] These nourishing and receptive substances are the latent matter actualised by visible species. The figure of ocular 'conception'—and colloquial references to the eye as a vulnerable, sexualised orifice—are thus consistent with Bacon's portrayal of the physiology of sight, if not with his mathematical perspectivism. While he takes us no further in this direction, Bacon would certainly have been cognizant of the sexual connotations of sight that peppered contemporary sermons, as well as secular literature.

Western science is often seen as having a special affiliation with the objectifying, emotionally detached *masculine* gaze. So the claim that medieval optics was a gendered discourse—or that the optical gaze was sexualised—is not in itself new. The problem is, the aspects of medieval optics discussed in this chapter do not conform to twentieth-century notions of scientific scrutiny. Bacon's account does not fit the stereotype of a male scientist 'having his way' with passive, feminised nature. For although extramission assumes the form of an active, probing, sometimes unmistakably phallic power of vision, the eye and the internal senses of the mind were feminine in their receptive capacity. Furthermore, intromission meant that the passive, feminised matter of the eye (or brain) was united as 'one flesh' to the formative essence of the visible world.[95] So if 'conception is the male having an idea in the female body', as Thomas Laqueur has argued,[96] then the world is the virile repository of ideas, while the human organism—our 'man of science'—is passive and pliant.

Bacon's assessment that vision is both active and passive effectively attributes masculine *and* feminine functions to the mechanism of sight. In this respect the optical gaze exhibits the same sexual-symbolic indeterminacy as the eroticised eye. Whether carnal or scientific, vision was a dynamic extension of the subject into the world and at the same time a penetration and alteration of the viewer's body by the object. This model of reciprocity—the idea that the eye can *act* and *be acted upon*—helps to explain the popularity and religious significance of devotional images: a point I shall return to in Chapter 6.

To conclude, Bacon's explanation of sight lends itself to two very different reproductive paradigms. Pictorial reproduction treats the world, eyes and mind as mathematical correlates in the interest of experimental science. Sight is the foundation of scientific knowledge because the eye and the visible world share the same geometrical language. But in order for seeing and knowing to coincide, the opaque, unpredictable, fallible conditions of human embodiment must be abstracted, elided or repressed. This part of the story is well known: the body becomes an object for taking pictures, while the self—now a disembodied inner eye—retreats into a realm of pure, immaterial intellection. Medieval optics thus anticipates the camera obscura and its symbolic territory, but only partially.

Bacon does abstract sight from the opacity and weight of corporeal matter and the thick 'fog' of the flesh; yet he retains the body as the ground of perception. Embodied sight and an enmattered mind are the medium of communication between self and world. If pictorial reproduction is compromised by the ever-changing matter of the body, sexual reproduction cannot take place without it. Nor does perceptual conception allow that critical distance between sensory representations (or 'raw' sense data) and an internal observer. Instead, it suggests an impregnation of the viewer by his or her objects. Not just in the sense that the eye and mind are *receptacles* for sense impressions or mental images, but because sensible species, ideas and emotions are realised in the matter of eye and mind in the same way that a foetus is formed out of—and not just carried around in—its mother's body.

Finally, perception involves a process of becoming, a period of gestation if you like, as the sensitive organs of the mind and body are assimilated with their objects.[97] It is not, as Lacan would have it, a question of recognising (or losing) oneself in the mirror of the world. The subject's relation to the visible universe does not necessarily bifurcate into moments of joyful identification and alienation, sameness and difference. Neither of these responses accounts for the fertile meeting of subject and object; or as Merleau-Ponty described it, the '*natal* bond between me who perceives and what I perceive' (emphasis added).[98]

Optical desire and the pleasures of science

Carnal vision was fundamentally an expression of the desires of the flesh; and in the final chapters of this book the desire to see—recast as spiritual longing—will become a precondition for redemption. But to what extent was the *scientific* gaze—like its carnal and spiritual counterparts—animated by desire? Post-Enlightenment science is premised on the exclusion of such comparisons: science is presumed to begin where religion and super-stition end. By extension, the ideal of dispassionate, detached scientific observation demands the suppression (or sublimation) of 'distorting' influences, most notably the subjective vicissitudes of human emotion.

The fact that we have been tracing the continuities between carnal vision and optical science already implies the coexistence of science and desire. On this evidence alone, one would expect the medieval scientist to be more comfortable with the presence of ocular desire. Yet Bacon is strangely reticent on the subject, beyond his celebration of visual 'delight'.[99] In order to answer our question about the relation between medieval *perspectiva* and desire we will need to read between the lines, while at the same time attending to Bacon's silence.

On the one hand, Bacon clearly wishes to *distance* sight from sensual pleasure and the vices associated with the desires of the flesh. We 'are called incontinent and blameworthy', he writes, 'more on account of taste and touch than because of the other senses, since we are overcome by the basest pleasures and by those in which we participate with the brutes'.[100] In the Aristotelian tradition, sight was the primary sense in the order of cognition, while touch was fundamental for human and animal survival.[101] There is something almost evolutionary about the hierarchy of the senses; with sight representing the human potential for knowledge, the capacity to transcend the particular through reason; and touch, the primordial sense, signifying brute animality. For Bacon, then, the 'higher' senses lead us towards noble objects, while touch and taste appeal to our 'lower' nature: the nature of not-quite-human flesh.

Despite this elevation of sight, Bacon is of his time (not Aristotle's) and is clearly familiar with contemporary sermonising on 'the lust of the eyes'.[102] In his treatise on mathematics, he provides an account of temptation and sin based on the multiplication of sensible species to the five senses. Because the senses are 'carried away' by the species of 'delectable things', Bacon's advice is to avoid encountering those species in the first place. His reasoning is clearly informed by an intromissionist perspective on sensation: objects and their species have the power to captivate and seduce us because they are agents and we are recipients. The examples he gives—Adam and Eve, David and Bathsheeba, Susanna and the elders—all involve looking at illicit objects (the apple and naked women respectively). It is a significant inconsistency, therefore, that Bacon again singles out touch and taste as the senses most likely to lead one astray. Righteous men, he says:

> turn away their senses as far as possible from all species of delectable things, and especially from those pertaining to the sense of touch and taste . . . lest the species multiplied into the senses should compel the spirit to serve carnal allurements . . .[103]

Conversely, we are aroused by 'visible instruments' to reflect on spiritual truths.[104] The possibility of redirecting or sublimating the natural human desire for sense experience to spiritual advantage was often cited in defence of religious images; but what is important here is that Bacon's passing references to visual desire are polarised into carnal and spiritual extremes. This polarisation leaves the gaze of science to occupy a neutral middle ground.

There are three possible reasons for this apparent absence of desire in the optical gaze. Firstly, most of Bacon's treatise on optics is concerned with elaborating an intromissionist theory of vision: that is, vision as a physical affect, rather than an expression of desire, curiosity or intent. Vision is both active and passive, but it is the passive component to which Bacon pays most attention. Secondly, he is less interested in the psychology of perception than in its physical and geometrical characteristics. One can extrapolate psychological implications from his account, but he is not expansive on such questions as the workings of memory, the role of attention, or indeed the complex relationship between desire or aversion and sensation. And thirdly, as I noted earlier, Bacon would have been aware of the literary, colloquial, theological and medical discourses feeding into the multi-faceted discourse of carnal vision. To mention desire and vision in the same breath would surely have been to call up such associations. The absence of desire in his theory of vision (as opposed to the occasional aside in discussions of mathematics or morality) may simply represent a convenient elision.

Bacon's silence on the subject of desire is all the more significant because it marks a departure from his two most illustrious sources: Aristotle and Augustine. For Aristotle, desire was a feature of all sensation. Where 'there is sensation', he wrote, 'there is also pleasure and pain, and, where these, necessarily also desire'.[105] In the context of experimental science, the desire for knowledge is grounded in the pure pleasure of sensory experience. In a passage echoed in the introduction to Bacon's *Perspectiva* (albeit without the reference to desire), Aristotle upholds the legitimacy of this epistemological 'desire' as well as sensory enjoyment:

> All men by nature desire to know. An indication of this is the delight we take in our senses; for even apart from their usefulness they are loved for themselves; and above all others the sense of sight.[106]

This is a long way indeed from the temptations of delectable species and the 'delights' of the flesh. For Aristotle, sight is the philosopher's friend; naturally inclined towards knowledge and utility. The desire to know coincides with the desire to see.

Augustine confirmed the conjunction of bodily sight and scientific knowledge, but in his case both were associated with carnal vision. The scientist's desire to observe and classify was simply lust by another name. There could be no such thing as dispassionate observation, for the gaze of science was a manifestation of the concupiscence of the eyes. To pursue sensory pleasures for their own sake, under the guise of science, would be to remain mired in the flesh. As Plato had so graphically put it, 'each pleasure and pain fastens [the soul] to the body with a sort of rivet, pins it there, and makes it corporeal . . .'[107]

Augustine, however, had spoken of ocular desire in another, more productive sense. He describes attention as a '*desire of seeing*'—an inclination or intention of the mind (or will) rather than a bodily appetite.[108] This desire is 'the power that fixes the sense of sight on the object . . .'[109] Of course, Augustine was approaching perception from an extramissionist and intellectualist position. Where Aristotle had attempted to explain the transmission and reception of sensible forms, Augustine was primarily concerned with the moral and psychological aspects of sight. His emphasis on intentionality or motivation is in keeping with these concerns because it enables him to elucidate our wilful investment in the material world, and therefore our culpability for sin. On the other hand, as Margaret Miles has shown, Augustine's understanding of bodily sight, with its emphasis on intentionality and emotional engagement, becomes one of the primary models for redemption.[110]

For Augustine, the desire to see is therefore by no means inherently bad; nor should we seek to eliminate it from our intercourse with the sensible world. But while sight cannot take place without desire, it is possible to direct that desire towards proper or improper ends. The 'rational soul lives disgracefully', says Augustine, 'when it applies to those things which form the sense of the body from without [i.e., extramental objects or their mental likenesses], not the laudable will by which it refers them to some useful end, but the shameful desire by which it has clung to them.'[111] If the 'laudable will' and 'shameful desire' are merely different orientations of the one power of attention then there is scope for a form of scientific inquiry that recognises its epistemological limitations. Rather than being an end in itself, science would be the means to a more 'useful end'. And for Augustine, the only truly useful knowledge was the knowledge required by the inner man.

Bacon satisfies Augustine's prescription, as of course he must, by arguing that science and its methods are indispensable to theology: 'it is impossible for the spiritual sense to be known without a knowledge of the literal sense', he writes.[112] Furthermore, in his treatise on moral philosophy he suggests that the desire for knowledge of the natural world will be sated only by going beyond it: 'human desire cannot have its limit in any good except in the highest good by which it is terminated; because the desire of the rational soul transcends all finite good and passes on to the infinite good.'[113] The crucial point, however, is that scientific inquiry, even when put to moral or spiritual use, does not cease to be driven by desire, even if this fact is cloaked in the more acceptable terminology of 'attention' or 'laudable will'. There is no suggestion, either in Aristotle or in Augustine, that vision can or should be detached from sensory pleasure or from the mechanism of desire: to rid sensation of these elements would be to extinguish sight itself. Scientific observation, then, cannot be dispassionate: knowledge, whether intellectual, empirical, spiritual or carnal requires the motivated, affective and transformative engagement of subject and object.

It is admittedly difficult to reconcile the rhetoric surrounding the objectivity and veracity of visual perception—the 'scientific visions' of Chapter 3—with the idea of sight as a 'passionate' encounter. Ultimately, however, the value of Bacon's synthesis may lie in this very ambiguity. By promoting the nobility and relative immateriality of sight in one sentence, then likening the eye to the skin or flesh in another, Bacon confuses the traditional separation of the senses and the epistemological alignment of seeing and thinking. Similarly, his acknowledgement of perceptual reciprocity unsettles—without actually displacing—the project of objective science. I am not arguing that this ambiguity is intentional. Rather, in his attempt to hold on to a number of apparent contradictions—that vision is both active and passive, that it happens 'out there' as well as inside viewing subjects, that it is reducible to geometrical coordinates but involves material changes—Bacon perhaps ends up telling us more about perceptual experience than we would glean from a more coherent or empirical account.

PART III

REDEMPTION

CHAPTER 5

THE CUSTODY OF THE EYES

you will touch with the hand of faith, the finger of desire, the embrace of devotion; you will touch with the eye of the mind.[1]

Bernard of Clairvaux

The final chapters of this book concern the relationship between vision and redemption. As such, they range over territory that is probably closer to modern notions of the Middle Ages than either carnal or scientific vision. 'Medieval vision' is likely to bring to mind enraptured saints and mystics, miraculous visitations and religious art (as the layman's visionary substitute): not the mundane spectacle of nature or the sensual pleasures of the fleshly eye. Yet the supermundane was only one aspect of redemptive vision. In this chapter and the next I will outline three basic kinds of spiritual discipline, each associated with particular techniques for regulating and exploiting the relationship between bodily and 'interior' sight. The first of these technologies of redemption involves the enclosure or custody of the bodily senses; the second uses forms of analogy to elevate the soul's gaze from sensory things to a realm of higher, transcendent truths. The third model of redemptive vision—the subject of Chapter 6—fosters a heightened sensitivity to sensory (and especially visual) experience as a means of communion with an increasingly human God.

While the first two paradigms of redemptive sight (enclosure and transcendence) existed throughout the Western Middle Ages, corporeal vision was rarely acknowledged as a means of actual *participation* in the divine before the twelfth and thirteenth centuries. That this development coincides with the burgeoning interest in optics as a scientific discipline is no coincidence. Chapter 6 will draw out the parallels between the reciprocal, affective aspects of Bacon's optics and these new patterns of medieval spirituality; especially their emphasis on the 'real' (causal, physiological) continuities between self and world, between motives and behaviour, body and soul, and ultimately between humanity and God. As such, we will find a certain consonance between carnal vision, the optical gaze of Chapter 4 and the 'ocular communion' of the final chapter.

My discussion of sensory enclosure and sublimation, on the other hand, should be read against the background of medieval dualism. The spiritual exercises we will look at in this chapter presuppose the denigration of the flesh; the visual subtext of original sin; and the fantasy of bodies purified of carnality. Redemption prior to the thirteenth century was primarily liberation *from* the flesh. Spiritual progress depended on the enclosure or sublimation of sensation and sensuality. The polarisation of reason and sensuality, spirit and flesh, heaven and earth underpins the redemptive visions of this chapter in other ways, too. Postlapsarian dualism provided a motivation for redemption: a rift to be mended. It also gave dialectical shape to humanity's spiritual pilgrimage: a journey towards perfect and eternal synthesis.

The present chapter, however, is about the journey itself, rather than its imagined end. As such, the oppositions and paradoxes we will encounter fall short of any final sublation. One such paradox is that spiritual vision throughout the Middle Ages was conceived as both the *opposite* and *analogue* of bodily sight. In the first instance, the polarisation of corporeal and spiritual vision gave rise to repressive or regulatory strategies. Bodily sight was to be 'cloistered'. On the other hand, the claim that invisible or spiritual things were manifest in the visible world meant that corporeal vision was crucial to humanity's return to God. One had to look *through* the world, not away from it. These different approaches to sight and embodiment sound like alternatives—restraint or repression versus sublimation. In practice, however, they worked on a continuum to draw the soul inwards and finally upwards, towards God. Following a brief introduction to polarity and analogy, I will turn to the paradox of sensory enclosure in St Bernard's sermon *On Conversion*; and then conclude with the practice of sublimating ocular desire. While the sublimation of desire represents a flight from fallen human nature (the body of flesh or fleshly body), its goal—the mystical or heavenly sublime—is curiously analogous to the flesh.

Polarity and analogy

In a sixth-century work promoting the study of the classical sciences as a vehicle for the cultivation of reason, Boethius wrote: 'there are certain definite stages and dimensions of advancement through which it is possible to rise and progress until *the eye of the mind . . . which has been*

submerged and blinded by our bodily senses, may be illumined once again . . .'
(emphasis added).[2] It is easy to gloss over the tangled metaphoric logic of
this statement, but I would like to attend to it for just a moment. Boethius
was, of course, drawing freely on a long and venerable tradition that treated
cognition as a kind of interior vision or 'insight'. But if the physical eye
and the eye of the mind are analogous, they are also pitted against each
other in the struggle between sense and intellect. The intellect as an 'inner
eye' is engulfed by the senses; blinded in effect by its bodily equivalent.[3]
This polarity is as ancient as the analogy between seeing and knowing.[4]

In his study of polarity and analogy in Greek thought, G. E. R. Lloyd
observes that forms of knowledge and belief tend to function according
to one of two dominant modes: either 'relating or reducing phenomena
to a pair or pairs of opposite principles, or . . . assimilating or likening one
(unknown) object to another that was or seemed to be better known'.[5]
Boethius, then, was employing both modes: the mind is *like* an eye; yet the
mind's eye and the bodily eye represent the opposing principles of reason
and sensation. Whereas Lloyd treats polarity and analogy separately,
as alternatives, Boethius weaves them into the one paradoxical image of
'enlightenment'. In doing so, he plays dualism (an extreme form of
polarity) against its resolution in analogy. The gulf between sensation and
intellection or flesh and spirit engenders a longing for mediation,
reconciliation, reunion; and the analogy between bodily sight and interior
vision provides a glimpse of redemption.[6]

Polarity and analogy, then, are ways of making the world meaningful.
In the context of medieval Christianity they help to articulate the cultural
ideal of a transcendent God whose creative power and essential goodness
are nevertheless visible in the creation; while at the same time accounting
for human fallibility, suffering and mortality. But the interaction between
polarity and analogy does not only have conceptual and ideological effects.
It structures religious expectations and practices by linking the denial
or denigration of sensuality to more productive spiritual exercises. In this
respect medieval configurations of polarity and analogy have something
in common with the operation of power described by Michel Foucault.
Foucault has shown that corporeal control is as likely to entail the *production* of desire as its repression or denial. Indeed, the two mechanisms seem
to be fundamental to the internal dynamic of power, insofar as power is
invested in—rather than exercised upon—the body.[7]

Enclosure, purification and censorship—all of which aim to contain
and immobilise sensuality, or to strip away the internal residue of sense
impressions—could be classed as 'disciplinary' techniques in Foucault's
terminology. They operate as mechanisms of self-constraint, internal surveillance and self-regulation. As such, these technologies stand in contrast

to the literary, artistic and devotional uses of analogy: envisaged not as a means of suppressing or repressing ocular desire, but as a way of stimulating and ultimately sublimating the sensory appetite: using the active openness of the flesh to apprehend God. I will be arguing in the rest of this chapter that mechanisms of sensory enclosure, cleansing and control serve to clear or create an interior space that might then, to quote Bernard of Clairvaux, be filled with 'a foretaste of the incomparable delights of love . . .'[8]

It is worth noting, before we return to *On Conversion*, that in Bernard's twelfth-century monastic milieu the standard Neoplatonic opposition of matter and spirit was refigured as a battle between reason and sensuality.[9] Sight, inner and outer, thus took its place alongside other binary oppositions. The theological and psychological significance of such radical polarisations is hinted at in Janet Coleman's observation that the 'divorce between flesh and spirit, body and soul, reason and intelligence, intelligence and God' in twelfth-century theology, amounted to a 'post-lapsarian dualism [that] could only be restored to unity by God's grace'.[10] Taking her insight a step further, one might see dualism as a precondition for medieval Christianity: a background or stage for the drama of sacrifice and salvation. Bernard, as we shall see, makes humanity's alienation from God the occasion of divine mediation; and the enclosure of the senses an opportunity for their penetration by God's love.

Bernard of Clairvaux and the cloistered gaze

Bernard's evocation of the delectable foretaste of heaven, painted in the sensual language of the Song of Songs, represents a pivotal moment in his sermon, *On Conversion*. The 'delights of love' are, he makes clear, granted only to those who have submitted themselves to an arduous process of introspection and purification. Most of his sermon is concerned with this preparatory process, and masterfully exploits the traditional alignment of sensation and the flesh. My analysis of the text in Chapter 1 focused on Bernard's contribution to the medieval understanding of carnality. Here we will look at his solution to the flesh: disciplinary and purgative techniques that prepare the vigilant convert for eventual induction into the lush, and highly sensual allegories of bridal mysticism.

For Bernard, preaching on this occasion to scholars in Paris rather than to the monks under his care at Clairvaux, enclosure was both a fertile metaphor and a compelling ideal. After all, the conversion about which he spoke—possibly in the cloister of Notre Dame—was not a conversion to Christianity, but to the monastic life.[11] For him, the life of the cloister represented a means of literally enclosing the senses. If sin—the life of the flesh—was above all about permeability and the intercourse between inside and outside, self and world, then salvation proceeded by way of withdrawal and enclosure.

Bernard shared this ideal with many of his religious contemporaries. The biographer of Stephen Obazine (d. 1158) was explicit about the spiritual benefits of physical enclosure. Referring to the nuns at Coyroux, he posed a question that, for him, was rhetorical: 'how can one sin', he asked, 'when the faculty of vision itself is enclosed?'[12] In a similar vein the author of the *Ancrene Wisse* urges his readers to be 'truly enclosed' and 'blind to the outside world'.[13] From the Biblical injunction to 'pluck out' your eye if it offends (Matt. 5.29), to less violent metaphors of enclosure, physical 'blindness' was a prerequisite for superior kinds of sight. If 'the cloister lies on the border of angelic purity and earthly contamination', as Peter of Celle claimed,[14] then the sensory 'windows' of the body were the gatekeepers.

Although the architectural 'blindfold' of the cloister was the ideal, it did not, as one might expect, correspond to a visually barren existence. For Bernard, and we can assume for the nuns of Coyroux and the anchoresses addressed in the *Ancrene Wisse*, the cloister was a space in which the bodily senses, turned inwards, were amplified, where desire increased.[15] So while monastic enclosure presented to the world the blank face of the tomb, its interior carried more vital associations: for instance, as womb the cloister or anchorhold was chaste but also fertile. To cloister the body's senses was thus to prefigure death, but also to secure the walled garden or the marriage chamber in which the soul as the bride of the Song of Songs might meet her beloved Christ.

Stephen Obazine's biographer implies that the enclosure of sight (rather than, say, touch, hearing or smell) will remove a major cause of sin. Did vision, then, have a special relationship to enclosure and its transgression? Although the majority of commentators advocated the custody, enclosure, or censure of sensation in general, they also tended to treat sight as exemplary. To repeat an example I have used previously, the preponderance of this ocular paradigm enables windows—traditionally homologous with eyes—to stand for all the senses.[16] It is my contention that carnal vision and medieval optics—not just undifferentiated sensation—lie behind the custody or enclosure of the senses. As an orifice *as well as* an active organ of the sensitive soul, the eye was doubly transgressive of corporeal or architectural borders. Add to this the spatialising capacity of sight—the vast 'reach' of the eye—and it is not surprising that this sense should so often define and disrupt medieval spaces.

In *On Conversion*, the individual's journey towards God is given shape and momentum through a dialectic of enclosure and permeability that is articulated primarily through lines of sight.[17] My reading of the text will focus on this visual substructure: its pivotal points and inversions. Enclosure, I will argue, was not just a physical reality of the monastic life; or even, taken figuratively, a spiritual ideal to strive towards. It was part of an economy of desire.

Bernard's sermon *On Conversion* opens with the acknowledgement that those being addressed have come 'to hear the Word of God'.[18] A humble servant of this Word, Bernard is quick to efface his own words: God must speak to the individual heart. 'I admonish you', he says, 'to lift up the ears of your heart to hear this inner voice, so that you may strive to hear inwardly what is said to the outward man.'[19] Yet having invoked the Word with the skill of a practised orator, having aroused the ears (outer and inner) of his audience, he shifts abruptly from speaking and hearing to seeing. God's inner voice is transformed into 'a ray of light'.[20] Hearing and seeing at first merge into one, then become the self-reflexive gaze of reason upon the interior landscape of the memory. The first 'audible' prick of conscience elicited by an inner voice thus gives way to introspection: a definitively visual operation. Illuminated by the Spirit, 'reason is enlightened and what is in the memory is unfolded as though set out before each man's eyes'.[21] The soul in these two 'persons'—reason and memory —is 'both gazer and that which is gazed upon, brought face to face with itself and overcome by the force of its realization of what it is seeing'.[22]

Self-knowledge, as the first step on the road to a conversion of the heart, takes the form of a visual examination. It is not, for Bernard, an enumeration of sins (which might be spoken by the conscience and heard by an inner judge), or a tactile 'probing' of invisible motives, fears, desires; but rather an instantaneous, visual and spatial apprehension of interiority. Illuminated by the Spirit and gazed upon by reason the knowable self (as distinct from the knowing, gazing self) is the memory: that 'repository' of sense impressions, or landscape of 'dirty footprints' accumulated over a lifetime; a 'cesspit'; a churning and bloated 'stomach'.[23] Bacon might have defined this aspect of the self in more neutral language, in terms of the sensitive soul's receptiveness to sensible species. For Bernard the world flows in; an inexorable torrent of polluting sensations. And the soul takes pleasure in 'wandering off' into the world through 'all the gates of the body'.[24]

Introspection is followed by a period of enforced enclosure. The convert is instructed to 'Close the windows, fasten the doors, block all entry carefully . . .'[25] What did Bernard hope to achieve by this celibacy of the senses, this sanctified blindness? Was he advocating the literal censorship of physical sight? In the context of this sermon, enclosure is an ideal: a measure against which failure is inevitable. Faced with such sensory deprivation the 'eye complains that it is told to weep and not wander'.[26] It is as though denial and containment were intended to sharpen the appetites, to throw the contours of the flesh into even sharper relief.

Far from containing the flesh, enclosure provokes a violent response in the form of Mistress Will. The soul is thrown open, the stomach of the memory distended in rebellion against Reason's attempts to deny and constrain the flesh. In an inversion of Bernard's closed windows and fastened doors, the body now becomes 'all eye', the members 'a gullet to eat with'.[27] As I suggested in Chapter 2, Bernard's Mistress Will is not only an allegorical figure: she is a vehicle for the literal enfleshing of the soul. Reason, looking inwards, 'sees the windows open to death and cannot close them because the will is still weak . . .'[28] Outward enclosure has thus elucidated the fatal openness of the soul. Confrontation with sin and death *within* the cloister serves to remind the novice of the necessity of humility: 'weakness is a benefit' when the flesh cannot be subdued by force.

Concluding his excursus on the vices of the flesh, Bernard returns to the theme of enclosure: not, this time, as a response to sin, but as a counterpoint to the divine gaze. We might suppose, he says, that our desires and motives are concealed from observers by the opacity of our flesh. Quite the contrary: 'Not even the wall of the body is impenetrable to the gaze of truth . . . All things lie bare to [God's] eyes, which penetrate more easily than a two-edged sword.'[29] By suturing the 'corruptible garment' of the flesh into an impermeable membrane we might stem the influx of the sensible world, but we can never withdraw into a place impenetrable to God's sight.[30] The interior thus becomes entirely exposed, as the envelope of the body is traversed by the penetrating and omnipresent gaze of the divine creator and judge.

Insisting 'that it is impossible for the sinner to hide',[31] Bernard invites comparison with the shameful visibility that followed the first sin. In the Genesis account of the fall, Adam and Eve's terrible awakening (the self-knowledge gained through their disobedience) is felt as an awareness of absolute visibility—nakedness—in the presence of God. Having looked with intent (Bernard has just given the examples of gluttony, lust and curiosity, all of which were present in Eve's desiring gaze at the forbidden fruit) every sinner is condemned to be *looked at*. Stripped bare before the piercing gaze of God, the convert is able, finally, to repent:

> Let his eyes pour out water. Let his eyelids not close in sleep. Truly, the eye which was in darkness before is cleansed by tears and its sight sharpened, so that it is able to gaze into the brightness of that most serene light.[32]

With these tears of repentance the influx of the world is reversed. But while Bernard is clearly referring to literal tears, the eye in this passage is inward and spiritual rather than corporeal. In an inversion of the reason versus sensation topos—which equated physical sensation with spiritual or mental blindness—the veil of tears obscures ('darkens') outward sensation and produces inner clarity. This unveiling of the inner eye heralds the soul's first glimpse of that 'most beautiful garden' of spiritual delights. The soul, in effect, is visually re-oriented: away from the sensible world and towards its spiritual source. What had once been vulnerable openings in the corporeal edifice are transformed into windows through which the soul receives divine illumination:

> From now onward, let him gaze upward through the window, look out through the lattice, and follow the guiding star with all his attention and, zealously imitating the Magi, let him seek the Light in the light.[33]

Enclosure once again serves to foreground its transgression: this time sanctified and redemptive instead of profane and polluting. Reversing the earthward pull of carnal vision, the soul's attentive gaze 'upward through the window' of its inner eye awakens a 'desire to contemplate heavenly things'.[34] Bernard is insistent that Mistress Will, though she could not be broken by force or swayed by logic, will be moved by Reason's description of the 'most beautiful garden. . . . not only to see the place', but 'to enter it, little by little, and make its dwelling there'.[35]

If sight is the sense most able to defy enclosure, it is also the sense most capable of 'leading' the will into the walled garden of the Song of Songs.[36] This transport of the soul's affections is also, however, a transformation from flesh into spirit: 'Do not think that this inward paradise of pleasure is corporeal', Bernard warns.[37] Furthermore, the enclosure and transformation of the will is a precondition for the body's 'subjection to it'.[38] On one level, this step-by-step realignment of reason, will and body under the 'guiding star' of the spirit could be construed as a means of corporeal control; but this does not seem to be Bernard's intention. His reference to subjection is almost in passing, sandwiched between the blossoming of the spiritual senses in their inner paradise, and a meditation on memory. It is as if the body had been entirely absorbed into its spiritual equivalent; transposed into the five inner senses. Bernard's objective, then, is the sublimation of carnal sensuality in an interior space where:

> continence shines and the vision of pure truth illuminates the eye of the heart. The most sweet voice of the inner Comforter brings joy and gladness to the ears. There the most lovely odor of a fruitful field . . . is carried to the

nostrils of hope. There a foretaste of the incomparable delights of love is enjoyed . . .[39]

If sublimation is Bernard's goal, a consummate exploitation of analogy is fundamental to his means of attaining it. Ann Astell makes the point that Bernard's sermons on Canticles,[40] like much of the twelfth-century devotional and courtly literature inspired by the Song of Songs, invest the allegorical interpretation of the text with the emotional charge of its literal, and highly sensual, language. So the physical attributes of the lovers, and the details of their courtship, do not simply translate into moral or doctrinal lessons, but provide an imaginative structure and a psychological mechanism for affective transformation. 'For exegetes and poets alike', Astell argues, 'reliteralizing Canticles meant joining its tenor (defined by the "spiritual" allegory) to its vehicle (the corporeal images of the Song *ad litteram*) in order to *affect* an audience with truth' (emphasis added).[41]

Finally, for Bernard the cultivation of one's spiritual garden is directly related to the notion of a purged or 'blanched' memory.[42] Unfurled before the soul's interior gaze, the memory constitutes a garden of very earthly delights, an ever-present landscape of sensation and desire.[43] The debased and polluting equivalent of Bernard's inner paradise, memories of the world outside the cloister compete with that spiritual garden for the soul's attention. If one garden flourishes, the other pales and withers. Bernard's meditations on the Song of Songs could be seen, then, as the perfected, claustral complement to *On Conversion*. Where the latter preaches conversion, enclosure and purification, Coleman notes that the sermons on Songs complete the process by 'converting private memories into communal, universal ones . . .'[44]

Having tamed the will and the body, Bernard writes, a 'third task remains and that is the hardest: to purify the memory and pump out the cesspit'.[45] As a storehouse of past sensations, the memory effectively brings the world into the cloister. Yet as Bernard himself asks, 'How can I forget my own life?' For the memory is not only a receptacle (a 'cesspit' or 'stomach'); it is also a sheet of 'parchment which has soaked up the ink with which the scribe has written on it'.[46] Imagined as a reservoir, the memory might conceivably be purged and sealed, but as an indelibly marked surface it becomes 'pointless . . . to try to clean it. The parchment would tear before the marks of wretchedness were removed.'[47]

Even if it were possible to forget—if a 'mental convulsion' were to literally and totally extinguish one's past, wipe the slate clean—this would not, Bernard suggests, be desirable.[48] For without memory of sin, there would be no awareness of its remission: no humility or gratitude. No, the more difficult question is: 'what keen edge can both clean my memory and keep it intact?'[49] Bernard's answer: the memory must be purged not of its contents, but of its power to *affect* us. If our memories can be disarmed, as it were—or 'blanched' of their emotional colour—then our past, including our past sins, 'will work together for good' rather than presenting the opportunity for further sin.[50] The key to this purgation of affect is not effort, but an act of God. God's pardon 'wipes out sin, not from the memory, but in such a way that what before was both present in the memory and rendered it unclean is now, although it is still in the memory, no longer a defilement to it'.[51]

One might well ask whether Bernard's programme of spiritual discipline had any relevance outside the cloister. After all, how can one shut one's windows and doors against incoming sensations while going about one's daily, worldly business? And if the world continues to flow in, how is it possible to cultivate that enclosed interior space in which universal memories might flourish? Part of the answer is that Bernard's architectural apertures—windows, doors, gates—are not just openings. Implicit in these metaphors is the conviction that one can 'close' the senses against the world.[52] The senses, then, are not just *enclosed* by the walls of a monastery or any other edifice: they can also be *closed*: averted from the world, turned inwards. This brings us closer to a psychological theory of enclosure, and to the possibility of being in the world while at the same time taking 'custody of the eyes'.

Distracting the flesh: Augustine's theory of attention

In the *Confessions*, Augustine makes the seemingly insignificant observation that certain objects, people, or events have a peculiar ability to command our attention. He admits, by way of example, that the unexpected sight of a dog pursuing a hare across a field 'might easily hold my attention and distract me from whatever serious thoughts occupied my mind'.[53] From an extramissionist point of view—according to which perception proceeds 'from a living body that perceives'[54]—this scenario raises an interesting problem. To suggest that the sensible world has sovereignty over our senses is to make a mockery of free will, as every medieval theologian well knew. Yet no one could deny that the sensible world was often seductive or compelling, sometimes repulsive: almost never a neutral object of the soul's indifferent attention. This paradox is foregrounded in Augustine's own involuntary attraction to the spectacle of the chase, his acute awareness of the force of attraction exerted by objects on our senses and our minds. Attention, in short, is both something that is 'caught' or 'drawn' by things in the world, and an intentional act—an act of the will—originating in the perceiver's mind.[55] It is at once a 'desire of seeing' initiated by the subject, and an appetite awakened by an object.[56]

The question is, can the will simply withdraw its attention from the sensible world? Is it possible to exercise or withhold the 'desire of seeing' at will, as it were? In the most obvious sense, certainly: all the bodily senses, as Augustine points out, can be literally blocked, shut or otherwise averted. The body may be used (by the will) to prevent the senses from 'combining' with sensible things.[57] But this literal—and surely impractical—version of sensory enclosure is not what Augustine has in mind when he advocates the custody of the senses. Far more important, and more difficult, is the care, cleansing and regulation of the *inner* eye.[58] This is mandatory, because 'even when the species of the body which was perceived corporeally has been taken away, yet a likeness of it remains in the memory, *to which the will may again turn its gaze . . .*' (emphasis added).[59]

Unlike the bodily senses, this inner eye cannot be shut in the face of its objects. And it is motivated not only by desire, but by fear as well. The very attempt to 'avoid' or 'guard against' undesirable—or dangerously desirable—memories or dreams is apt to sharpen both one's appetite, and the clarity, the immediacy of the resulting image.[60] Dreams, and their physiological effects, are an acute and humbling reminder of the futility of such prohibition—at least for a male celibate like Saint Augustine.[61]

As both Augustine and Bernard realised, the discipline and deprivation of one's sensual appetites can have quite the opposite effect, inflaming rather than extinguishing desire. Their solutions, not surprisingly, are similar. Augustine envisages the withdrawal not of sensation, but of attention—the glue that binds the bodily sense to its object. Without this hook of attention or desire, the senses slip over their objects without adhering to them. That sight or hearing, indeed any of the bodily senses can exist passively, without the desire or intent to see or hear, is quite apparent, says Augustine: think of all the times we 'hear' someone without *really* hearing them 'because we were thinking of something else . . .' His explanation is that 'we did hear, but we did not remember, because the speaker's words slipped immediately away from the perception of our ears, being directed elsewhere by a command of the will which is wont to fix them in the memory.'[62]

If one can be distracted from one's metaphysical musings by the sight of a hare pursued by a dog, so too might distraction work in reverse, to censor the sensible world. This conclusion brings us very close to Bernard's garden of spiritual delights in which the fleshly soul is sated and subdued, where one's 'tender and intimate' love of Christ as the Bridegroom of Canticles 'oppose[s] the sweet enticements of sensual life', and where

'Sweetness conquers sweetness as one nail drives out another.'[63] For Bernard and Augustine the appetites of the flesh are a perversion of spiritual love; and bodily sensations are a pale substitute for something more perfect and ultimately more fulfilling.[64] When the body and soul are turned towards God in contemplation and longing, it follows that the world's allure, its ability to seduce and captivate the senses, will diminish proportionately.

The re-direction or re-investment of one's sensory appetite, attention or desire is a recurring theme in medieval theology: we will see this principle at work in the 'transports' of analogy and the associated mechanism of sublimation. First, however, I would like to discuss one final means of regulating the bodily senses. The 'internal censor' has two functions: it screens out unwanted or undesirable sensations; but it also plays a productive role in the individual's spiritual progress, as the guardian of beneficial sensations and memories.

The internal sense as censor

In his exposition of optics for preachers, Peter of Limoges (d. 1306) notes that the internal sense (which he locates in the 'common nerve' at the front of the brain) enables us to be 'morally informed so that we avoid a misleading judgment and do not judge things as they first appear . . .'[65] The intervention of this sense ensures that we 'have recourse to the deliberation of the internal censor'.[66] Scholars of optics, including Peter's contemporary Roger Bacon, were understandably concerned to distinguish between truthful perceptions and optical illusions, dreams or hallucinations. Indeed, Peter makes use of the standard repertoire of optical illusions to establish the existence of an internal judge.[67] His aim, however, was not to prove the scientific utility of sight. Rather, what he offered was a *moral* interpretation of the new optical science; a 'morality based on the scientific observation of nature'.[68] To this end he extends the jurisdiction of the internal censor considerably. If this interior judge is capable of intervening between object and intellect in the case of optical illusions, then surely, he implies, all sense impressions might be interrupted, and sensations judged to be 'wrong'—morally *or* logically—might be rejected.[69]

Peter's notion of an internal censor is not dissimilar to the Stoic understanding of the internal sense as a faculty of judgement that could be honed and strengthened.[70] What distinguishes his approach is an emphasis on morality as technique; a factor that probably accounts for the enduring popularity and relatively wide dissemination of *De Oculo Morali*.[71] It is an eminently practical work: its purpose is not to describe or speculate, but to instruct individuals in the cultivation of a 'moral' eye. In keeping with this objective, there is more to the internal censor than censorship, an essentially repressive activity. Like the metaphor of sensory 'doors' and 'windows' in a corporeal edifice, Peter's internal sense is both a barrier and an opening. As well as preventing the passage of harmful or misleading species, the internal censor ensures that useful and edifying impressions are retained and then properly interpreted. Whereas Bernard imagined the apertures of the body shut fast against the world, Peter—writing with preachers and their lay audiences in mind—not only makes allowances for the ongoing influx of worldly sensations; he places bodily sight on a continuum with interior modes of perception.

When Peter says that 'Man ought to shift his eye's gaze from exterior things to interior things',[72] it is implied that this introspective and redemptive trajectory has a physiological basis. In other words, spiritual progress begins with outward, bodily sight and moves inward, just as sensible species originating in the world enter the eyes and then pass through the interior organs of the sensitive soul. This perceptual continuum is conceived by Peter, as it is by Bacon, as a process of dematerialisation. Only the bodily eye (*oculus corporis* or *oculus carnalis*) and the inner eye (*oculus interior*, including memory, imagination and interior censor) actually 'see' the world as a picture. With the mind's eye (*oculus mentis*) the soul is led 'to truths that no longer depend on physical images'.[73] Finally, by means of the purest gaze of the heart (*oculus cordis*) the soul is assimilated to its object.

In the perspectivist tradition, the geometrical essence of the world was isolated from its material substance in the interests of scientific knowledge. Peter is concerned with the abstraction of *moral* truths, but the operation is essentially the same. In both contexts the mind's eye (or for Bacon the agent intellect) gazes upon bodily organs of sensation and cognition in which extramental species have real, physical existence. For Bacon, the embodied soul and mind comprised 'an intelligible world' in which the transcendent, active intellect could behold 'the form of the whole universe . . .'[74] Peter implies similarly that the traces of extramental objects— seen in their moral aspect by the inner eye—can provide a focus for devotion and meditation:

The opening (*foramen*) that we ought to gaze upon most frequently is the wound of Christ who was pierced on the cross . . . Anyone can enter into the interior of his conscience and meditate in his mind's eye on Christ's wound, so that he conforms to Christ's sufferings through his model.[75]

The soul is effectively transported 'through' Christ's wound as the visible image gives way to a deeper, moral truth. And when the eye of the heart grasps the very essence of the crucified and redemptive body, the viewer is assimilated to Christ. Not only does the movement from bodily to interior sight follow the transformative multiplication of sensible species; the *passio* of sensation in this instance is united with the Passion of Christ.[76]

Peter's example must surely have brought to mind medieval devotional images of the crucified Christ, with their emphatic presentation of the wounds, particularly the side wound as gateway to the sacred heart (see Figs 6.1 to 6.4 in the next chapter). Indeed, many of the eventual recipients of his advice would have been able to look at such an image while listening to the sermon. There is another reason, however, why this example may have appealed to Peter. Both St Hilary (c. 315–c. 368) and St Augustine had described the relationship between the first and second persons of the Trinity in terms of species. The Son was the species or image (*imago*) of the Father. Commenting on this idea in his *Summa Theologica*, Thomas Aquinas wrote:

> The term *species* as Hilary put it into the definition of image connotes a form derived in one thing from another. In such a usage an image means the species of something in the way that anything made like another is said to be in the form of the other, namely by having a like form.[77]

Bacon's theory of species, as we have seen, provided for the continuity of an object's form or essence through successive material bodies: the intervening medium, the skin or eye, the corporeal chambers of the brain. It explained how something could be outside, in the world; and at the same time inside, in the viewer's sensory apparatus. The idea that the Son is the species or image of the Father suggests that Christ brings the 'essence' of God into material existence; and that this essence can be extended to individual Christians in a real and transformative way.

Even without the scientific detail of Bacon's optics, the operation of species offered a useful way of thinking about the mysteries of the incarnation and the sacrament of the mass. William of Auxerre, writing between 1215 and 1229, used the analogy of a mirror to explain how Christ was wholly present in each part of the consecrated host, both before and after it was broken.[78] In the fourteenth century—probably with the benefit of Bacon's *Opus Majus*—John Wyclif equated Christ's sacramental presence in the eucharist with the multiplication of sensible species: 'Just as the optical writers say a body is multiplied intentionally, and is truly present wherever its species acts, and has the power of acting there; so God can make his body to be sacramentally present at every point of the host, and act there spiritually.'[79] The union of divine form and human flesh, Christ was the archetypal mediator. Through his sacramental and pictorial images, a transcendent God could participate in—and redeem—humanity.

To sum up, the internal censor—as gateway and gatekeeper—had a significant role to play both in the avoidance of sin and in personal devotions. On the first count, sight could no longer be said to lead inexorably to sin, looking to lusting: seductive 'forms' might be judged and deflected in the same way one discredits the bent appearance of a stick in water. Secondly, optics provided a scientific foundation for moral perception: progressively stripped of its corporeality, the phenomenal world was first 'moralised' then distilled to its spiritual essence.

It should be clear by now that the custody of the eyes involved more than the repression of bodily sight. Bernard of Clairvaux, Augustine and Peter of Limoges all approached the regulation or censorship of bodily sensation as a means of stimulating internal, spiritual sight. And although the inner and outer senses were often mapped onto the dualistic principles of reason and sensation (bodily sight, for example, being equated with spiritual blindness), they were also analogous: thus it was taken as given that the science of optics could shed light on the soul's interior 'vision'. In the next section we will look more closely at this relationship of signification between corporeal and spiritual modes of sight; and between the visible world and its invisible analogue.

The transports of analogy

An appropriate starting point is John Scotus Eriugena's much quoted claim that 'there is nothing among visible and corporeal things which does not signify something incorporeal and intelligible.'[80] In this sentence the ninth-century philosopher and theologian encapsulated a principle of analogy between material things and immaterial ideas that had the potential to turn every sensation to spiritual advantage.[81] His message is characteristic of the medieval proclivity for looking beyond—literally *seeing through*—the sensible world to a parallel realm of unchanging and universal truths. Eriugena does not speak of the imaginative movement from things to pure ideas in terms of a *visual* ascent, but the passage from matter to spirit was often articulated through modes of vision. This might take the form of a perceptual 'ladder' stretching from sensual to higher understanding; or it might exploit the Platonic language of analogy, transforming the split between humanity and divinity into a mirror.[82]

Medieval scholars distinguished between different kinds of analogy. The most widely used formula identified four levels of signification: a literal or historical sense, an allegorical sense, a tropological or moral sense, and an anagogical sense.[83] The literal sense does not concern us here, as it remains

by definition within the material, earthly realm; and the art of reading a
text or object in terms of its moral significance has been covered in relation to Peter of Limoges, who offered a tropological interpretation of
optical science. That leaves us with allegorical and anagogical interpretation. According to Guillaume Durand (who was writing his *Rationale
Divinorum Officiorum* around 1285–92) the difference between the two is
that allegories are relationships between two *visible* things; while what is
signified anagogically is 'invisible and heavenly'.[84] Durand illustrates this
distinction by comparing the etymologies of the two terms. Allegory, he
says, 'is derived from the Greek *allon*, which means *foreign*, and *gore* which
is *sense*: it is essentially a '*foreign sense*'.[85] 'Anagogue', on the other hand, 'is
so called from *ana*, which is upwards, and *gogue*, a leading: as it were an
upward leading. Whence the anagogic sense is that which leadeth from
the visible to the invisible . . .'[86]

Allegory, tropology and anagogy can all be grouped under Lloyd's more
general heading of analogy: each uses what is known (the literal meaning
of a text, for instance) to explain something that is more elusive or unknown. What interests me in Durand's schema is the vertical momentum
of the highest level of signification (other commentators, as we shall see,
attribute the same power to allegory). This particular form of analogy is
not so much a mode of symbolic *translation*, as a means of *transportation*.
Abbot Suger's description of the reconstructed and sumptuously re-
decorated abbey church of St Denis is a particularly famous example of
anagogical elevation:[87]

> When—out of my delight in the beauty of the house of God—the loveli-
> ness of the many-coloured stones has called me away from external cares,
> and worthy meditation has induced me to reflect, transferring that which is
> material to that which is immaterial, on the diversity of the sacred virtues:
> then it seems to me that I see myself dwelling, as it were, in some strange
> region of the universe which neither exists entirely in the slime of the earth
> nor entirely in the purity of Heaven; and that, by the grace of God, I can
> be transported from this inferior to that higher world in an anagogical
> manner.[88]

Often cited as one of the definitive statements of the medieval aesthetic
sensibility,[89] Suger's account also speaks of the confluence of verbal and
visual processes. Both anagogical interpretation and redemptive vision
locate the viewer or reader somewhere *between* worldly experience and
transcendent mysteries or hidden meanings. Medieval writers referred
to the figural surface of texts as *involucrum* or *integumentum*, suggesting a
'covering' or 'wrapping' of invisible meaning by visible words. In the same

way, the material world became a veil that revealed, but also concealed its interior truth.[90] For as Peter Abelard observed, every analogy, every resemblance—particularly that between spiritual things and their material representations—is 'dissimilar in some respect'.[91]

Like the play between identity and difference that motivates and 'moves' the senses, a gap between word and meaning or creation and Creator is fundamental to the transpositions of analogy.[92] The experience evoked by Suger is one of suspension or syncopation: between heaven and earth, matter and the immaterial. Instead of lifting him beyond the visible world, the anagogical ascent leaves Suger straddling the irreconcilable poles of medieval dualism, as it were. This, perhaps, is the source of his wonder and his sense of strangeness. It is also more broadly characteristic of Christian mysticism.

Michel de Certeau has argued that mystical experiences are fundamentally paradoxical:[93] at once hidden and 'phenomenal;' unutterable and given to voluble expression; transcendent and immanent. 'Mysticism', he concludes—and Suger seems to confirm this conclusion—'cannot be reduced to either of the aspects that always comprise this paradox. It is held within their relation. It is undoubtedly this relation itself.'[94]

Durand and Suger single out the anagogical sense as that most able to bring human minds within reach of the divine mysteries, but other writers are less particular in their approach to the poetics and technologies of redemption. Gregory the Great, for example, described allegory as a 'machine' capable of lifting up the soul towards God.[95] Similarly, in Bonaventure's *Journey of the Mind to God* the perceptual ladder is ascended by means of a series of analogies, directing the soul's attention from earthly to spiritual things.[96] To begin with:

> the soul was led to God by going out to external things to admire in them the work of God's creative power. Then, looking at creation, the soul beheld God's footprints upon the world's surface: the material world became a mirror in which it beheld its God. Next, turning its attention inward to itself, the soul began to reach God from a consideration of itself as God's created image, and then a further step was made when it began to behold God in the mirror of its renovated being. Whereupon, the soul was led to raise its gaze above and beyond itself, seeking, as it were, the light of God's countenance . . .[97]

Each 'step' in the pilgrimage towards God takes place, as it were, through the mirror of analogy; or rather through a series of mirrors of diminishing materiality. Cast in this redemptive role, vision is no longer polarised into two, incommensurable gazes. Instead, there is a continuum of gazes, or rather continuous aspects of the one gaze: first the bodily sight of God's creation, then the progressively introspective vision of a soul no longer tethered to the sensible world, and finally the contemplative gaze 'above and beyond'. As with Peter of Limoges's vision of Christ's side wound, the focus shifts from corporeal to incorporeal reality along an axis that follows the trajectory of sense perception itself. In the same text Bonaventure writes of the soul's 'threefold progress' through a series of 'outlooks', the first being 'toward corporeal things without', the second occurring when the soul 'enters in within itself to contemplate itself'.[98] The third and final stage is the 'upward glance' which takes the soul 'beyond itself'.[99] The bodily eye is both the model and the vehicle for the inward and upward looking gaze which will eventually be re-incorporated into the divine Light.

The idea of spiritual ascent through progressive stages of vision acknowledges, even if only implicitly, the necessity of bodily sight; just as the theory of analogy vindicates words and images as signifiers of the ineffable. Analogy and the idea of a hierarchy of perception share the same structure, the same productive tension between identity and difference, and a common goal of imaginative motility. Through analogy the mind might be 'carried away to contemplation' or 'enlarged' by understanding,[100] in the same way that one is 'moved' and altered by visible things.

Sublimating sensation and the ocular sublime

In his sermons on the Song of Songs, Bernard often starts out by describing the bride of Canticles from the perspective of a human lover. The male auditors of these sermons (which were probably written to be read rather than spoken) are encouraged to identify with the Bridegroom in his longing, to visualise the bride's face and body and imagine going to meet her in the enclosed garden of Canticles.[101] Repeatedly, however, Bernard insists that his words are not to be taken in their carnal sense; and the imaginative movement beyond the literal meaning of the text corresponds to an *identification* with the bride, who yearns to be united with her heavenly spouse.[102] For Astell, Bernard thereby 'provides a way for an awakened eros to be sublimated into the love of God and neighbour'.[103] This is possible, she explains, because 'there is only one love, not two'. Lust is simply 'a blinded *charitas*, what Etienne Gilson calls "a love of God become unaware of itself." '[104]

Although Freud's comments on sublimation do not constitute a theory, they have had an enormous influence both within and outside the field of psychoanalysis (Astell's passing reference being a pertinent example).[105] Freud describes sublimation as a 'certain kind of modification of the aim and change of the object, in which our social valuation is taken into account . . .'[106] The sexual instincts are singled out for this purpose of diversion or transferral because these instincts, according to Freud, are 'noticeable to us for their plasticity, their capacity for altering their aims, their replaceability . . . and their readiness for being deferred . . .'[107] Thus diverted, the libido is placed at the service of non-sexual activities, and directed towards the 'higher' interests of self and society. Artistic, scientific and intellectual pursuits, along with religion, are, for Freud, paradigmatic of this process, although on a more basic level sublimation is held to be fundamental to the formation of the ego or socialised subject.[108] As the mechanism by which primal drives are re-directed to socially constructive ends, sublimation becomes responsible for self and for civilisation.[109]

It is significant that the mechanism of sublimation corresponds so closely to the rhetorical devices of analogy and allegory, with their ability to transport the imagination from corporeal signifiers to an incorporeal signified. Indeed, the Latin *sublimis*, from which the English 'sublimation' and 'sublime' derive, means 'lofty' or 'raised on high':[110] making the action of sublimation identical to the medieval allegorical 'machine'. And if bodily lust may be sublimated—raised up—to spiritual love, so too corporeal sight might be diverted into spiritual vision. Rather than *transcending* embodiment and everything associated with it, spiritual vision would originate from the same source, the same drive, as its carnal, sensual other. In the remainder of this Chapter I will use Julia Kristeva's re-reading of Freudian sublimation to reopen the problem of the flesh and its relation to the gaze 'above and beyond'.

It was not until the seventeenth century, according to Hans Loewald, that the term 'sublimation' was used figuratively in the current sense of 'elevation to a higher state or plane of existence; transmutation into something higher, purer, or more sublime'.[111] In the Middle Ages 'sublime' referred to either physical transmutation—in *The Canterbury Tales* Chaucer writes disparagingly of alchemists' efforts 'to sublime' base metals into gold[112]—or to mystical states. Bonaventure's description of the 'sublime' glimpse of eternity enjoyed by the mystic is a typical example of the latter.[113] Whether alchemical, mystical or psychoanalytic, however, sublimation is imagined as a process of de-materialisation; a conversion of 'base' materiality, carnality or the sexual instincts into something 'purer'.[114] What is behind these fantasies of transcendence? For Kristeva, the answer to this question has everything to do with the Judaeo-Christian notion of the flesh.

Kristeva brings Freud's understanding of sublimation into contact with the medieval sublime by grounding both in the 'carnal overflow' of the flesh.[115] The flesh, as we have seen, is a site of permeability and pollution: a vast suppurating ulcer or a brimming sewer, to repeat Bernard of

Clairvaux's metaphors. Unable to be contained within the imagined boundary of the self, but equally impossible to separate from the self, the penetrated and penetrating 'border' of flesh engenders nausea, even horror.[116] The encounter with flesh is in this sense an encounter with the abject.

For Kristeva, this vertiginous slippage or dissolution of the boundaries between inside and outside, self and other, can only be kept at bay through endless attempts at separation and sublimation. The dividing reflex is an attempt to externalise the abject as object: 'Necessarily dichotomous, somewhat Manichaean, [the subject] divides, excludes . . .'[117] Abjection could thus be said to give rise to the polarising impulse that sets flesh against spirit, reason against sensation: a battle in which the lines are constantly being redrawn. If the desire to divide underpins *polarising* discourses, then sublimation—as we have seen—finds its discursive equivalent in *analogy*. Though equally partial and imperfect, sublimation seeks ultimately to unite opposites, by reabsorbing the abject into the self, or by losing oneself in the other.[118] A 'land of oblivion' that is 'edged with the sublime', abjection is the unimaginable coexistence of opposites—a collision, perhaps, more than a fusion—a 'flash of lightning . . . the moment when revelation bursts forth'.[119]

Kristeva's segue from sublimation into the sublime obscures an important difference between the two terms. Sublimation is the means by which 'I keep [the abject] under control'; yet the sublime is typically experienced as a *loss* of control, equal parts wonder and terror, pleasure and pain.[120] Similarly, while sublimation underwrites all intellectual endeavour, thereby enabling the acquisition of knowledge, reason and knowledge fall away in the face of the sublime. Speaking of the abject (and thus of its sublime 'edging') Kristeva insists: 'One does not know it, one does not desire it, one joys in it [*on en jouit*]. Violently and painfully. A passion.'[121] It would seem, then, that even as one is lifted up, 'sublimed', away from the abject, it returns in the form of the sublime, in ecstasy or what the French call *jouissance*.

How can we account for this paradox, by which the end—the 'flash of lighting', the mystical collision of opposites—unravels the very means by which it was reached? In making abjection the site of the sublime, Kristeva implies that sublimation is no ladder out of embodiment or language, no transcendental machine, but the trajectory by which one is returned to the threshold of the flesh.

This is not to say, however, that one is returned to one's self or one's senses. The passage from sublimation into the sublime is characterised not only by a loss of mastery, but by a loss—or at least suspension, marginalisation or displacement—of self. As Richard of St Victor writes: 'human understanding increases from the greatness of its enlarging so that it is no longer itself (not that it is not understanding, but that it is no longer *human*) when in a marvellous manner and by an incomprehensible change it is made more than human . . .'[122] If we read this through Kristeva's assertion that the abject/sublime is not the *object* of desire or knowledge, but a borderland that 'one joys *in*' (my emphasis) we can begin to rethink transcendence.[123] In one respect, the interpenetration of one's desire with an object or other does indeed place one beyond, outside or 'beside' one-self, as the term ecstasy—literally 'displacement'—implies.[124] Just as there occurs, in the act of seeing, an assimilation of the percipient subject to the visible object, so the contemplative is 'transformed' through a steadfast gaze of spiritual longing 'into [God]'.[125]

There is still a thread, however tenuous, of continuity in this quintes-sential fantasy of transcendence. Even at the point of 'immeasurable and absolute elevation of soul, forgetting all created things and liberated from them', there remains the unbroken trajectory of the gaze.[126] The sublima-tion of ocular desire through successive levels of seeing and understanding may ultimately 'lift' the soul's gaze beyond the visible or desirable object, but not beyond vision or desire itself. Both subject *and* object, vision tra-verses the distance between time and eternity, earth and heaven, humanity and God. So when Bonaventure says 'the soul was led to raise its gaze above and beyond itself . . .' he is locating transcendence in a 'gaze' that is at once a subjective power of attention and affect, and an attribute of God. For Kristeva, this experience of being in two places at once—which I have mapped on to a specifically medieval model of vision—is definitively sublime:

> the sublime is a *something added* that expands us, overstrains us, and causes us to be both *here*, as dejects, and *there*, as others and sparkling. A divergence, an impossible bounding. Everything missed, joy—fascination.[127]

Finally, as a 'divergence' (rather than loss or transcendence) of self, and as the fruit of sublimated desire, redemptive vision repeats the feminine poetics of carnal and optical sight. Richard of St Victor describes how the inward-turned soul is penetrated by a 'great beam' of divine light, and from it 'conceives the flame of longing for the sight of God . . .'[128] By 'longing', he continues, the soul 'goes into labor; and the more longing increases, the closer it comes to giving birth'.[129] Vision in its libidinal, maternal aspect is the site of spiritual 'rebirth', in the same way that visible forms, actualised in the humours of the eye and internal senses, enable ideas to be conceived in the mind. And just as Bacon had used the Aristotelian concept of passive potency to explain how matter (whether sense-organs, mind, or intervening medium) is actualised by species, here Richard emphasises the soul's desire and expectation as active elements of humanity's openness to God.[130]

If sight is experienced and theorised as a compound of and movement between subject and object; if it is felt to be at once outside the body, and an organ of the sensitive soul; and if vision is inextricably bound up with desire, then 'transcendental' vision is something of a misnomer. As a state of suspension on the threshold between self and other and a condition of active, desiring permeability, the sublimated gaze still maintains the pulse (though not the core) of a 'self'. In the next chapter we will encounter this sublime threshold between self and other, humanity and divinity in a different context: not as the product of an anagogical elevation above the 'slime of the earth', but in the unsublimated flesh of the Redeemer and in the gaze of communion. For as the opportunities for seeing Christ's body increased in the thirteenth century, the need for anagogical 'transport' diminished. To rephrase Bernard's opening words, one could touch and embrace the Saviour with one's bodily eyes.

CHAPTER 6

OCULAR COMMUNION

It is often observed that from the thirteenth century, visual experience of the sacred played an increasingly central role in both private devotions and communal religious life.[1] A proliferation of public and devotional images; dramatic re-enactments of Biblical stories; the exhibition of relics and other cultic objects; the elevation of the host within the mass and its extraliturgical display in the monstrance: all of these developments, as Hans Belting points out, speak of a 'need to see'.[2] If previously God's ultimate invisibility and unrepresentability were proof of his transcendent divinity, Belting contends that the daily possibility of beholding Christ, the Virgin and saints came increasingly to 'fulfill the postulate that reality attains to full existence and is proven only in visibility'.[3]

One of the questions addressed in this chapter is *why* did visibility become the proof and locus of God's existence?[4] For Belting, the answer has to do with the 'communicative function' of the new visual forms.[5] The transformed host raised for all to see, the character in the mystery play, and the sacred image or exhibited relic could convey doctrinal lessons; but more importantly they invited participation. Each of these developments helped to redefine devotion (*devotio*) as an 'intersubjective relation', a relationship of reciprocity.[6] In the process the viewer could expect to be transformed, but so too was God. Where Richard of St Victor felt himself become 'more than human' through contemplation,[7] Belting notes that the thirteenth-century devotional image 'drew the sacred into the human sphere . . .'[8]

This does not, however, explain why *visibility* should be a privileged signifier or site of divine reality, rather than, say, hearing or touching. After all, seeing was not believing for Doubting Thomas. Reciprocity might just as easily take the form of a mutual touch or an interior dialogue as an 'exchange of gazes' (*Blickaustausch*), to borrow A. Neumeyer's term.[9] In order to understand why bodily sight became the primary means of experiencing spiritual reality, it is necessary to consider the relationship between thirteenth-century developments in optical theory and the changing spiritual ideals mentioned above. The omission in Belting's account is *medieval* vision: optical, carnal, redemptive. While he makes the reciprocal gaze central to late medieval devotion, vision itself is treated as common historical ground, a universal given. My argument in this chapter is that sight, as it was defined by Bacon and his contemporaries, offered a means of *communion* that exceeds Belting's model of 'communication' or 'dialogue'.[10] The visual relationship—more than any other sensory interaction—allowed for bodily participation in the divine.

Sight alone—as a visual palpation or a deep, interior 'touch'—would probably have dispelled the doubt of a medieval Thomas. But the 'need to see' to which Belting refers was motivated as much by desire as by doubt. If the spiritual ideals discussed in the last chapter echo Bacon's vision of a disembodied 'veridical eye', the redemptive visions described in this chapter have more in common with the bodily and affective aspects of optical science, and the ocular interpenetrations of carnal vision.[11] The continuities between Bacon's optics, carnal vision and late medieval devotional practices are not apparent if vision is equated with distance, mastery and objectification. If, however, sight is conceived in terms of physical and affective proximity—and imagined as a mutual engagement or interpenetration—then we can begin to understand why the emotional and physical communion with God was often envisaged as an *ocular* communion.

I will begin by examining two of the key features of late medieval piety: the doctrine of *imitatio Christi*—increasingly interpreted as a transformative *visual* identification with a visible Redeemer—and the rise of 'ocular communion' as an alternative to sacramental communion during the mass. The remainder of the chapter is a case study of a popular devotional image: the Man of Sorrows or *Imago Pietatis*. As a pictorial 'incarnation' of Christ, the Man of Sorrows reflects, and no doubt contributed to the reorientation of vision in the thirteenth century.[12] This particular group of images is also the focus of Belting's investigation, and it is his figure of 'reciprocity' that provides me with my point of departure.

Each of these developments, I will argue, assumes a reciprocal gaze at once potent and intimate; a gaze consistent with the aspects of Bacon's optics discussed in Chapter 4. And in each case, the devotional relationship—as a form of visual and bodily *communion*—can be distinguished from verbal or psychological *communication*. These conclusions have significant implications for the study of devotional art. Art history as a discipline might be seen as the product of modern ocularcentrism. Its clear delineation of spectator and image; the delimitation of more or less discrete stylistic or symbolic entities; more recent attempts to view these objects in their historical, cultural or economic 'perspective':[13] these ways of making sense of material culture are also ways of seeing. And they are ways of seeing that approximate the abstractive, mathematical branch of optical science. This chapter will begin to negotiate this gap between the vision of art history and medieval visual culture by focusing on the shared flesh of vision in which communion takes place.

Imitatio Christi

In the account of her sixteen 'showings' or revelations (completed in around 1393), the anchoress Julian of Norwich mentions that she prayed for 'a bodily sight' of Christ's Passion, 'in which I might have more knowledge of the Saviour's bodily pains . . .'[14] Years later, gravely ill, she asks once again to experience with her own body the 'passion' of her Redeemer. Gazing at the crucifix held before her eyes by an attendant priest, she asks that her 'body might be filled full of recollection and feeling of his blessed Passion . . . that his pains might be my pains, with compassion which would lead to longing for God'.[15]

The desire to be identified with Christ in his suffering, death and resurrection has its Biblical precedent in the words of the Apostle Paul: 'I have been crucified with Christ; it is no longer I who live, but Christ lives in me . . .'[16] Paul, however, speaks of an interior transformation. Julian's *imitatio Christi* involved bodily memory: the transcription of Christ's every pain on to her own flesh. Elsewhere she refers to spiritual vision, and to the 'eye' of her understanding.[17] Her vision of Christ, however, and her participation in his Passion are unambiguously and gloriously corporeal. Mystical union, as Julian saw it, occurs in the shared flesh of Christ and his bride.

For Julian, God was an immediate reality, not a transcendent mystery. The primary site of religious experience was not the inner, spiritual senses but the five senses of the 'outer man' (though as we have seen, this 'man' typically wore the feminine garments of the flesh—a point I will return to).[18] There is a profound difference between the 'uplifting' anagogical function of images discussed in the last chapter and the kind of visual encounter with God described by Julian. Like the sight and taste of Christ's 'flesh' in communion, the potent physical presence of a saint in a reliquary, or the conviction that Christ or the Virgin animate their painted or sculptural likeness, Julian's visions are unsublimated.[19] The sense of the divine that emerges from these practices and convictions is not unitary, autonomous and heavenly, but embodied in a diversity of sacred objects.[20] To be sure, most theologians spoke of images—whether mental or material— as the necessary means to an end: not an end in themselves.[21] But for many

Christians, spiritual and corporeal sight were one and the same. To quote Richard Trexler, 'the sacred was very much in and about this world'.[22]

The shift in religious experience away from the word—or its pictorial equivalent—as a signifier of transcendent truth, towards an embodied, visual or visionary encounter with the divine can be tracked through saints' lives or *vitae*, as well as through accounts of miracle-working images. By the twelfth century, anthologies of miracles and *exempla* were in circulation, developing into a genre of popular religious literature that flourished through to the fifteenth century.[23] Coinciding with the dissemination of these legends, the role of sight in religious conversions became more common. By the fourteenth century, according to Margaret Miles, visionary conversions—often involving a specific crucifix or paint-ing—outnumbered those brought about by oral or scriptural revelation.[24] Catherine of Siena (d. 1380), for example, was said to have received a vision of St Dominic 'in that form in which she had seen him painted in the church'[25] and both Gertrude of Helfta (d. 1301 or 1302) and Julian of Norwich (d. 1423) reported that their visions of Christ were inspired by crucifixion images.[26]

Angela of Foligno says at one point in her *Memorial* (which she dictated to a scribe between 1292 and 1296): 'whenever I saw the Passion of Christ depicted in art, I could not bear it: a fever would overtake me and I would become sick. For this reason, my companion carefully hid all pictures of the Passion from me.'[27] The crucifix is a recurring image in her spiritual journey. Following the death of her husband, children and mother, Angela entered the Third Order of Saint Francis. Shortly afterwards, during a pilgrimage to Assisi in 1291, she had a vision prompted by the sight of a painting. She tells her confessor and scribe that on entering the church: 'I saw Saint Francis depicted in the arms of Christ. And He said to me, "I will hold you this closely, even closer than the eyes of the body can see". Then I looked so as to see Him with the eyes of my body and of my mind.'[28] Following her vision, in which outward and inward sight converge, she realises that she bears an impression of the cross 'within my body'.[29]

St Francis of Assisi's own conversion before the crucifix is probably the most famous of these legends. As a paradigmatic instance of *imitatio Christi*—the intense and transformative identification with Christ—the stigmatisation of St Francis makes vision a corporeal event. Seeing was not only believing, but being assimilated with Christ's flesh and blood through a visual interaction. This new ideal of affective and bodily identifica-tion with the Saviour reflects the influence of Franciscan thought on thirteenth- and fourteenth-century spirituality. Franciscan incarnational theology embraced on the one hand the simple humanity of Christ, and on the other the spiritual potential of sensory experience. In David

Jeffrey's words, 'Enjoyment derived from the senses is the primary Franciscan aesthetic experience.'[30] Roger Bacon's 'visual delight' was undoubtedly inflected by this Franciscan sensibility, as was his commitment to what Jeffrey has called 'the science of ordinary things'.

It is possible to explain St Francis's encounter with Christ in terms of an intense psychological identification; to read Julian of Norwich's pains and paralysis as psychosomatic symptoms, her visions as hallucinations. The alternative is to approach visionary literature in its historical context: to ask why *imitatio Christi* was so plausible as a spiritual ideal. It may be stating the obvious to say that vision is crucial to Angela's *Memorial* and Julian's *Showings*, and to visionary mysticism in general. Little, however, has been written on the subject beyond the observation that religious images frequently served as a stimulus and focus for visions.[31] Julian's 'revelations' are a case in point, interspersed as they are with references to the seemingly ubiquitous presence of a crucifix. Her Second Revelation, for example, begins with the words: '. . . I looked with bodily vision into the face of the crucifix which hung before me, in which I saw a part of Christ's Passion . . .'[32] Jesus appears before her bodily eyes, and it is his corporeal, visible presence which precipitates her own physical and emotional 'passion'.

Julian of Norwich and Angela of Foligno would not have explained the changes in their bodies in terms of an intense psychological identification, but they would certainly have thought of sight—ordinary or miraculous— as a *physical* activity. My argument is that miraculous visions and mystical revelations merely amplify the 'transmutations' and 'passions' of ordinary sight as understood by Bacon and his commentators. Similarly, the functions and significance of medieval images (both mental and extramental) reflect a specifically medieval understanding of vision. It is no coincidence, therefore, that the phenomenon of *imitatio Christi* shares a number of basic principles with Bacon's optics, most importantly an emphasis on physical transformation.

Vision, in the medieval world, did not leave the viewer untouched or unchanged. The consequences of looking when one *shouldn't* were well rehearsed; but one could also expect to be positively changed by judicious looking. Given that perception was defined as assimilation,[33] the objects of one's attention were of critical importance. To see was to become similar to one's object. Devotional texts repeatedly instruct their readers to visualise the Virgin with her child, to recollect every detail of Christ's Passion; to gaze at his wounds and, through extended meditation, to identify with his suffering and with his mother's sorrow.[34] One of the most popular texts in this genre was the late thirteenth-century *Meditations on the Life of Christ*.[35] This early Franciscan devotional handbook, written by a friar

living in Tuscany, was translated into Middle English seven times during
the following century, as well as into other European vernaculars. In the
chapters covering the Passion the reader (or perhaps more correctly, the
viewer) is urged to imagine they are present at the crucifixion, following
the events recounted in the text with their 'innere eye'.[36] By visualising
Christ's death and resurrection, the meditator could expect to be led 'to a
newe state of grace'.[37] Angela's visions are remarkable in their enactment
of these instructions, as her gaze lingers on Christ's throat, the individual
hairs of his beard, his closed eyes, the wound in his side:[38]

> At the tenth step . . . [God] took pity on me and often appeared to me, both
> when I was asleep and awake; each time, he appeared hanging on the cross.
> He told me that I should look at His wounds . . . He even showed me the
> hairs of His beard, eyebrows and head, which had been plucked out, and He
> counted every blow of the whip, pointing to each one, and then he said, 'All
> this I endured for you'.

The emphatic display of Christ's wounds in pictorial representations of
the Passion, the elevation of the host, and the exhibition of relics in transparent ostensories performed a similar function. To use Belting's expression, they presented the object of devotion with 'exclamation marks'.[39]
Belting's model of visual rhetoric takes its bearings from modern psychology and semantics. However, interpreted in light of medieval (rather than
modern) theories of perception, the visual apprehension of Christ's self-
sacrificing love or the Virgin's grief emerges as something other than a
process of verbal or non-verbal 'communication'. Communication implies
the existence of a meaning (emotional or conceptual), and its understanding. But grief, passion, longing: these states are often about the absence or
suspension of meaning or understanding; and they are certainly experienced as physical conditions. It is significant that Belting himself uses an
example that implies far more than a psychological 'dialogue'. He quotes
from the liturgical commentary written at the end of the twelfth century
by Sicard of Cremona:

> In some [mass] books the majesty of the Father and the cross of the cruci-
> fix are portrayed so that it is almost as if we see at present the one we are
> calling to, and the Passion which is depicted imprints itself on the eyes of
> the heart.[40]

If we read this literally, in terms of medieval theories of vision, rather
than figuratively, as an account of emotional projection or affective
response, the two senses of 'passion'—Christ's Passion and the perceptual

passio—come together. Bacon used the term *passio* to denote the 'transmutation' produced in the body of the recipient (viewer) by the agent
(object or species).[41] For him, 'passion' was synonymous with the idea of
a deep, 'interior' impression: analogous to the imprint of a seal in wax, but
altering all of the wax and not just its surface.[42] Like the maternal body,
the organs of the sensitive soul provided the latent, receptive matter in
which the pure species of the Son of God might be realised. Far from
being a 'dead weight', this sensitive matter was described by Bacon (following Aristotle) as existing in a paradoxical state of 'active potency'.[43]
One might almost say that matter is expectant of form, as the worshipper
is expectant of God's grace. *Passio* was the realisation of that expectation.

Passion, then, is born of the anticipated (desired) assimilation of subject
to object. It entails a certain violence to the self, as one becomes 'like' one's
object; and yet this decentring or partial dissolution of self is also a source
of pleasure. (Compassion—literally 'with suffering'—is similarly bitter-
sweet in its suspension of self, and identification with the other.) Jacopone
da Todi's description of the stigmatisation of St Francis is illustrative. For
this thirteenth-century Franciscan poet and mystic, Francis of Assisi was
both an exemplary bride of Christ and visible proof that it was possible to
be bodily transformed into the image of Christ through the fusive power
of love:

> Love has this function of uniting two forms into one; it transforms Francis
> into the suffering Christ . . . Divine love, most high, embraced him with
> Christ; his deeply burning passion so incorporated him into him [Christ], it
> softened his heart like wax for the seal, and impressed on it that one [Christ]
> into whom he was transformed.[44]

Later in the chapter, I will discuss Christ's reciprocal assimilation to his
human 'spouse'. What I want to emphasise here is that this love that
unites—like the wounding gaze of courtly romance—is a way of seeing.
No less than sexual lust, redemptive love is articulated through sight: it
penetrates, inflames and transforms, leaving an indelible impression on the
beholder's soul. In pictorial representations of St Francis's stigmatisation,
this divine love is conventionally depicted as rays of light emanating from
the wounds of the winged seraph to pierce Francis's own body.[45] Visible
light thus becomes an expression of the divine light of creation; the
eternal 'gaze' of God.[46]

St Bonaventure's 'official' biography of St Francis, the *Legenda maior*,
describes this transformation in the most detailed and naturalistic terms.[47]
Written between 1260 and 1263, the *Legenda* was used by Giotto for his
frescoes of the life of St Francis in the upper church at Assisi. Again, the

stigmata are referred to as 'sacred seals'.[48] Francis's flesh becomes 'wax', moulded into the image of the crucified Christ:

> [A]s the vision disappeared, it left in his heart a wondrous glow, but on his flesh also it imprinted a no less wondrous likeness of its tokens. For his hands and feet seemed to be pierced through the midst with nails, the heads of the nails shewing in the palms of the hands, and upper side of the feet, and their points shewing on the other side; the heads of the nails were round and black in the hands and feet, while the points were long, bent, and as it were turned back, being formed of the flesh itself, and protruding therefrom. The right side, moreover, was—as if it had been pierced by a lance—seamed with a ruddy scar, wherefrom ofttimes welled the sacred blood, staining his habit and breeches.'[49]

The 'image' of Christ received by St Francis is more than a pictorial likeness: it is a sculptural reproduction. In fact Bonaventure mixes his metaphors. God is the divine sculptor, 'fashioning' the image of Christ out of flesh;[50] but he is also the Word, writing his creation into existence. St Francis bears the marks of the crucifixion *written on his members of flesh by the finger of the Living God* (my emphasis).[51] This ambiguity surrounding the mode of representation (writing or sculpting) is not confined to theological discussions of *imitatio Christi*. As Mary Carruthers has shown, it was central to medieval discussions of memory, where the archetypal metaphors were writing/reading and picturing/viewing.[52] Either way, memory was conceived as a physical process; a bodily imprint as real as St Francis's stigmata. In this sense, the devotional practice of identification with Christ mirrors (and no doubt exploits) the medieval 'art of memory', with its emphasis on bodily sight, interior visualisation, and the mnemonic articulation of memory images.[53]

To gaze, like Francis and Julian of Norwich, at a crucifix, or to meditate on an image of the Man of Sorrows would have been to enter into this fabric of associations and expectations. I would like to turn now to another dimension of this visual incorporation of the individual beholder with Christ's flesh: the practice of viewing, rather than eating or drinking the consecrated bread and wine of the eucharist.

Ocular communion

At the Fourth Lateran Council of 1215 it was decided that for the laity, annual communion was both obligatory and sufficient. The majority of Christians, in other words, received the eucharistic host only once a year, at Easter, after confession, penance and absolution from their sins.[54]

Cautionary tales about inadequate preparation acted as a deterrent to regular communion; and as sacramental communion decreased, the attractiveness of eucharistic substitutes increased.[55] *Seeing* the miraculously transformed bread and wine became a substitute for 'tasting' Christ: an *ocular* communion.[56] If original sin began with a visual transgression, before the forbidden tasting of the fruit (Fig. 2.1),[57] redemption could, it seemed, similarly begin with a look (Fig. 6.1).

Transubstantiation, ratified as dogma at the same Lateran Council, dictates that the sacramental bread and wine of the mass are the actual body and blood of Christ. The doctrine is founded on a literal interpretation of the words uttered by Christ at the Last Supper: 'unless you eat the flesh of the Son of Man and drink His blood, you have no life in you. Whoever eats My flesh and drinks My blood has eternal life . . .'[58] The nature of Christ's instruction to the Apostles on the eve of his crucifixion, and its theological ramifications, were the subject of controversy from the ninth century until the resolution of 1215. But behind the question of what exactly was contained in the wafer and wine was the issue of church authority. As Miri Rubin points out, debate over the eucharist intensified in the eleventh century, a period in which the popes were attempting to consolidate their power and 'enforce claims of primacy and universality . . .'[59] Shoring up the position of the clergy as the ordained mediators between individual Christians and their God was central to the construction of the 'universal church'.[60] Rubin explains:

> Whereas early Christianity looked to holy men and early medieval society turned to saints to effect the connection between God and humankind through prayers of intercession, a different order was now emerging. It was embedded in procedures and mediating practices, in neatly defined mystery, rather than in the inspiration of charismatic and exemplary figures.[61]

Within this context the eucharist was a valuable commodity and a privileged symbol: the principal means of access to salvation, grace and the divine mysteries.[62] In theory, it was a commodity that could be strictly controlled by clerical mediation; however, in practice this was not always the case.

From the late twelfth century, elevation of the host came to mark the moment of its consecration. The rationale behind this innovation is expressed by Bishop Quivil of Exeter:

> Since it is by the words *Hoc est corpus meum* ['This is my body'] and not by others that the bread is transubstantiated into the body, the priest should not elevate the Host beforehand . . . And the Host is thus raised high so that it

Figure 6.1.   Elevation of the host, initial of the Corpus Christi mass (detail).
Roman missal.

can be contemplated by all surrounding believers. And by this the devotion of believers is excited, and an increase in their faith is effected.[63]

It was not until the thirteenth century, however, that the cultic appeal and theological importance of the eucharist was fully realised, against the physical backdrop of a new liturgical art form: the altarpiece.[64] Pictorial representation of the crucified Christ found its most common expression in altarpieces, visually framing and dramatising the reincarnation of the body and blood of Christ during the mass.[65]

It is not surprising, given these conditions, that the 'impulse to look at the body of Christ' intensified;[66] or that the elevation of the host gradually assumed what Rubin describes as 'sacramental efficacy'.[67] As Bishop Quivil intimates, this 'staging' of Christ's transubstantiation made the miracle come alive for the congregation. On the other hand, Guillaume Durand lamented the fact that many people ran to mass only after hearing the elevation bell;[68] and judging by attempts to regulate attendance it was common to leave after seeing the body of Christ.[69] Although 'spiritual communion' was generally regarded as beneficial,[70] it was repeatedly stressed that gazing was insufficient in itself. In a work written around 1220, Alexander of Hales articulated this difference in terms of two kinds of 'eating': 'eating by taste' (*manducatio per gustum*), which was sacramental; and 'eating by sight' (*manducatio per visum*), which was not sacramental.[71]

Like the display of Christ's wounds in images of the Passion, and their invocation in sermons and devotional literature, the presentation of the host—whether during communion, or in the monstrance outside of the mass—invited participation on the part of the viewer.[72] Extra-liturgical showings of the host began in the early fourteenth century, by which time the *corpus Domini* had acquired the associations and trappings of a holy relic. Paraded in the feast of *Corpus Christi* (as early as 1264 in Liège), the exhibition of the host became a focus for private devotion and cultic ritual.[73] The reliquary was undergoing a similar transformation, from the traditional bejewelled casket, through the 'talking reliquary' which expressed the bodily derivation of the relic, to the ostensory. The latter, first appearing in the early thirteenth century, made use of glass or crystal containers to 'showcase' their contents.[74]

The Church's condemnation of the figurative interpretation of the eucharist (as the sign rather than the substance of the Saviour's flesh and blood) coincided with an increasing emphasis on the humanity of Christ. As Christ's physical presence came into focus in the mass, there was a corresponding pictorial shift away from the promise of future glory symbolised by the risen, exalted Redeemer, to the suffering, crucified Christ of the Passion.[75] The image of the Man of Sorrows exemplifies this transition, drawing God into the sphere of human emotion, and opening up the possibility of redemption in and through the flesh.

The Man of Sorrows

The Man of Sorrows is a contradictory image. In it, Christ bears the marks of human suffering and death, as well as his triumph over death as the living God. He stands upright, sometimes against the cross, sometimes partially supported by his mother or other members of the mourning party. His arms may be outstretched as if expectant of an embrace, but also in order to display his wounds: the indisputable 'proof' of his sacrifice. In transalpine examples Christ often points to or touches his wounded side, inviting us to drink of his blood, and showing the way to the sacred heart.[76] With his eyes often fully or partially open, Christ as Man of Sorrows is, as Leo Steinberg aptly put it, a lively corpse.[77] At once living and dead, human and divine, this representation of the Son of God embodies, and extends to the viewer, the possibility of mediation and reconciliation. As such, the efflorescence of this devotional type in the thirteenth and fourteenth centuries stands as an eloquent answer to the postlapsarian dualism that alienated humanity from God; all the more effective because it made the viewer an equal participant in his or her redemption.

The origins of this image have long been the subject of legend. A famous mosaic panel of the Man of Sorrows in the pilgrimage church of Santa Croce in Gerusalemme in Rome is said to be the true and original likeness of Christ, dating from his miraculous appearance during Pope Gregory's mass.[78] As Hans Belting notes, however, the events recounted in the legend—including the transformation of a host into the actual body of Christ—pre-date the image by some seven centuries. The panel in Santa Croce is now thought to have been brought to Rome from Constantinople around 1380.[79] Though factually inaccurate, the story is illuminating for several reasons. In the first place, it highlights the identification of the Man of Sorrows with the flourishing cult of the eucharist. Secondly, the fictitious association of the *Imago Pietatis* with the Roman Pope Gregory (c. 540–604) is significant in its elision of the central importance of the Byzantine icon to the development of the Western devotional image.

The real Eastern prototypes of the Man of Sorrows probably found their way to Italy around 1200,[80] and by the end of that century had been widely disseminated, both in the Mediterranean area and north of the Alps. Absorbing this influence, the Western devotional image combined the cultic status, timelessness and psychological intimacy of the icon with a condensed iconographic language derived from the traditional *historia* or narrative cycle.[81] The result was a conventionalised, yet highly personal 'open' narrative in which the viewer could be, was indeed expected to be, an active participant.[82]

Belting makes a distinction between the application of mathematical perspective to the *historia* in fifteenth-century Italy, and the 'psychological perspective' of the devotional image.[83] The latter, he says, assumes the presence of an *external* participant: its composition and narrative structure are definitively 'open'. In his view, the 'closed reference system' of the *historia*:

> which rationally arranged the parts of the image according to optical laws, moved farther and farther away from the open reference system on which the devotional image was dependent. Here *open* means incomplete in the factual narration, unconnected within the internal pictorial syntax, while being bound to an external viewer.[84]

If Belting is right, then the ability of a devotional image to move or engage the viewer is in no way dependent on a convincing illusion of reality.[85] His assessment marks a significant departure from the commonplace belief that the more 'realistic' an image, the greater its affective power.

Erwin Panofsky's periodisation of medieval and Renaissance art is a case in point. Equating pictorial naturalism with an unmediated experience of reality, Panofsky claimed that Northern and Italian art of the fifteenth century 'shared . . . one basic premise which did not apply in the Middle Ages: on both sides of the Alps, art had become a matter of direct and personal contact between man and the visible world'.[86] Medieval art, in contrast, is held to separate reality from experience: Panofsky writes of a 'curtain' of convention that might be 'lifted now and then but could not be removed'.[87] Even if 'realism' and 'reality' are not confused, there has been a tendency to associate pictorial naturalism with emotional directness, and to ascribe a 'conceptual' or 'symbolic' role to medieval art.[88] This particular historical construction implies that medieval images are 'read' or decoded while Renaissance art is truly 'seen'.[89]

The idea of devotion as a 'psychological perspective' or 'exchange of gazes' cuts across this schema. None of the images reproduced in this chapter could be described as naturalistic, though all are expressive. There is no sense that the figures occupy a space analogous to or continuous with ours. One is acutely aware of the materiality of the image: whether mosaic tiles, the rough surface of a wall or carved wood (Fig. 6.4), or the page of a book (Figs 6.2 and 6.3). These are not illusory 'windows' into a parallel world that one might step through. Yet all of these images require an external viewer for compositional and psychological closure. How, then, should this devotional 'perspective' be defined, if not geometrically?

Figure 6.2.   Imago Pietatis. Manuscript illumination, Franciscan prayer book.

I mentioned earlier that the characteristic singled out by Belting is reciprocity;[90] and that this could take a number of forms. Reciprocity can be a dialogue between the individual and Christ; an 'exchange of gazes';[91] or an empathic identification. Indeed, the Latin term *Imago Pietatis*—

Figure 6.3. Miniatures from The Rothschild Canticles. Fol. 18v: (above) Christ embracing the Sponsa in the garden; Christ and the Sponsa entering the garden; (below) the Sponsa as Caritas. Fol. 19r: Christ as Man of Sorrows.

image of piety—conveys this double meaning. *Pietas* refers to the sacrificial act of Christ performed out of compassion and mercy, so that the *Imago Pietatis* might be rendered: 'image of self-sacrificing love'.[92] Yet the term also describes the piety of the individual worshipper in his or her attitude towards the image/Christ.[93] As Belting notes, both participants are altered by this mutual affect:

> The images were expected to reciprocate the believer's mood, and, if possible, even generate it. The viewer and the person depicted in the image were related to one another mimetically. The viewer tried to assimilate himself to the depicted person and demanded back from the latter the quality of aliveness which he himself possessed. This mimesis, which was intended to bring about the ecstasy of the individual viewer, nevertheless in the long run drew the sacred into the human sphere . . .[94]

The rest of this chapter takes Belting's argument for a devotional perspective and maps it on to medieval vision. This strategy will enable us to move beyond his psychological explanation, and provide a more historically specific account of physical and affective reciprocity.

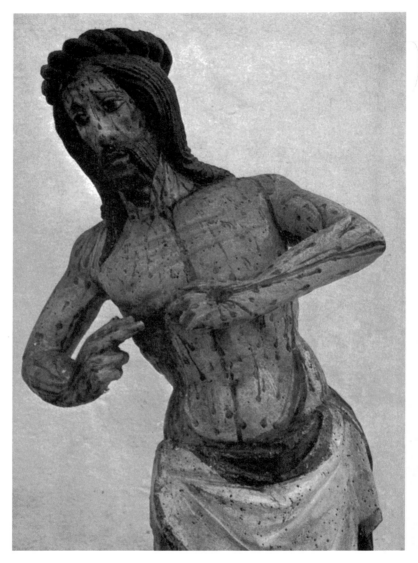

Figure 6.4.   Man of Sorrows 'Barmherzigkeit' (detail).

The devotional relationship, I will argue, is informed by optical principles; yet it cannot be reduced to mathematical precepts. It is not a 'perspective' in the sense of a stable, unitary point of view. Nor is it a method
of epistemological abstraction; a redemptive *mathesis*. On the contrary, it is

a way of seeing that exploits the ambiguities of thirteenth-century *perspectiva*, including the mutual 'gaze' of subject and object that results from Bacon's synthesis of intromission and extramission. But late medieval spirituality also redeploys the sensual, libidinal attributes of carnal vision. In this sense, we are dealing with a perspective of the flesh.

The kind of ocular communion offered by the Man of Sorrows is both violent and sexualised. In its exemplary form, the intercourse between the wounded Christ and his human 'bride' follows the tropes of ocular erotica developed in the secular romance: the gaze they exchange is an articulation of their shared carnality as it overflows the limits of individual bodies. The medieval understanding of flesh is therefore central to my reconfiguration of devotion and the devotional image. Before we turn to the *visual* dimension of communion, I would like to look more closely at the paradox of the incarnation. For Christ as Man of Sorrows not only assumes human form, or a human body: he becomes flesh. It is as God-made-flesh that he fulfils the role of archetypal mediator.

Carnal mediations

In his second sermon on the Song of Songs, Bernard of Clairvaux makes Christ's descent into human flesh the basis of humanity's return to God. 'If the mediator is to be acceptable to both parties', he writes, 'then let him who is God's Son become man . . . It is impossible that I should be spurned by him who is bone from my bones, and flesh from my flesh.'[95] But what exactly did it mean for the Son of God to take on human flesh? Bernard's words belie the theological complexities of this question, and the amount of scholarly attention that has been devoted to it over the centuries. Quite apart from the permutations of the theological debate— which are beyond the scope of this study—it is necessary to situate Christ's humanity in relation to the medieval distinction between *flesh* and *body*.

I argued in Chapter 1 that the *flesh* was conceived both as condition of corporeal permeability and as an active, libidinal force. Moreover, the openings, penetrations and appetites of the flesh were typically sexualised, often following the imaginary contours of the female body. Because it was associated with sensuality and the feminine, the flesh was invariably opposed to reason and intelligence. Responsible for retarding or cloaking the mind's eye, the flesh represented confusion and disorder. Carnal vision (the subject of Chapter 2) introduced an intersubjective dimension to the flesh. In its optical mode, carnality became the flow of desire between and through bodies.

The postlapsarian *body*—especially the female body—existed in a state of carnal entropy, to the extent that the terms 'flesh' and 'body' are often used interchangeably. Unlike the bodies enjoyed by Adam and Eve before the fall, or the 'restored' bodies of the resurrection, the fleshly body was mutable and vulnerable, subject to ageing, death and decay. Nevertheless, as an ideal or a metaphor distanced from the realities of the flesh, the human *corpus* signified the potential for a stable and harmonious hierarchy in which each part was defined in relation to a whole. While the flesh was by definition amorphous and illegible, in its 'pure' state the body was coherent, both anatomically and semantically. The body was also distinguished from the flesh by its passivity and instrumental status in relation to the sovereign mind or will. If the flesh was its own master (or rather, its own mistress), the body was both a dutiful handmaiden and a fluent expression of the soul.

A number of factors suggest that in the later Middle Ages the body of the incarnate Christ was *fleshly* rather than passive, bounded and stable. In the first place, Christ's body is semantically unstable. It signifies excessively. And it is literally fluid in its outpouring of redemptive blood: an attribute often associated with the 'maternal Jesus'. More than this, the body of Christ is eroticised in the context of a visual encounter identical to that of the courtly romance. So while the body of the Redeemer is not, properly speaking, an erotic *object*, it derives its potency from a sexualised and libidinally motivated exchange of gazes. I will expand on each of these points in turn; but first let me respond to an obvious objection. The Son of God was human, but blameless,[96] so surely the flesh of Christ is not the same flesh that was born of original sin, the flesh defined by St Bernard as a 'sinful body'.[97]

Although Jesus was not born into sin, in dying he became, in Peter Damian's words, 'the victim who has drawn all to himself', 'the victim who by his immolation purges the guilt of the world'.[98] Jaroslav Pelikan explains that redemption rested on these two basic principles: 'that Christ had taken the sins of mankind on himself and that he had made expiation for them'.[99] Furthermore, 'expiation consisted in "the sacrifice of his flesh", whose effects were then applied to the sins of those who believed in him'.[100] As Man of Sorrows, Christ is innocent—the immaculate sacrificial lamb—yet he assumes humanity's guilt by voluntary substitution; he represents the wages of sin as well as the promise of atonement. No theologian would imply that Christ had sinned, yet in the later Middle Ages there is an increasing theological, devotional and pictorial interest in the Redeemer's physical and emotional suffering, his vulnerability and the humanness of his death: all marks of the fleshly, mortal, postlapsarian body.

Another perspective on Christ's fleshliness is suggested by anthropological and psychoanalytic theories concerning the proximity of the sacred and profane. I am thinking in particular of Victor Turner's account of the liminal phase in rites of passage, and Julia Kristeva's work on abjection, discussed briefly in Chapter 5 in the context of sublimation.[101] In the following elaboration of these ideas, I will use Turner's analysis of liminality to elucidate the sexual and symbolic indeterminacy of the Redeemer's body; while Kristeva's emphasis on the *maternal* origins of the abject and sublime will serve to complicate the figure of Jesus as mother.

Victor Turner and the liminality of the flesh

Although Turner is concerned with the socio-cultural function of ritual, his description of liminality as a period of dangerous but potent 'structurelessness' bears some striking parallels to the image of Christ as a living corpse, and to the medieval understanding of flesh as unbounded, volatile corporeality.[102] In the liminal period the ritual subject is 'betwixt and between' states, whether those states are biological (unborn and born, child and adult, living and dead), social (Turner mentions 'initiation' into college fraternities or sororities) or environmental (such as rituals associated with agricultural cycles). Because the dissolution of the subject's existing social identity is a precondition for his passage to a new identity, liminality is associated both with death, decay and pollution; and with regeneration, growth, gestation and birth.[103] It is a condition marked above all by 'ambiguity and paradox'.[104] The neophyte, for example, is often represented as both corpse and embryo or suckling infant: a conjunction that brings to mind certain *Pietàs* in which a diminutive crucified Christ is cradled by his mother.[105] Alternatively, the subject's 'interstructural' state may be manifest in the symbolic erasure of sexual characteristics, or in sexual ambiguity or androgyny.[106] As Turner writes, initiates 'are symbolically either sexless or bisexual and may be regarded as a kind of human *prima materia*—as undifferentiated raw material'.[107]

These aspects of ritual liminality are clearly applicable to the Man of Sorrows. Christ is both dead and alive. He is physically and emotionally 'raw', dissolved into naked and abject suffering. Yet he remains alert, upright, claiming his victory over pain and death. More than just a union of opposites, however, the Man of Sorrows converts the polluting power of the corpse into spiritual potency; the grief associated with death into hope and the promise of a new birth.[108] Christ's body is also sexually ambiguous. For Guerric of Igny, Christ is mother, father and spouse. 'The Bridegroom', he says, 'has breasts, lest he should be lacking any one of all duties and titles of loving kindness. He is a father in virtue of natural creation . . . and also in virtue of the authority with which he instructs. He is a mother, too, in the mildness of his affection, and a nurse.'[109]

There has been considerable interest in Christ's sexuality in the wake of Caroline Bynum's work on the maternal Jesus and Leo Steinberg's documentation of what he terms the '*ostentatio genitalium*' (or genital display) in Renaissance images of the infant and crucified Christ.[110] What is striking in these accounts is that the Redeemer's body lends itself to such divergent interpretations; that it can be read as both masculine (Steinberg) and feminine (Bynum). Their point of agreement is that Christ's sexuality, masculine or feminine, is fundamental to his humanity.

Steinberg contends that the exhibition, or conspicuous concealment of Christ's genitals amounts to a display of credentials equal in significance to the *ostentatio vulnerum* or 'showing forth of the wounds'. By drawing the viewer's attention to the genitals, and hence the sexuality of Christ, the artist, in Steinberg's view, is displaying proof of Christ's humanity.[111] Furthermore, this visible sexualisation of the Redeemer's body is coupled with an emphasis on his physical suffering and death; mortality and sexuality being the defining characteristics of the postlapsarian human condition—the condition that Christ takes upon himself, and ultimately triumphs over in his redemptive act of sacrificial love.[112] For Steinberg, in short, 'sexuality' is an anatomical category, and Christ, by virtue of his concealed or revealed genitals, is definitively male.

While Steinberg reads sexuality as masculine and genital, Bynum argues along the lines of the twelfth-century nun Hildegard of Bingen, that 'man represents the divinity of the Son of God and woman his humanity'.[113] The Saviour's 'humanation', in other words, is expressed through his feminisation.[114] Specifically, it is in his bodily suffering, in the shedding of blood that cleanses and gives succour to his 'children', and in his compassion for sinners that Christ's humanity finds its most complete, and maternal, expression.[115]

As Bynum and others have observed, the medieval body seems altogether more ambiguous, more 'elastic' than its modern counterpart.[116] Leo Steinberg's reading of the body of Christ presupposes that male and female bodies are intrinsically and unambiguously different, and that sexual difference is anatomically legible. But this is to overlook the complexities of sex and gender in the Middle Ages. In his book *Making Sex*, Thomas Laqueur argues that from classical antiquity through to the Enlightenment, 'male' and 'female' were mapped on to a corporeal, sexual continuum.[117] Rather than two inherently different sexes, male and female were conceived as 'more and less perfect versions' of one sex: one set of reproductive organs, one material substance in different forms, one libido.[118] I do have a few reservations about Laqueur's compelling—if rather sweeping—argument, which I will mention shortly. Let me first outline his key points.

Measured against a normative male anatomy and physiology, 'normal' women were congenitally weaker and cooler. As a result, their genitals were retained, 'unborn' within the body rather than externalised.[119] Biological sex hung in a delicate balance: a balance that might be upset by inappropriate behaviour, illness, or even a change in the weather.[120] It was 'observed', for example, that women menstruate less in summer than in winter, and that female dancers and those 'engaged in singing contests' often stopped menstruating altogether.[121] Men, on the other hand, might become cooler, moister, softer, more feminine if engaged in unmanly pursuits, or too often in the company of women.[122] Reports of male lactation, even pregnancy, seem to confirm this condition of biological precariousness.[123] Conversely, according to one authority 'women have changed into men' when 'the heat, having been rendered more vigorous, thrusts the testes outward'.[124]

Laqueur admits that the connection between 'scientific' accounts of lactating men and devotional meditations on a maternal Saviour is far from clear. Whether intended as metaphors or empirical phenomena, however, such events 'suggest that, in the world of one sex, the body was far less fixed and far less constrained by categories of biological difference than it came to be after the eighteenth century'.[125] Reversing the familiar (post-Enlightenment) notion that biological sex determines gender, Laqueur contends that in the pre-modern period, 'sex, or the body, must be understood as the epiphenomenon, while gender, what we would take to be a cultural category, was primary or "real"'.[126] One's social identity as 'masculine' or 'feminine' literally gave form and meaning to one's body. And the transgression of one's prescribed role or behaviour could precipitate a corporeal transformation.

This reading of the relationship between sex and gender is useful, up to a point. Medieval bodies do seem to have been more open to biological 'reassignment' than modern ones. Laqueur does not ask why this should be so (or at least why medieval writers believed it to be so). One explanation is that there was an established 'scientific' basis for the body's responsiveness to its environment. The principles of Aristotelian intromission discussed in Chapters 3 and 4 suggest that bodies were actively produced at the level of visual and spatial culture (bearing in mind that species were thought to be vehicles of meaning as well as physically 'formative' agents). In this sense I would argue, with Laqueur, that gender played a significant part in constructing and regulating sexed bodies. At the same time, though, physiology was often presented as the basis of personality, behaviour and social status. Albertus Magnus, for example, attributes woman's fickle nature to her physiological constitution: 'Woman's complexion is more humid than man's', and as a result, she 'receives an impression easily but retains it poorly. The humid is readily mobile, and thus women are unconstant and always seeking something new.'[127] I think it would be more correct to say that sex and gender were mutually constituting in the Middle Ages. Gender was inferred from physiological and anatomical models *and* bodies were thought to be moulded by their social and sensory environments.

Laqueur's interpretation of the sexual continuum is also somewhat limited. His 'one-sex/one-flesh' model is supported by theological discussions of *unitas carnis*, in addition to the medical theories cited above. But there is also abundant evidence of sexual dimorphism in medieval discussions of sex and gender. Even where male and female bodies are *in principle* mapped on to a biological continuum, medieval writers tend to use the language of binary opposition.[128] The ambiguous 'middle ground' between male and female was socially and semantically policed. Masculine women and feminine men were—in ordinary circumstances—regarded as deviant and even deceitful. In a twelfth-century bestiary, such duplicity is attributed to the hyena:

> Its nature is that at one moment it is masculine and at another moment feminine, and hence it is a dirty brute . . . Since they are neither male nor female, they are neither faithful nor pagan, but are obviously the people concerning whom Solomon said: 'A man of double mind is inconstant in all his ways'.[129]

To some extent, of course, a duplicitous nature is symptomatic of the postlapsarian condition: think of Augustine's commentary on the 'splitting' of the subject as a result of the fall, and the idea that every individual—male or female—was made up of feminine (sensuous) and masculine (rational) components.

Gender was mobilised in many different ways (and for many different purposes) in the Middle Ages, and my analysis differs from Laqueur's in emphasis, if not in substance. Medieval bodies, I have suggested, articulated multiple gender roles *internally*, just as the body was often viewed as a microcosm of society. To understand gender in terms of biological, social or symbolic *entities* is to overlook these internal relationships. That said, the Saviour's body was certainly more fluid than the bodies of ordinary men or women, for whom gender—one's place and role in society—was rigidly defined, if vulnerable to transgression. And in the sense that flesh was the antithesis of the ordered, stable and socially productive body, Christ's body was more fleshly, more biologically and semantically 'elastic' than others.

As masculine (the divine second person of the Trinity and heavenly Bridegroom) *and* feminine (formed out of the immaculate flesh of his virginal mother and identified with her in his intercessory and nurturing role) the Son of God embodies the possibility of integrated and harmonious being. If ordinary bodies were homologous with social and cosmological hierarchies,[130] Christ's incarnation enacted the miraculous union of flesh and spirit, masculine and feminine, human and divine. In the Augustinian sense, this interior melding of natures—rendered oppositional with the fall—represents a promise of mystic marriage available to the individual; a union in which the disjunction of desire and will, body and soul, female and male, is finally annulled.

Julia Kristeva and the feminine borders of redemption

The unthinkable union of opposites in Christ's flesh is characteristic of the liminal and the sublime, but it is also interlaced with violence and pain. The Passion is after all horrific; and those who, like Julian of Norwich or St Francis, receive a bodily 'memento' of the Passion suffer terribly in their ecstasy. For Kristeva, the abject and the sublime, horror and *jouissance*, spring from a single source: the child's early (pre-Oedipal and pre-linguistic) relation to its mother. It is this relationship—fusive, *dis*organised, symbiotic, definitively corporeal—that must be excluded in order for the child to become a stable and bounded speaking subject. But the subject's ongoing efforts to police the border between self and (m)other, inside and outside (indeed all binary oppositions), are only ever partially successful. Abjection, the expelled maternal bond, is like an abyss at the margins of subjectivity and language: it threatens the dissolution of self and signification, even while it remains the precondition of both. Hence the nausea and fear, as well as fascination and seduction.

For the thirteenth-century Flemish poet and beguine, Hadewijch, redemption takes place in the space between self and other, inside and outside, flesh and spirit:

> He came in the form and clothing of a Man, as he was on the day when he gave his Body for the first time . . . he gave himself to me in the shape of the Sacrament, in its outward form . . . After that he came himself to me, took me entirely in his arms, and pressed me to him; and all my members felt his in full felicity, in accordance with the desire of my heart and my humanity. So I was outwardly satisfied and fully transported . . . for a short while, I had the strength to bear this; but soon, after a short time, I lost that manly beauty outwardly in the sight of his form. I saw him completely come to nought and so fade and all at once dissolve that I could no longer

distinguish him within me. Then it was to me as if we were one without difference.[131]

On one level, this is a romance to rival the Song of Songs in erotic intensity. As such, the passage can be read as a condensed narrative of two (sexed) bodies becoming one (undifferentiated) flesh. Yet the interpenetration Hadewijch describes—at once sexual and eucharistic—entails a dissolution of self that is hardly compatible with Augustine's image of marital harmony, tranquillity and productivity. If the 'good wife' always defers to the primacy of reason, Hadewijch evokes the sensual abandon of unbounded flesh.[132] The question is: if this carnal borderland of redemption ultimately lies beyond that manly form, on maternal ground, how is Christ's role different from that of the Virgin Mary?

The idea of Jesus as mother—nurturing, protective, the fount of love—tends to obscure an important difference between the bodies of Christ and his mother. As Kristeva observes of the Virgin:

we are entitled only to the ear, the tears, and the breasts. That the female sexual organ has been transformed into an innocent shell which serves only to receive sound may ultimately contribute to an eroticization of hearing and the voice, not to say of understanding. But by the same token sexuality is reduced to a mere implication.[133]

It is as though the Virgin's sexuality, her absent flesh, has in the imagery of the Passion been displaced on to the body of her son. In his vulnerable nakedness Christ is emphatically, often distressingly corporeal. Mary is a face and neck, two hands and sometimes a breast. In late medieval paintings these fragments of a body—almost relics—float in a sea of drapery or hover over a gilded surface. And whereas Christ's Passion entails the violent opening of his body, his mother's remained closed even during childbirth.[134] Guibert of Nogent urged his readers to contemplate 'the sublime dignity of the way she gave birth'.[135] The fourteenth-century Carthusian prioress Marguerite of Oingt described Christ's 'labour' on the cross in altogether more bloody terms:

who ever saw a mother suffer such a birth! For when the hour of your delivery came you were placed on the hard bed of the cross . . . and your nerves and all your veins were broken. And truly it is no surprise that your veins burst when in one day you gave birth to the whole world.[136]

Christ's femininity clearly exceeded the serene, domesticated maternity allowed the Virgin Mary. And if the Virgin's role of intercessor placed her in an erotic economy of the ear and the voice, Christ offered himself up to the desires of the eye according to the erotic conventions of carnal vision.[137] Even in the absence of accounts like Marguerite's, it could be argued that the ocular penetration of Christ's wounds by the viewer carries the same sexual connotation as the eye pierced by Love's arrows. In this sense, too, the feminised body of Christ unsettles the maternal emblem of the nourishing breast (which now coincides with the displaced 'vagina' through which humanity is born anew), and transgresses the virginal ideal of the sealed body.

So far I have considered the liminal characteristics of the Redeemer's body, using Kristeva to shed light on the relationship between flesh, femininity and the potent margins of corporeal identity. But the notion of corporeal 'elasticity' or fluidity can arguably be extended to the relationship *between* bodies. The final part of this chapter moves into the intersubjective domain of image devotion and mystic eroticism, situating the Man of Sorrows in this expanded field of the flesh. Christ's body is not only fleshly and liminal in itself; it is a threshold ('liminal' is from the Latin *limen*, meaning 'lintel' or 'threshold') for others. The sacred blood flows out of its corporeal envelope to purify the supplicant; and the viewer is invited to enter into the side wound as through a door or gateway. Naked and opened up, the body of Christ is a space of ritual, the physical setting for the believer's own redemptive rite of passage.

Interpenetration: the perspective of the flesh

For Mechtild of Hackeborn, a nun at the Saxon monastery of Helfta in the second half of the thirteenth century, Christ and the soul meet as the lovers of the Song of Songs on the marriage-couch of the cross:

> On this couch of love he is still waiting for thee with desire unutterable. But if thou desirest to be his bride, thou must utterly renounce all delight and approach him on his little bed of sorrow, on which the Lord has placed Him, and join thyself to his side, which Love has wounded.[138]

The theme of the mortally wounded bridegroom—in this case literally transfixed by desire—suggests a convergence of the Man of Sorrows with the bridegroom of the Song of Songs. Mechtild may well have had access to a painting or sculpture similar to the examples reproduced in this chapter. By identifying with the bride of the Song of Songs, she would have 'completed' the picture. Christ's wounded side, then, could be taken as a metonym for the open structure of the devotional image itself, requiring an external viewer for closure and consummation.

For religious women in particular, nuptial mysticism provided an intensely personal context in which images of Christ (mental or visual) could 'come to life'.[139] What this means for us, however, is that we are left with only half of a picture: we can see the bridegroom, but the bride is a ghostly presence at best. A rare exception is a pair of manuscript illuminations from the early fourteenth-century *Rothschild Canticles* (Fig. 6.3), a small devotional handbook intended for personal use, possibly by a nun or canoness attached to one of the convents in the Rhineland or Flanders.[140] The text of the handbook comprises quotations grouped around themes, drawn from a variety of sources including the Bible, the liturgy and Patristic literature. As the manuscript's sobriquet suggests, particular emphasis is given to motifs and metaphors derived from the Song of Songs (or Canticles). An example of the popular medieval literary form known as *florilegium*—'bunch of flowers'—the text served as a stimulus for private devotions rather than a statement of dogma or a set of formal instructions for spiritual improvement.[141] The illuminations (including 50 full-page miniatures) supplement and extend this function, with the result, to quote Jeffrey Hamburger, that the 'visual provides a simulacrum of the visionary'.[142]

The Song of Songs miniatures exemplify this process of imaginative association. In the folios reproduced here, Christ as Man of Sorrows invites his own wounding at the hand of the Sponsa. It is significant that the bride is depicted as a nun, perhaps the owner of the handbook, or at least a type with which she could readily identify. I mentioned earlier that the *Imago Pietatis* is generally isolated from the Passion story. Here the image of Christ, crucified but living, is partially reintegrated into a narrative framework, but not that of the *historia*—the historical events surrounding Christ's death and resurrection. As with many images of the Man of Sorrows, these events are signified, in shorthand, by the instruments of the Passion.[143] While the spatially distinct and self-contained scene on the right-hand page represents the historical space and time of the crucifixion, Christ's gesture and the inclination of his head and eyes beyond the frame point to a more inclusive and open narrative. His gaze is returned by the nun on the left-hand page, and the point of her 'love' lance penetrates the decorative border, spatially and temporally linking the two figures in its upward thrust towards Christ's side. Because the act of transfixion is both the focal point and dramatic climax, the facing images of bride and bridegroom are drawn together across the charged void of the central margin.[144] Above the nun, lovers embrace in the enclosed garden of the Song of Songs. As a vision or visualisation of spousal union, this scene transforms the nun's cell into Bernard's 'most beautiful garden'.[145]

Mechtild refers to Christ's wound as the mark of Love. In the *Rothschild Canticles* miniature, however, it is the Sponsa herself who wounds: the lance becomes a metaphor for her own love and desire. Hamburger has documented a number of texts and images in which Christ is wounded by his bride, or by a feminine personification of Caritas.[146] The following dialogue is a typical example, based on an original believed to be contemporaneous with the *Rothschild Canticles*:

Sponsa:	I will fire upon him / so that I may enjoy him there.
Christ:	My heart is wounded, / There, my love, you have pierced me, / So that I must do your will, / That will probably be to your good.
Sponsa:	O Lord, so make open my heart / And let us flow with one another there, / so that you may satisfy me.[147]

The title of this text—*Christus und die minnende Seele* ('Christ and the loving soul')—indicates the extent to which bridal mysticism and the secular love lyric had converged by the fourteenth century. *Minnende* refers specifically to courtly love (*Minne*). It is hardly surprising, then, to find a shared repertoire of motifs; the wounds of love being but one example. In the *Rothschild Canticles* images the bride's eye becomes an active agent in the amatory drama. If one follows the gestures of the protagonists, it is her eye that wounds Christ's side in a re-enactment of Song 4.9: 'You have wounded my heart, my sister, my spouse; you have wounded my heart with one glance of your eyes . . .'[148] The lance signifies her love, of course, but more specifically it is a literalisation of the penetrating, desiring gaze.[149]

The parallels between devotional literature and courtly love are well established.[150] This literary cross-fertilisation—together with the unambiguous representation of a 'wounding gaze' in the *Rothschild Canticles* miniatures—suggests that by the fourteenth century ocular desire was no longer associated exclusively with sin or secular love. To what extent, then, did the erotic configuration of the fleshly eye as a 'penetrating orifice'—at once phallic and vulvic, aggressive and vulnerable—structure the believer's encounter with God?

Commenting on Mechtild's vision of spousal union, and the Song of Songs images in the *Rothschild Canticles*, Hamburger mentions the 'role reversals' evoked by the figure of 'the Sponsa penetrating Christ with her phallic spear'.[151] But if Christ's body is 'wounded', so too is the bride's. She is transfixed by God's love, just as he is by hers. The *inter*penetration of Christ and the soul is a recurring theme in bridal mysticism. In *Christus und die minnende Seele* both hearts are opened to enable the lovers to 'flow with one another there'. For the thirteenth-century Franciscan theologian and mystic, Bonaventure, the soul's assimilation to her beloved precipitates a mutual wounding. Addressing his 'sisters' (in a spiritual handbook intended specifically for nuns) he writes:

> Draw near, O handmaid, with loving steps to Jesus wounded for you . . . Gaze with the Blessed Apostle St Thomas, not merely on the print of the nails in Christ's hands; be not satisfied with putting your finger into the holes made by the nails in his hands; neither let it be sufficient to put your hand into the wound in his side; *but enter entirely by the door in his side and go straight up to the very Heart of Jesus.* There, burning with love for Christ Crucified, be transformed into Christ . . . [T]ransfixed by the lance of the love of your inmost heart, pierced through and through by the sword of the tenderest compassion, seek for nothing else, wish for nothing else except dying with Christ on the Cross.[152]

While these examples of interpenetration are not specifically ocular, there are textual and iconographic clues in the *Rothschild Canticles* that the Sponsa's *eyes* are points of entry (and therefore potentially 'channels' of affect) as well as the active and seemingly phallic implements of love.

On the pages preceding those reproduced above, the scribe has paraphrased Revelation 3.20 ('Behold, I stand at the gate and knock. If any [will come] to me, I will come in to him, and sup with him, and he with me') alongside Song 4.9.[153] Noting that the wound in Christ's side is often described as a door or gate (by which one gains entry to the sacred heart), Hamburger concludes that in this instance the 'side-wound is the door at which the soul knocks and desires entry'.[154] But in the verse from Revelation, it is Christ who knocks. Hamburger's interpretation reverses this action.

It makes more sense, I believe, to read the textual accompaniment to the Song of Songs miniatures in terms of interpenetration and mutual affect. As we have seen, the senses—in particular the eyes—were commonly signified by architectural apertures. It is possible, surely, that the nun's gesture refers both to the verse from the Song of Songs, and to Revelation 3.20. As well as an 'organ' of desire capable of traversing Christ's wound, her eye is a privileged point of entry. She cannot, after all, literally touch or taste her bridegroom on the facing page: he comes to her through her physical eyes or their internal equivalent.[155]

There is a further sense in which visual principles informed the affective encounter between Christ and the individual: the side wound and the sacred heart sometimes exhibit peculiarly optical qualities. In Chapter 5, I quoted a passage from *De Oculo Morali* in which Christ's wound was identified with the pupil of the eye. The author of the text used the term *foramen* ('hole' or 'opening') for both orifices. Why? Because both open-ings—the bodily eye and the aperture in Christ's flesh—share a privileged relation to the heart. Just as the eye is 'the heart's gatekeeper', Christ's wounded side is the gateway to the sacred heart.[156] The eye was also the closest organ to the heart in the anatomy of love: to receive Love's arrows in the eye was to be inwardly penetrated by desire.[157] There existed a causal relationship between eyes and hearts that finds condensed, iconographic expression in the 'ocular' wound in Christ's side. Enjoined to gaze at the wounds, to enter within Jesus's parted flesh, to be enraptured and trans-formed by mutual desire, the worshipper enacts a ritual that is both erotic and distinctively visual.

Christ's 'breast' thus doubles as an eye as well as a vagina; the sacrificial body empties itself out in an eternal flow of blood, but it is also a womb that can be re-entered (Fig. 6.4). Jesus as mother gives birth through his side, and re-envelops his children in the deep crevices of his flesh.[158] The viewer—as bride—adopts a masculine, penetrative, role in response to Christ's nominally masculine, but carnally feminine body. She is also, however, feminised in her identification with Christ, and penetrated by his love.

So far we have considered the ocular associations of Christ's side wound as a point of entry, a 'way in' for the Sponsa's embodied, desiring gaze. But just as the eye is both a vulnerable orifice and a physical force of extension and penetration, the wound is also capable of wounding. Jesus's reciprocal penetration of the bride follows the amatory conventions of mutual wounding, as in the pseudo-Augustinian *Liber meditationum*:

> I ask you by those saving wounds of yours . . . wound this sinful soul for the sake of whom you deigned to die: wound her with the fiery and most powerful dart of your exceeding charity.[159]

While there is no direct reference to ocular intermediaries or agents here, it is telling that the dart of Christ's love draws 'copious tears' from the recipient's heart.[160] In other accounts light is seen to radiate from the wound or wounds, further cementing the equation of sacred heart, the *oculus cordis* (eye of the heart) and the bodily eye with its visual rays.[161] Gertrude the Great, for example, received a vision in which love's arrow assumed the form of a ray of light. After taking communion, and retiring to her cell to pray, she reports:

> it seemed to me that I saw a ray of light like an arrow coming forth from the wound of the right side of the crucifix, which was in an elevated place,

and it continued, as it were, to advance and retire for some time, sweetly attracting my cold affections.[162]

Behind Gertrude's vision is an understanding of the divine light as a kind of transformative, disembodied gaze. Robert Grosseteste had claimed in his treatise *On Light* that the heavenly spheres were set in motion by the creator's 'glance'.[163] Gertrude's God is no less potent, but his glances are more intimate. In the same work she likens her union with Christ to the marriage of light and air. Just as 'the air receives the brightness of the solar rays', she will be penetrated 'so intimately' by her spouse.[164] Standing in for the optical arrow of Love, this is light as desire: passionate, inflaming and fusive. It is also light as flesh, the medium of Gertrude's eucharistic communion; and as blood, as it flows in a luminous stream from Christ's wounded side.

By the time Gertrude was writing her *Revelations* in the Saxon monastery of Helfta at the close of the thirteenth century, vision had become a means of feeling, knowing, even tasting God and, reciprocally, the means by which one was touched, moved or transfixed by God. I have argued that these technologies of redemption, unlike the sublimations and transports of analogy discussed in the last chapter, exploit the carnality of vision. As the physical flow of desire between the individual and Christ, the redemptive gaze is definitively of the flesh. And the flesh shared in this communion (ocular or otherwise) is none other than the flesh of Christ: open, fluid and polysemic.

There are two intermediaries in these visions of redemption. One, the Son of God, is the product of human flesh and a divine Father. The other, sight itself, mediates between each supplicant or communicant and the visible presence—whether pictorial, eucharistic, mental or visionary—of an incarnate Redeemer. Communion, as a 'sharing' in the flesh, is, however, not to be confused with undifferentiated union or unity. Gertrude, Julian of Norwich, or the nun of the *Rothschild Canticles* identify with and participate in the Passion of Christ; they are not identical with Christ. Redemptive vision, conceived as a mutual assimilation and interpenetration, knits together the desires and perspectives of humanity and God into 'one flesh', without thereby dissolving them into one being.

Rethinking ocularcentrism

As an ideal, the model of spectatorial reciprocity developed in this chapter is as different from the now dominant formulations of the 'male gaze' or 'Western ocularcentrism' as it is from the desire for visual transcendence examined in Chapter 5. If we are to retain the concept of ocularcentrism then it needs to be opened up, both historically and conceptually, in order to accommodate changes within and across cultures, as well as internal contradictions and tensions.

In terms of the history of vision, the thirteenth century was clearly a period of transition; but not in the sense that vision and the visual were rediscovered or reawakened (from obscurity or slumber). Augustine's custody of the eyes and Bernard of Clairvaux's sublimation of sensation attest to a need (indeed desire) to see as intense as any in the thirteenth century. The difference was that for Augustine, for Bernard of Clairvaux, and for many clerics and theologians in later centuries, ocular desire was something that required constant regulation, restraint and sublimation. One thing is certain: there was no sudden dawning of sight, or unexpected arousal of ocular desire in the later Middle Ages. What occurred during this period was, rather, a *reorientation* and *discursive elaboration* of the visual sense. Attention and desire could now linger, unsublimated, in the universe of bodily sensation. And images, previously absorbed into the mechanism of allegory, were increasingly liberated from this 'uplifting' function. Where ocular desire had previously been denigrated or redirected 'up' the ladder of perception; where the visible creation had occasioned contemplation of an invisible creator; now God could be seen in the flesh.

It has not, however, been my intention to write a history of medieval vision; certainly not one that would polarise into two periods, neatly straddling the year 1200. Rather, I have explored the tensions and alignments *within* late medieval visuality; the relationship between ocularphobia and visual delight, between science and redemption, and between knowledge and desire. As we have seen, none of these terms is fixed in relation to the others. For example, the discourses of science and redemption outlined in Chapters 3 and 5 exploited the abstractive, moral and anagogical potential of sight. Yet in this final chapter, redemption was grounded in the inter-subjective flesh of carnal vision (discussed in Chapters 1 and 2) and in the more fleshly aspects of thirteenth-century optics (Chapter 4), rather than in fantasies of transcendence or geometrical essence. Unlike the 'clear', rectilinear operations of optical sight, or the mystic's gaze 'above and beyond' the sensible world, the bride's vision is sensual; an intimate and highly physical language of desire.

If there is a constant presence behind the many (often incompatible) 'ocular desires' expressed in these pages it is surely the body; or rather the myriad permutations of human embodiment: fleshly, useful, sensuous and sublime. Sight articulates the desires of the flesh, but it is also the hand-maiden of an embodied mind. It is binding and blinding—a paralysing 'fog' of flesh—yet also illuminating and as swift, as subtle as light. By look-ing one could travel outside oneself or throw open one's bodily 'windows' to earthly pleasures. A look could be a sublimation of carnality; or a sharing in the flesh. Ocularcentrism accounts neither for these vicissitudes of medieval visuality; nor for the impoverishment of a more 'rational', less ambiguous way of seeing.

NOTES

Introduction

1. M. Jay, 'Vision in Context: Reflections and Refractions', in *Vision in Context: Historical and Contemporary Perspectives on Sight*, ed. T. Brennan and M. Jay (New York: Routledge, 1996), 3. As Jay notes, the term 'optical unconscious' was first used by Walter Benjamin, and serves as the title for R. E. Krauss's recent book The *Optical Unconscious* (Cambridge, MA: MIT, 1993).

2. Jay, 'Vision in Context', 3, referring to W. J. T. Mitchell's 'The Pictorial Turn', *Picture Theory: Essays on Verbal and Visual Representation* (Chicago: University of Chicago Press, 1995). The following titles are evidence—though by no means exhaustive—of this burgeoning interest in vision: *Languages of Visuality: Crossings between Science, Art, Politics and Literature*, ed. B. Allert (Detroit: Wayne State University Press, 1996); *Modernity and the Hegemony of Vision*, ed. D. M. Levin (Berkeley: University of California Press, 1993); *Sites of Vision: the Discursive Construction of Sight in the History of Philosophy*, ed. D. M. Levin (Cambridge, MA: MIT Press, 1997); *Vision and Visuality*, ed. H. Foster, DIA Art Foundation Discussions in Contemporary Culture 2 (Seattle: Bay, 1988); *Vision in Context*, ed. Brennan and Jay; *Visual Culture*, ed. C. Jencks (London: Routledge, 1995); J. Crary, *Techniques of the Observer: On Vision and Modernity in the Nineteenth Century* (Cambridge, MA: MIT Press, 1990); M. Jay, *Downcast Eyes* (Berkeley: University of California Press, 1994); and V. Sobchack, *The Address of the Eye: a Phenomenology of Film Experience* (Princeton: Princeton University Press, 1992).

3. J. F. Hamburger, *Nuns as Artists: the Visual Culture of a Medieval Convent* (Berkeley: University of California Press, 1997). A few notable excursions into the subject are Jay's introductory comments on medieval vision in *Downcast Eyes* (of which more will be said later), and Janet Martin Soskice's essay on 'Sight and Vision in Medieval Christian Thought' in *Vision in Context*. Soskice does not, however, include medieval optics in her analysis. Suzanne Lewis goes further than most in relating medieval theories of vision and cognition to the visual culture of the late Middle Ages, while at the same time engaging with current thinking on visuality and textuality. See her *Reading Images: Narrative Discourse and Reception in the Thirteenth-Century Illuminated Apocalypse* (Cambridge: Cambridge University Press, 1995).

4. I owe this observation to Jill Bennett.

5. U. Eco, 'Living in the New Middle Ages', *Travels in Hyperreality*, trans. W. Weaver (London: Picador, 1987), 73–85.

6. M. Camille, *The Gothic Idol: Ideology and Image-making in Medieval Art* (Cambridge: Cambridge University Press, 1989), xxvii.

7. M. A. Holly, 'Vision and Revision in the History of Art', *Theory Between the Disciplines: Authority/Vision/Politics*, ed. M. K. and M. A. Cheetham (Ann Arbor: University of Michigan Press, 1990), 157.

8. At the culturalist end of the spectrum, for example, Marx W. Wartofsky insists that 'human vision is itself an artefact, produced by other artefacts, namely pictures'. From 'Picturing and Representing', in *Perception and Pictorial Representation*, ed. C. F. Nodine and D. F. Fisher (New York: Praeger, 1979), quoted in Jay, *Downcast Eyes*, 5.

9. See, for example, S. Y. Edgerton, Jr, *The Renaissance Rediscovery of Linear Perspective* (New York: Basic Books, 1975) and J. White, *The Birth and Rebirth of Pictorial Space*, 3rd ed. (Cambridge, MA: Belknap, 1987). Although neither of these works purports to be a history of vision, both authors single out Renaissance perspectivism as evidence of a change in the way people actually viewed the phenomenal world.

10. I am quoting D. M. Levin, *The Opening of Vision: Nihilism and the Postmodern Situation* (New York: Routledge, 1988), 164. His argument is discussed at greater length later in this chapter.

11. 'The life of medieval Christendom is permeated in all aspects by religious images', writes Huizinga, and as a consequence, 'everything intended to awaken a consciousness of God rigidifies into terrible banality . . .' J. Huizinga, *The Autumn of the Middle Ages*, trans. R. J. Payton and U. Mammitzsch (Chicago: University of Chicago Press, 1996), 174. Hans Belting's comment about the late medieval 'need to see' provides the point of departure for Chapter 6.

12. S. Ringbom, 'Devotional Images and Imaginative Devotions: Notes on the Place of Art in Late Medieval Private Piety', *Gazette des Beaux-Arts*, 73 (1969): 159–66.

13. P. de Bolla, 'The Visibility of Visuality', in *Vision in Context*, ed. Brennan and Jay, 65.

14. T. Brennan, ' "The Contexts of Vision" from a Specific Standpoint', *Vision in Context*, ed. Brennan and Jay, 219. See, for example, Freud's comments in 'Instincts and Their Vicissitudes', *The Standard Edition of the Complete Psychological Works of Sigmund Freud*, ed. J. Strachey, trans. J. Strachey et al., 24 vols (London: Hogarth, 1957), 14: 109–40.

15. Brennan notes that both Freud and Lacan acknowledge an active component of sight, while maintaining a 'split' between 'psychical and physical effects'. 'Contexts of Vision', 219.

16. M. Merleau-Ponty, *The Visible and the Invisible*, ed. C. Lefort, trans. A. Lingis (Evanston: Northwestern University Press, 1968), in particular Chapter 4: 'The Intertwining—the Chiasm', 130–55. Lewis similarly compares Merleau-Ponty's 'ontology of embodied vision' to the medieval notion of

continuity between the phenomenal world (the visible realm) and language (the invisible), *Reading Images*, 9. While I think the comparison is illuminating (on both sides), it is important to acknowledge Merleau-Ponty's resistance to the kind of causal thinking inherent in the idea of an original (invisible) creator and a secondary (visible) creation.

17. In *Phenomenology of Perception* Merleau-Ponty makes the body the 'meaningful core' not only of the 'biological world', but also the 'the cultural world'. M. Merleau-Ponty, *Phenomenology of Perception*, trans. C. Smith (London: Routledge, 1962), 146.

18. For these and similar metaphors, see in particular Merleau-Ponty, 'The Intertwining—the Chiasm' in *The Visible and the Invisible*.

19. The relationship between nature and culture has been taken up by a number of Australian feminists in an attempt to rethink sexual difference somewhere between the untenable positions of biological essentialism ('nature') on the one side, and radical culturalism on the other. Elizabeth Grosz, for example, has described the body as 'a hinge or threshold between nature and culture' (8). As such, the body (and the same could be said of vision, as a bodily process) cannot be regarded as an historical constant, an organism that science simply gets better at describing: 'the body is not inert or fixed. It is pliable and plastic material' (3). Grosz, 'Notes Towards a Corporeal Feminism', *Australian Feminist Studies*, 5 (Summer 1987). More recently, Sue Best has explored the 'intertwining' or 'imbrication' of feminine terms and the female body via Derrida, Irigaray and Merleau-Ponty. Best, 'Sexualising Space', in *Sexy Bodies: the Strange Carnalities of Feminism*, ed. E. Grosz and E. Probyn (London: Routledge, 1995), 181–94. Bodies and texts, actuality and discourse, can in this way be conceptualised as inextricable, without collapsing one term into the other (i.e., making nature a product of culture, or seeing culture as built upon the immemorial bedrock of nature).

20. Martin Jay has questioned the cause and effect model that dominates much of the thinking about the relation between vision and its contexts. See his 'Disciplinary Prisms: Responding to My Critics', *Comparative Studies in Society and History*, 38.2 (Apr. 1996): 389. Jay's point—which is equally applicable to this thesis—is that a discourse on vision cannot be read in any straightforward way as political or social commentary.

21. I have not mentioned Gothic architecture here, as it is not discussed at any length in this book. It would, however, be possible to extend my argument in Chapter 5 (on redemptive vision) through a spatial and optical analysis of ecclesiastical architecture. Otto von Simson gestures in this direction in his discussion of light in *The Gothic Cathedral: Origins of Gothic Architecture and the Medieval Concept of Order*, Bollingen Series 48, 2nd ed. (New York: Pantheon, 1962), 50–8. A broader, and more recent, survey of the relationship between medieval visuality and Gothic architecture is provided by Michael Camille in *Gothic Art: Visions and Revelations of the Medieval World* (London: Orion, 1996): 'New Visions of Space', 27–68.

22. I am quoting David d'Avray, 'Some Franciscan Ideas about the Body', *Modern Questions about Medieval Sermons: Essays on Marriage, Death, History and Sanctity*, ed. N. Bériou and D. L. d'Avray et al. (Spoleto: Centro Italiano di Studi Sull'Alto Medioevo, 1994), 156.

23. Jay, *Downcast Eyes*, 34–6.

24. Febvre locates the turning point at the end of the sixteenth century, Mandrou somewhat later: 'Until at least the eighteenth century, touch remained . . . the master sense.' R. Mandrou, *Introduction à la France moderne 1500–1640: Essai de Psychologie historique*, quoted by Jay, *Downcast Eyes*, 35.

25. L. Febvre, *The Problem of Unbelief in the Sixteenth Century: the Religion of Rabelais*, trans. B. Gottlieb (Cambridge, MA: Harvard University Press, 1982), quoted in Jay, *Downcast Eyes*, 34.

26. This conceptualisation of medieval art (symbolic, the 'Bible of the illiterate') in contrast to Renaissance art (naturalistic, emotionally appealing, grounded in direct observation) is fairly common. For example, in *Meaning in the Visual Arts* (Harmondsworth: Penguin, 1970), Panofsky writes of the 'curtain' of tradition intervening between the medieval artist/viewer and the visual world, in contrast to the Renaissance doctrine of 'experience . . . as the root of art' (321). An interesting variation on the theme is proposed by Jean Paris, who describes the passage from Byzantine icons to Renaissance painting as the 'transformation of a sacred *surface* [deflecting our transgressive look] into a profane *volume*', *Painting and Linguistics* (Pittsburgh: Carnegie-Mellon University, 1975), 69. The interpolation is Levin's (*Opening of Vision*, 114), amplifying Paris's point that prior to the Renaissance, one was 'seen' by sacred images of Christ, the Virgin and the saints, rather than 'seeing' them as objects.

27. Levin is following Samuel Edgerton in this assertion, *Opening of Vision*, 102.

28. Levin, *Opening of Vision*, 3.

29. Levin, *Opening of Vision*, 164.

30. M. Heidegger, 'The Age of the World Picture', *The Question Concerning Technology and Other Essays*, trans. W. Lovitt (New York: Harper, 1977), 131, discussed in Levin, *Opening of Vision*, 257–9.

31. Paraphrasing Heidegger, Levin writes: 'In the first age [pre-Renaissance] we are in *God's* picture: the world is a picture seen only by God. In the second age, of Renaissance and Enlightenment, we usurp God's place: the world is pictured, but what the picture represents is what is visible *to us*.' *Opening of Vision*, 119.

32. Levin, *Opening of Vision*, 257.

33. 'What would a vision be like', asks Levin, 'if it "remembered" its ontological beholdenness?', *Opening of Vision*, 258. Elsewhere (165–6) he makes a similar point with regard to Galen's theory of extramission.

34. Edgerton, *Renaissance Rediscovery of Linear Perspective*, 22. Edgerton does qualify this theory, stating that 'the mind . . . of the medieval European Christian . . . is not to be thought of as a mere preliminary or deficient version of the adult in modern Western society. Instead, it is a *qualitatively* different and homogeneous entity' (22). Notwithstanding this note of

caution, however, the simple fact that the 'rediscovery' of linear perspective is compared to the normal development of spatial awareness in children is enough to fix perspective securely within a progressive, normative paradigm.

35. E. H. Gombrich, 'Achievement in Mediaeval Art' (1937), trans. M. Podro, in *Meditations on a Hobby Horse and Other Essays on the Theory of Art* (London: Phaidon, 1963), 74.

36. Murray Krieger observes similarly that Gombrich, in contrasting Renaissance naturalism to the 'pictographs' or 'conceptual images' of medieval art, invokes a model of historical progress in which the development of illusionistic art represents 'a gradual movement to an absolutely true (that is, more "correct") representation, one that requires fewer codes for us to see it'. Krieger, 'The Ambiguities of Representation and Illusion: an E. H. Gombrich Retrospective', *Critical Inquiry*, 11.2 (Dec. 1984): 189. The text he is referring to is Gombrich's 'Illusion and Art', in *Illusion in Nature and Art*, ed. R. L. Gregory and E. H. Gombrich (London: Duckworth, 1973). See also E. H. Gombrich, 'The "What" and the "How": Perspective Representation and the Phenomenal World', in *Logic and Art: Essays in Honour of Nelson Goodman*, ed. R. Rudner and I. Scheffler (Indianapolis: Bobbs-Merrill, 1972). In this essay Gombrich contends that as well as representing *what* we see with a high degree of accuracy (i.e., the objective world), perspective pictures approximate the perceptual process itself: *how* we see. For these reasons, he argues, perspective representation is widely regarded as 'better' (truer, more natural) than other methods (148).

37. U. Eco, *The Aesthetics of Thomas Aquinas*, trans. H. Bredin (Cambridge, MA: Harvard University Press, 1988), 138.

38. Eco, *Aesthetics of Thomas Aquinas*, 141.

39. Eco, *Aesthetics of Thomas Aquinas*, 141.

40. Eco, *Aesthetics of Thomas Aquinas*, 138.

41. Panofsky regarded this chronological gap as evidence that there was 'a curious dichotomy between optic theory and artistic practice' in the Middle Ages, *Renaissance and Renascences*, 138. This fairly common misconception stems from a reductive (not to mention retrospective) understanding of optical theory. My discussion of devotional images in Chapter 6 draws on a more complex analysis of medieval optics, developed in Chapters 3 and 4.

42. Edgerton, *Renaissance Rediscovery of Linear Perspective*, 21. W. V. Dunning paraphrases this argument (without crediting Edgerton) in *Changing Images of Pictorial Space: a History of Spatial Illusion in Painting* (Syracuse, NY: Syracuse University Press, 1991), 12–13.

43. The inability to distinguish figure from ground—or the tendency to integrate them—has been identified as a feminine characteristic in several spatial studies. See, for example, I. M. Young, 'Throwing Like a Girl' in *Throwing Like a Girl and Other Essays in Feminist Philosophy and Social Theory* (Bloomington: Indiana University Press, 1990), 153. Edgerton's conceptualisation of the medieval artist—and the 'neurotic' paradigm generally—could be read as implicitly feminine, by virtue of the traditional alignment of

femininity with subjectivism and the emotions (as against male reason), and maternal non-differentiation (versus masculine individualism).

44. For Panofsky, too, focused perspective provides the perceptual and intellectual 'distance between the eye and the object' necessary for 'a total and rationalized view', *Renaissance and Renascences*, 108.

45. Edgerton, *Renaissance Rediscovery of Linear Perspective*, 21.

46. Brennan, 'Contexts of Vision', 224.

47. C. Erickson, *The Medieval Vision: Essays in History and Perception* (New York: Oxford University Press, 1976), 33.

48. Erickson claims, for instance, that 'Visions erased the shear line between the known and the unknowable', and that 'accepting a more inclusive concept of reality, [medieval subjects] saw more than we do', *Medieval Vision*, 28, 29.

49. Erickson, *Medieval Vision*, 5.

50. Eco, *Aesthetics of Thomas Aquinas*, 141.

51. N. Klassen, *Chaucer on Love, Knowledge and Sight*, Chaucer Studies XXI (Cambridge: D. S. Brewer, 1995), 24.

52. Jay, *Downcast Eyes*, 38.

53. Jay, *Downcast Eyes*, 44.

54. Klassen, *Chaucer on Love*, x, 2.

55. Jay, *Downcast Eyes*, 34. Soskice also writes of 'a central ambivalence in Christian attitudes towards vision from the patristic through the medieval periods and beyond'. 'Sight and Vision in Medieval Christian Thought', 31.

56. D. Boyarin, 'The Eye in the Torah: Ocular Desire in Midrashic Hermeneutic', *Critical Inquiry*, 16 (Spring 1990): 532–50.

1   Flesh

1. Alan of Lille, *The Plaint of Nature* (? 1160–75), trans. J. J. Sheridan (Toronto: Pontifical Institute of Mediaeval Studies, 1980), 183–4 (13).

2. Papias the Lombard, *Elementarium Doctrinae Erudimentum* (c.1060), quoted in J. B. Friedman, *The Monstrous Races in Medieval Art and Thought* (Cambridge, MA: Harvard University Press, 1980), 111. Pliny lists over thirty 'incredible' races in Book 7 of the *Natural History*, ed. T. E. Page et al., trans. H. Rackham, 10 vols (London: Heinemann, 1942), vol. 2.

3. From Thomas of Cantimpré's encyclopaedia *De Natura Rerum* (c.1245), quoted in Friedman, *Monstrous Races*, 183.

4. The argument is Thomas of Cantimpré's, as cited in Friedman, *Monstrous Races*, 183.

5. Friedman, *Monstrous Races*, 103.

6. Hugh of St Victor (c.1096–1141), quoted in M. C. Pouchelle, *The Body and Surgery in the Middle Ages*, trans. R. Morris (Cambridge: Polity, 1990), 118.

7. Caesarius, bishop of Arles, quoted in J. Le Goff, *The Medieval Imagination*, trans. A. Goldhammer (Chicago: University of Chicago Press, 1992), 101.

8. Le Goff, *Medieval Imagination*, 101.

9. *The Opus Majus of Roger Bacon*, trans. R. B. Burke, 2 vols (New York: Russell, 1962), 2: 672 (7.3.3). Underlying such judgements was the medieval understanding of an individual as a 'psychosomatic unity—a self in which part can stand for whole and in which an imbalance between parts leads to evil'. C. W. Bynum, *The Resurrection of the Body in Western Christianity, 200–1336* (New York: Columbia University Press, 1995), 328 n.38.

10. In Roman Latin *monstrum* and *portentum* were interchangeable. Although in the Middle Ages *monstrum* became associated with things *contra naturam* (against nature), the application of the term to the races of men retained something of its original meaning. Friedman, *Monstrous Races*, 108–9.

11. Of the races described by Pliny and represented in medieval literary and pictorial sources, the following exhibit displaced, deformed or unnatural sensory apparatus: the 'owl-eyed' Albanians, the Astomi (thought to sustain themselves entirely by smell), the Blemmyae, the Cyclopes or Monoculi ('one-eye'), the Epiphagi (closely related to the Blemmyae, having eyes in their shoulders), the Maritime Ethiopians (sometimes depicted with four eyes or four pupils, representing their keen sight), and the Panotti (literally 'all ears').

12. Plato, *Timaeus* in *Timaeus and Critias*, trans. D. Lee (Harmondsworth: Penguin, 1971), 97 (38.69). Alan of Lille repeats Plato's tripartite division of the body (*Timaeus* 97–100 (38.69–72)) in his allegory of the 'perfectly organised state'. Wisdom reigns in the 'citadel of [man's] head', with the 'heart . . . in the middle of the earthly city', and the 'loins like the city's outskirts, giv[ing] the lower portions of the body wilful desires', *Plaint of Nature*, 121 (6).

13. Plato, *Timaeus*, 97 (38.69–70).

14. Henri de Mondeville (d. c.1320), quoted in Pouchelle, *Body and Surgery*, 120.

15. N. G. Siraisi, *Medieval and Early Renaissance Medicine* (Chicago: University of Chicago Press, 1990), 80–1, 107–9. On the primacy of the heart (as opposed to the head) in the corporeal hierarchy of Antiquity through the Middle Ages, see: E. Jager, 'The Book of the Heart: Reading and Writing the Medieval Subject', *Speculum*, 71.1 (Jan. 1996): 1–26. As Jager notes, however, Galen located perception and cognition in the brain—which may explain why schematic medical illustrations typically represent the head as *prima regio*. Examples of the latter are included in M. Camille, 'The Image and the Self: Unwriting Late Medieval Bodies', *Framing Medieval Bodies*, ed. S. Kay and M. Rubin (Manchester: Manchester University Press, 1994): 62–99.

16. Siraisi, *Medieval and Early Renaissance Medicine*, 106.

17. A detailed explanation of these functions is provided by Siraisi, *Medieval and Early Renaissance Medicine*, 107–8.

18. Bynum cites Clement of Alexandria (d. c. 215) and Abbot Nilus (d. 430) as representative of the patristic culture of fasting. She traces this tradition to the Pythagorean and Neoplatonic denigration of matter in general (including food), and corporeality in particular: a view amply demonstrated by Clement's pronouncement that 'Fasting empties the soul of matter and makes it, with the body, clear and light for the reception of divine truth'. *Holy Feast and Holy Fast: the Religious Significance of Food to Medieval Women* (Berkeley: University of California Press, 1987), 36.

19. Gerald of Wales (c.1145–c.1223), *The Jewel of the Church: a Translation of Gemma Ecclesiastica by Giraldus Cambrensis*, trans. J. J. Hagen, 2 vols (Leiden: Brill, 1979), 2: 199 (2.19). On Gerald in general, see R. Bartlett, *Gerald of Wales*, Oxford Historical Monographs (Oxford: Clarendon Press, 1982).

20. Gerald of Wales, *Jewel of the Church*, 2: 182–3 (2.16). For Gerald, carnal vision is sexualised, and therefore a locus of sin, but it is not associated with the nutritive or reproductive functions of the lower body. Interestingly, it is in the context of anatomy and physiology (discussed in Chapter 4) that the eye is described in terms that suggest the nourishing, maternal body.

21. The long tradition of visual primacy is discussed in Chapter 3.

22. In the sense that a woman's 'head' was her husband or father, she lacked the necessary social and symbolic organs to represent the entire corporeal hierarchy. Instead, defined primarily by her reproductive function, she served as man's body, both literally and metaphorically. My analysis of Augustine and Bernard of Clairvaux later in this chapter will elaborate on the symbolic link between femininity and flesh.

23. Hostiensis (d. 1271), commentary on the fifth book of the Decretals, quoted in Camille, 'The Image and the Self', 72. In this essay, Camille looks at the multiple symbolic dimensions of the medieval (principally fourteenth-century) body, including its function as a microcosm of the universe and the 'body politic'. On the latter, see also J. Le Goff, 'Head or Heart: the Political Use of Body Metaphors in the Middle Ages', trans. P. Ranum, *Fragments for a History of the Human Body, Part III*, ed. M. Feher, R. Naddaff and N. Tazi, 3 vols (New York: Zone, 1989), 13–26; and Pouchelle, *Body and Surgery*, 117–20.

24. For a seminal anthropological formulation of the body as a 'medium of expression' see M. Douglas, 'The Two Bodies' in *Natural Symbols: Explorations in Cosmology* (London: Barrie, 1970), 93–112. Pouchelle discusses the reciprocal metaphors of body/society and body/architecture in Part II of *Body and Surgery*.

25. R. E. Latham, *Dictionary of Medieval Latin from British Sources* (London: Oxford University Press, 1975), 1: 497–9.

26. Hélinand of Froimont, *Verses on Death*, quoted in Le Goff, *Medieval Imagination*, 84.

27. St Bernard of Clairvaux (1090–1153), *On Conversion*, in *Bernard of Clairvaux, Selected Works*, trans. G. R. Evans, Classics of Western Spirituality Series (New York: Paulist Press, 1987), 89 (17.30). The relevant passage is quoted in full later in the chapter.

28. P. Brown, *The Body and Society: Men, Women and Sexual Renunciation in Early Christianity* (London: Faber, 1990), 434.

29. Le Goff, *Medieval Imagination*, 83.

30. Le Goff, *Medieval Imagination*, 96.

31. New Testament sources for Augustine's outer and inner man include Col. 3.9–10 and 2 Cor. 4.16.

32. St Augustine, *Eighty-three Different Questions*, trans. D. L. Mosher, Fathers of the Church, 70 (Washington DC: Catholic University of America Press, 1982), 85 (Q. 51).

33. St Augustine, *The Trinity*, trans. S. McKenna, Fathers of the Church, 45 (Washington DC: Catholic University of America Press, 1963), 315 (11.1); 343 (12.1); 355 (12.8).

34. Eleanor Commo McLaughlin, for example, refers to a 'platonized patristic anthropology that defined the human being as a soul imprisoned in the materiality of the flesh'. McLaughlin, 'Equality of Souls, Inequality of Sexes: Woman in Medieval Theology', *Religion and Sexism: Images of Woman in the Jewish and Christian Traditions*, ed. R. R. Ruether (New York: Simon and Schuster, 1974), 216. Janet Coleman gives a more detailed (and more measured) account of medieval dualism in her *Ancient and Medieval Memories: Studies in the Reconstruction of the Past* (Cambridge: Cambridge University Press, 1992).

35. C. Bynum, 'Why All the Fuss About the Body? A Medievalist's Perspective', *Critical Inquiry*, 22 (Autumn 1995): 6. Bynum cites a number of examples of this style of historical analysis, including Le Goff's work, quoted above, 6 n. 19.

36. Bynum, 'Why All the Fuss About the Body?', 7.

37. Bynum, 'Why All the Fuss About the Body?', 7.

38. Pouchelle, *Body and Surgery*, 204.

39. Pouchelle, *Body and Surgery*, 204.

40. By contrast, d'Avray thinks that 'a great of early medieval writing could be described as dualist . . . in feeling, if not in definite thought, and negative, if not actually hostile, in its attitude to the body'. 'Some Franciscan Ideas about the Body', 161.

41. Bynum, 'Why All the Fuss About the Body?', 13.

42. Bynum, 'Why All the Fuss About the Body?', 13.

43. Bynum, 'Why All the Fuss About the Body?', 14–15.

44. Bynum, 'Why All the Fuss About the Body?', 15.

45. Bynum, 'Why All the Fuss About the Body?', 16.

46. Augustine, *Literal Meaning of Genesis*, 2: 191 (12.11.22). In addition to the tripartite division of sight into corporeal, spiritual and intellectual modes in Book 12 of *The Literal Meaning of Genesis*, we find a trinity of object, attention and vision in *The Trinity* (11.2); and a trinity of memory (mental simulacra of extramental objects), will and internal vision (11.3–4). Unless otherwise indicated, I have used the following translations of these texts: St Augustine, *The Literal Meaning of Genesis*, trans. and annotated by J. H. Taylor, 2 vols (New York: Newman, 1982); and McKenna's translation of *The Trinity*.

47. Augustine, *Literal Meaning of Genesis*, 2: 186 (12.7.16).

48. Augustine, *Literal Meaning of Genesis*, 2: 190, 216 (12.10.21; 12.26.54).

49. Augustine, *Literal Meaning of Genesis*, 2: 214 (12.24.51).

50. St Bonaventure (1221–74), for instance, reiterates Augustine's categories, substituting the term 'internal sense' or 'imagination' for spiritual vision.

Cited in D. L. Clark, 'Optics for Preachers: the *De Oculo Morali* by Peter of Limoges', *The Michigan Academician* (Winter 1977): 339. In this treatise on the 'moral eye' (which I discuss in later chapters) Peter of Limoges extends the tripartite Augustinian model in such a way that the intermediary imagination is retained as the internal sense, along with a demarcation between reason and contemplation. The resulting quadripartite scheme comprises: the carnal or bodily eye, the inner eye or internal sense, the mind's eye and the heart's eye (338).

51. Augustine, *Literal Meaning of Genesis*, 2: 190 (12.9.20). J. H. Taylor notes that *spiritus*, as it is used in this context, is comparable to the Neoplatonic idea of *pneuma* (2: 301 n. 13).

52. Manicheans and Platonists are named by Augustine as proponents of the theory that the body is essentially evil, and is shed by the soul in its ascent to God. *Concerning the City of God, Against the Pagans*, trans. H. Bettenson (Harmondsworth: Penguin Classics, 1984), 524–9 (13.16); 554–5 (14.5). Unless otherwise indicated, all quotations are from this translation.

53. Further examples are listed in A. C. Thiselton, 'Flesh', *The New International Dictionary of New Testament Theology*, ed. C. Brown, 3 vols (Exeter: Paternoster, 1975), 1: 672. On the relation between flesh, fallenness and redemption in the Hebrew Bible and New Testament, see also D. Welton, 'Biblical Bodies', *Body and Flesh: a Philosophical Reader*, ed. D. Welton (Oxford: Blackwell, 1998), 243–55.

54. Thiselton, 'Flesh', 1: 673.

55. Unless otherwise indicated, all Old Testament and New Testament quotations are taken from the New King James Version of the *Holy Bible* (Nashville: Nelson, 1982).

56. Insofar as ' "All flesh" is mankind, and to strive after evil is inherent in man (Gen. 8.21)', flesh and evil are related. However, flesh is not interpreted as 'the actual cause of sin'. Thiselton, 'Flesh', 1: 673.

57. Thiselton, 'Flesh', 1: 674.

58. Thiselton, 'Flesh', 1: 674.

59. Thiselton, 'Flesh', 1: 680. Günther Bornkamm remarks similarly that for Paul, flesh 'designates man's being and attitude *as opposed to and in contradiction to God and God's Spirit'*. *Paul*, trans. D. M. G. Stalker (London: Hodder, 1975), 133.

60. The body–tomb analogy is facilitated by the similarity of the terms *soma* and *sema*. This observation, and the quotation, are from Bornkamm, *Paul*, 130.

61. Bornkamm, *Paul*, 130–1.

62. See: Rom. 7.14, 18; 8.6–8, 12–13; Gal. 5.16, 24. Bornkamm, *Paul*, 133.

63. Latham, *Dictionary of Medieval Latin*, 284.

64. A. Souter, *A Glossary of Later Latin to 600 AD* (Oxford: Clarendon, 1949), 40.

65. As Margaret Miles observes, Augustine's views on the body changed considerably during the course of his life, although they were characteristically 'inconsistent'. While his early writings preserve the Pauline distinction between body and flesh, his mature works move towards a reconciliation of flesh and

body in the concept of the *resurrectio carnis*, *Augustine on the Body* (Missoula: Scholars, 1979) 108–18. For my purposes, it is precisely Augustine's inconsistency and ambivalence, rather than the chronological development of his thought, that is of interest.

66. Human existence is divided into two cities, 'one city of men who choose to live by the standard of the flesh, another of those who choose to live by the standard of the spirit'. Augustine, *City of God*, 547 (14.1).

67. Augustine divides Paul's 'works of the flesh' (Gal. 5.19–21) into two categories: those 'concerned with sensual pleasure', and vices like jealously, animosity, enmity and envy, which originate in the mind rather than in the body. Augustine, *City of God*, 549 (14.2).

68. Augustine, *City of God*, 574–5 (14.15).

69. Augustine, *City of God*, 551 (14.3). See also 525 (13.16).

70. Augustine, *City of God*, 479–80 (12.7).

71. Augustine, *City of God*, 511–13 (13.3).

72. Augustine, *City of God*, 522 (13.13).

73. In addition to expulsion from the garden of Eden, the punishments listed in Genesis are: toil and death, and for women, pain in childbirth and subjection to men.

74. Although Augustine does not make this point himself, it does account for his seemingly unconscious oscillation between the two terms when he is discussing the postlapsarian body: the body, that is, of his own experience. This ambiguity stands in marked contrast to his careful delineation of the terms where he reconstructs the 'pure' prelapsarian body, or writes of the glorified body of the resurrection.

75. Augustine, *City of God*, 522–4 (13.13–15).

76. Augustine, *City of God*, 576 (14.15).

77. Augustine, *City of God*, 577 (14.16). Paraphrasing Augustine, the twelfth-century theologian Peter the Chanter stated: 'In the heat of lust, the whole man is so absorbed that he can neither do nor think of anything else. . . . The pleasure of the body totally captures and enslaves the mind.' Quoted in J. W. Baldwin, 'Five Discourses on Desire: Sexuality and Gender in Northern France around 1200', *Speculum*, 66.4 (Oct. 1991): 801.

78. Augustine speculates that in the absence of sin, sexual relations between man and wife would be a tranquil affair, incurring 'no impairment of [the] body's integrity'. *City of God*, 591 (14.26).

79. For a more extensive discussion of the connection between sexuality and death, see Brown, *Body and Society*, 404–8.

80. Augustine, *Enarrationes in Psalmos*, as quoted in K. Lochrie, *Margery Kempe and Translations of the Flesh* (Philadelphia: University of Pennsylvania Press, 1991), 19. Because Augustine often refers to the 'marriage' of body and soul, I have given these terms in parentheses rather than Lochrie's 'flesh and spirit'. See also Peter Brown's rendering of this passage, *Body and Society*, 426. For a slightly different configuration of the same metaphor (Adam and Eve are likened to 'virile reason' and the 'soul's appetite'), see St Augustine, *On Genesis, Against the Manichees* 2.11.15, in *St Augustine on Marriage and*

Sexuality, ed. E. A. Clark, Selections from the Fathers of the Church 1 (Washington, DC: Catholic University of America Press, 1996), 39–40.

81. Alan of Lille, *Plaint of Nature*, 117–18 (6).

82. Richard of St Victor, *The Mystical Ark* (probably written between 1153 and 1162) in *The Twelve Patriarchs, The Mystical Ark, Book Three of the Trinity*, trans. G. A. Zinn, Classics of Western Spirituality Series (London: SPCK, 1979), 200 (2.17). Meister Eckhart is less optimistic about the relationship between sensuality and the 'inner man', preferring 'the soul [that] draws to itself all its powers it had loaned to the five senses'. Meister Eckhart, 'German Works', *Meister Eckhart: the Essential Sermons, Commentaries, Treatises, and Defence*, trans. E. Colledge and B. McGinn, Classics of Western Spirituality Series (New York: Paulist Press, 1981), 290. See also 'German Works', 108.

83. Alan of Lille, *Plaint of Nature*, 170 (12). As her name suggests, Bacchilatria personifies the supreme worship of wine.

84. Lochrie, *Margery Kempe*, 20.

85. See, for example: J. Butler, *Bodies That Matter: On the Discursive Limits of 'Sex'* (New York: Routledge, 1993); H. Cixous, 'Sorties', *New French Feminisms: an Anthology*, ed. E. Marks and I. de Courtivron (New York: Schocken, 1981), 90–8; P. Deutscher, 'The Evanescence of Masculinity: Deferral in Saint Augustine's *Confessions* and Some Thoughts on its Bearing on the Sex/ Gender Debate', *Australian Feminist Studies*, 15 (Autumn 1992): 41–56; L. Irigaray, *Speculum of the Other Woman*, in particular 'How to Conceive (of) a Girl' and 'Une Mère de Glace', trans. G. C. Gill (Ithaca, NY: Cornell University Press, 1985), 168–79; G. Lloyd, *The Man of Reason: 'Male' and 'Female' in Western Philosophy* (London: Methuen, 1984).

86. McLaughlin, 'Equality of Souls', 216.

87. St Augustine, *The City of God*, trans. G. G. Walsh and D. J. Honan, Fathers of the Church 8 (New York: Fathers of the Church, 1954), 483 (22.24).

88. Bynum, 'Why All the Fuss About the Body?', 15–16.

89. Bynum, 'Why All the Fuss About the Body?', 15. Bynum's examples of 'deliberate misreading' include Butler's *Bodies That Matter* and Irigaray's *Speculum of the Other Woman*. To clarify and extend Bynum's rather cursory observation: strategic (mis)interpretation of a text may involve reading against the grain of the author's intentions, identifying unspoken tensions or contradictions, or investing significance into the seemingly insignificant. In this limited sense, both Butler and Irigaray are intentionally 'unfaithful' to their sources.

90. Echoing this idea, Augustine uses the agricultural metaphor of the male seed being sown in the 'fertile soil' of the female body. For references, and discussion of this motif, see K. E. Børresen, *Subordination and Equivalence: the Nature and Role of Woman in Augustine and Thomas Aquinas*, trans. C. H. Talbot (Washington, DC: University Press of America, 1981), 41–4.

91. Aristotle, *Generation of Animals*, 2.4.738b. Unless otherwise indicated, I have quoted from *The Complete Works of Aristotle: the Revised Oxford Translation*, ed. J. Barnes, Bollingen Series, 2 vols (Princeton: Princeton University Press, 1984). On the union of female matter and male form see also: *Generation of*

Animals, 1.20.729a ff. The metaphor is discussed in Lloyd, *Polarity and Analogy*, 264, 369. For Aristotle's influence on medieval theories of sexuality and human physiology, see: Cadden, *Meanings of Sex Difference in the Middle Ages: Medicine, Science, and Culture* (Cambridge: Cambridge University Press, 1993); and D. Jacquart and C. Thomasset, *Sexuality and Medicine in the Middle Ages*, trans. M. Adamson (Princeton, NJ: Princeton University Press, 1988).

92. 'The truth is that what desires the form is matter, as the female desires the male . . .' Aristotle, *Physics*, 1.9.192a.

93. Jacquart and Thomasset, *Sexuality and Medicine*, 14. Tellingly, *mollities* could refer to weakness of mind, sexual immorality, luxury and effeminacy (when applied to men), in addition to softness, tenderness and pliancy.

94. On the passivity of the body in relation to the soul, see Augustine, *De musica*, 6.5.8: 'Nullo modo igitur anima fabricatori corpori est subjecta materies'. Quoted in *The Cambridge History of Later Medieval Philosophy: From the Rediscovery of Aristotle to the Disintegration of Scholasticism 1100–1600*, ed. N. Kretzmann et al. (Cambridge: Cambridge University Press, 1982), 443 n.11. See also Augustine, *Literal Meaning of Genesis*, 2: 200 (12.16.33).

95. St Augustine, *Confessions*, trans. R. S. Pine-Coffin (Harmondsworth: Penguin, 1961), 344 (13.32). Unless otherwise indicated, all subsequent quotations are from this translation. For additional commentary on this passage, see: Børresen, *Subordination and Equivalence*, 30–4; Deutscher, 'Evanescence of Masculinity', 45–7; and Lloyd, *Man of Reason*, 29–33. One could also trace the idea of a gendered soul through John Scotus Eriugena's *Periphyseon (The Division of Nature)*, written in c. 865. In Book 2, the Irish philosopher and theologian writes: 'the spiritual sexes are understood to exist in the soul—for *nous*, that is intellect, is a kind of male in the soul, while *aisthesis*, that is sense, is a kind of female'. Quoted in Bynum, *Resurrection of the Body*, 145.

96. Men, by extension, are masculine by virtue of their reasoning minds, and feminine in their sensuality. For example, in *The Trinity*, 355 (12.8) Augustine likens the appetite to Eve in its ability to lead the mind (its 'spouse') astray.

97. Isidore of Seville, quoted in Jacquart and Thomasset, *Sexuality and Medicine*, 14. The popular twelfth-century text, *De secretis mulierum*, attributed women's appetite for sex to the heat generated by the accumulation of menstrual blood. *Women's Secrets: a Translation of Pseudo-Albertus Magnus' De Secretis Mulierum with Commentaries*, trans. H. R. Lemay (New York: State University of New York Press, 1992), 122 (ch. 7).

98. J. W. Baldwin, *The Language of Sex: Five Voices from Northern France around 1200* (Chicago: University of Chicago Press, 1994), 134. Baldwin's source is the *Dragmaticon* of Guillaume de Conches, written in 1146–9. See also Jacquart and Thomasset, *Sexuality and Medicine*, 81–2.

99. Cadden, *Meanings of Sex Difference*, 178.

100. Cadden, *Meanings of Sex Difference*, 178.

101. Cadden, *Meanings of Sex Difference*, 178.

102. As Jean Leclercq notes, this 'ability to interpret everything symbolically was greatly developed in the monastic milieux of the high middle ages, and

doubtless also among the clerics, and, though probably to a lesser extent, among the laymen'. *Monks and Love in Twelfth-Century France: Psycho-Historical Essays* (Oxford: Clarendon, 1979), 34.

103. My basic comparative framework here—focusing on the concept of 'flesh' as understood by Augustine and Bernard of Clairvaux—follows the structure of Karma Lochrie's argument in *Margery Kempe*, 19–23. While my interpretation of these authors accords with Lochrie's analysis on most points, there are a number of divergences or differences of emphasis. Most notably, my reading of Augustine more clearly delineates body (as 'good' wife) from flesh (as rebellious wife). As well, Bernard's emphasis on the permeability of the flesh—in contradistinction to the chaste, enclosed body—is given an ocular twist in later chapters.

104. Bernard of Clairvaux, *On Conversion*, as quoted by Lochrie, *Margery Kempe*, 21.

105. The corporeal matter of the body is to the incorporeal soul 'a rod of fatherly correction (Prov. 29.15) and a purgation of the heart (Ps. 44.7)'. Similarly, 'where there is no body there is no possibility of action (Matt. 24.28)'. Bernard of Clairvaux, *On Conversion*, 69 (3.4), 71 (5.6).

106. Bernard of Clairvaux, *On Conversion*, 89–90 (17.30). References cited in text: 2 Cor. 5.6; Rom. 7.24; Rom. 6.6; Rom. 7.23, 25. Note that where parenthetical references are given in the original text, I have listed this information after the citation details, in the order in which the references appear in the sermon.

107. Bernard of Clairvaux, *On Conversion*, 74 (6.10).

108. Bernard of Clairvaux, *On Conversion*, 74 (6.10). Cited in text: Isa. 1.6. This inventory would not appear out of place in a moralising account of the Plinian races.

109. Lochrie, *Margery Kempe*, 4. The enclosure and extension of sight in *On Conversion* is discussed in Chapter 5 of this book.

110. I have used the definition of 'passio' in the *Mediae Latinitatis Lexicon Minus*. In subsequent chapters I will extend this definition through Roger Bacon's reference to the 'passion' of sensation, and (in Chapter 6) the devotional 'Passion portrait' of Christ.

111. Bynum writes of the 'fear of aging and putrefaction' evident in thirteenth-century mystical and devotional texts. *Resurrection of the Body*, 331.

112. Bynum, *Resurrection of the Body*, 174.

113. Bernard of Clairvaux, *On Conversion*, 89 (17.30).

114. See also Richard of St Victor, *Mystical Ark*, 179 (2.4). The 'eye of reason', according to Richard, is 'blinded under a fog of error' and 'surrounded by a cloud of sin'.

115. Augustine, *Eighty-three Different Questions*, 43 (Q.12). See also: Augustine, *Soliloquies* (14.24), where the fleshly body is described as a condition of darkness, and the senses as 'sticky lime;' and *Confessions*, 43 (2.2).

116. Joseph Goering, 'The *De Dotibus* of Robert Grosseteste', *Mediaeval Studies*, 44 (1982): 83–109. An edition of the text is appended to Goering's article, and the date of the treatise is discussed on pages 94–5.

117. Like Augustine, Grosseteste conceives of this perfection within a hierarchy in which the soul is subject to God, and in turn exercises its rightful dominion over the body. Goering, *De Dotibus*, 97.
118. Goering, *De Dotibus*, 98.
119. Alan of Lille, *Summa* (ch. 34), quoted in Bynum, *Holy Feast*, 44.
120. *The Ancrene Riwle* (The Corpus MS *Ancrene Wisse*), trans. M. B. Salu (London: Burns, 1963), Part 3: 62.
121. Plato, *Timaeus*, 102–3 (40.74–5).
122. Plato, *Timaeus*, 103 (40.75).
123. *Ancrene Wisse*, Part 2: 41.
124. See also Umberto Eco's treatment of *claritas* in relation to scholastic theories of beauty and proportion, in *Aesthetics of Thomas Aquinas*, 102–21.
125. Robert Grosseteste, *Hexaemeron*, quoted in R. W. Southern, *Robert Grosseteste: the Growth of an English Mind in Medieval Europe*, 2nd ed. (Oxford: Clarendon, 1992), 219.
126. Although light exists in the order of corporeal things, it has 'greater similarity than all bodies to the forms that exist apart from matter, namely, the intelligences'. Grosseteste, *On Light*, trans. C. C. Riedl (Milwaukee, WI: Marquette University Press, 1978), 10.
127. Otto of Freising, *Chronica sive historia de duabus civitatibus*, quoted in Bynum, *Resurrection of the Body*, 182. Otto studied in Paris before joining the Cistercians in 1133. The work quoted from here was begun in the 1140s.
128. This definition of *impassibilitas* is from J. F. Niermeyer, *Mediae Latinitatis Lexicon Minus* (Leiden: Brill, 1976), 513. See also Bynum's discussion of the dowering of the body in *Resurrection of the Body*, 121 ff. (especially 135–6).
129. A. Boureau, 'The Sacrality of One's Own Body in the Middle Ages', trans. B. Semple, *Corps Mystique, Corps Sacré: Textual Transfigurations of the Body from the Middle Ages to the Seventeenth Century*, special issue of *Yale French Studies*, 86 (1994): 7.
130. Peter [the] Lombard, *Sentences*, 4.49.4 (1157–8). Peter is borrowing from Augustine, *Literal Meaning of Genesis*, 12.35, quoted in Bynum, *Resurrection of the Body*, 132.

2   The Eye of the Flesh

1. St Augustine, *Confessions*, trans. V. J. Bourke, Fathers of the Church, 21 (New York: Fathers of the Church, 1953), 60 (3.6).
2. Pseudo-Dionysius, *The Mystical Theology* in *Pseudo-Dionysius: the Complete Works*, trans. C. Luibheid, Classics of Western Spirituality Series (New York: Paulist, 1987), 138 (2.1025a).
3. I am using the term 'gaze' here in its broadest sense, not as Lacan defines it: as something prior to and outside viewing subjects, and thus quite distinct from ordinary sight. J. Lacan, 'The Split Between the Eye and the Gaze', *The Four Fundamental Concepts of Psycho-Analysis*, ed. J.-A. Miller, trans. A. Sheridan (New York: Norton, 1978), 67–78.

4. Gen. 3.4–7.

5. For biographical and contextual information on Peter the Chanter (d. 1197), see J. W. Baldwin, *Masters, Princes, and Merchants: the Social Views of Peter the Chanter and His Circle* (Princeton: Princeton University Press, 1970), vol. 1: 3–16.

6. Peter the Chanter, paraphrased in Baldwin, *Language of Sex*, 118.

7. I discuss Augustine's commentary on Genesis 3 in Chapter 1.

8. The passage is quoted in full below. Gerald of Wales, *Jewel of the Church*, 2: 182 (2.16).

9. The *Ancrene Wisse* enjoyed a large lay readership in the fourteenth century, and has been the subject of a number of recent studies, including: L. Georgianna, *The Solitary Self: Individuality in the Ancrene Wisse* (Cambridge, MA: Harvard University Press, 1981); J. Grayson, *Structure and Imagery in the Ancrene Wisse* (Hanover: published for the University of New Hampshire by the University Press of New England, 1974); and E. Robertson, 'Medieval Medical Views of Women and Female Spirituality in the *Ancrene Wisse* and Julian of Norwich's *Showings*', *Feminist Approaches to the Body in Medieval Literature*, ed. L. Lomperis and S. Stanbury (Philadelphia: University of Pennsylvania Press, 1993). I have used the translation of *The Ancrene Riwle* (The Corpus MS: *Ancrene Wisse*) by Salu for quotations.

10. *Ancrene Wisse*, Part 2: 23.

11. 'Your mother Eve leaped after her eyes had leapt . . .' *Ancrene Wisse*, Part 2: 23. Georgianna notes that 'Looking, though seemingly innocuous and certainly passive enough, can abruptly become leaping in [the] tiny but concentrated spiritual landscape [of the anchorhold]'. *Solitary Self*, 64. For reasons that will become more apparent in the course of this chapter, I would take issue with the assumption that sight is a universally (or naturally) passive phenomenon.

12. H. A. Kelly traces the tradition of the 'maiden-faced serpent' to Peter Comestor's commentary on the Book of Genesis in his *Historia Scholastica* of c. 1170, although the earliest iconographic examples date from the 1220s and 30s. 'The Metamorphoses of the Eden Serpent During the Middle Ages and Renaissance', *Viator*, 2 (1971): 308, 321. The theme is also discussed in Camille, *Gothic Idol*, 91; and J. A. Phillips, *Eve: the History of an Idea* (San Francisco: Harper, 1984), 61–2.

13. Peter Comestor, *Historia Scholastica*, 1.21, quoted in Kelly, 'Metamorphoses of the Eden Serpent', 308. Kelly notes that Peter's reference to Bede is erroneous (309).

14. Richard of St Victor, *Mystical Ark*, 200 (2.17).

15. St Thomas Aquinas (c.1225–74), *Summa Theologiæ* (begun c.1265), 1a Q.81.1. I have used the Blackfriars parallel text edition for quotations (London, 1964–81). Augustine gives a number of symbolic interpretations of the serpent in *The Trinity*, 12.11–13, including 'the five-fold sense of the body', 362 (12.13.20).

16. 'Serpens gets its name because it creeps (*serpit*) by secret approaches and not by open steps. It moves along by very small pressures of its scales.' *The Book*

of Beasts: Being a Translation from a Latin Bestiary of the Twelfth Century, ed. and trans. T. H. White (New York: Dover, 1984) 165. See also Augustine, The Trinity, 357–8 (12.11.16).

17. Augustine, City of God, 522–3 (13.13). The relevant passage is quoted in Chapter 1.
18. Augustine, The Trinity, 358 (12.11.16).
19. Aquinas, Summa Theologiæ, 1a Q.81.1.
20. Jay, Downcast Eyes, 307 n.143.
21. Aquinas, Summa Theologiæ, 1a Q.81.1. Aquinas's theory is essentially one of Aristotelian intromission, and should be distinguished from Augustine's extramissionist understanding of sensation as an act of the soul.
22. Bernard of Cluny, quoted in R. H. Cline, 'Heart and Eyes', Romance Philology, 25.2 (Nov. 1971): 288.
23. See Cline ('Heart and Eyes', 285–6) for the relevant passages in the Patrologia Latina, with the exception of Gerald of Wales (discussed below) and Peter the Chanter, whose comments on Matt. 5.28, are cited in Baldwin, Language of Sex, 118.
24. Peter Abelard, Ethics, quoted in M. Lapidge, 'The Stoic Inheritance', A History of Twelfth-Century Western Philosophy, ed. P. Dronke (Cambridge: Cambridge University Press, 1988), 98. D. E. Luscombe remarks that sin, for Abelard, 'lies neither in being tempted to do nor in doing what is wrong; it lies between these two moments, in consenting to the initial temptation'. 'Peter Abelard', in the same volume, 305.
25. Lapidge, 'Stoic Inheritance', 90.
26. Peter Abelard, quoted in Lapidge, 'Stoic Inheritance', 98.
27. Gerald of Wales, Jewel of the Church, 2: 182 (2.16).
28. See for example Ovid's Metamorphoses, 1.490; 2.726f; 3.370f, 413–17; 8.324–7; 14.350f. The influence of the Ovidian theme of love at first sight on medieval literature is widely acknowledged, though Cline points out that this topos is quite distinct from that of the wounding or aggressive gaze. 'Heart and Eyes', 277, 289 ff. John Baldwin discusses the influence of Ovid on Andreas Capellanus's twelfth-century work, De amore, in Language of Sex, 137–43.
29. Eneas: a Twelfth-Century French Romance, trans. J. A. Yunck (New York: Columbia University Press, 1974), 217. Cline concludes from this passage that Eneas's glance wounds Lavine ('Heart and Eyes', 293). This interpretation is not, however, supported by Yunck's translation, in which Love is named as the perpetrator of the wounding glance.
30. As Cline notes ('Heart and Eyes', 276–7), eyes in classical Latin poetry sometimes burn with passion, and in Seneca's Hippolytus, Phaedra's eyes cast darts at her love-object. But the eye that wounds another's eye is absent, with the one exception of a scene in Apuleius's Golden Ass (10.3).
31. In Ovid's Ars amatoria the narrator is 'skewered' by Love's 'bowshots', and seared by his flaming torch. Ovid, The Art of Love, in The Erotic Poems, trans. P. Green (Harmondsworth: Penguin, 1982), 166 (1.21, 22). Additional examples of Cupid's arts are given by Cline, 'Heart and Eyes', 276–7.

32. 'He seized me here at the window from which I was gazing at the Trojan', Lavine recounts in *Eneas*, 216.
33. *Eneas*, 215.
34. Sarah Spence makes the important observation that Lavine's complaints are 'all standard symptoms of the evil eye'. ' "Lo Cop Mortal": the Evil Eye and the Origins of Courtly Love', *The Romantic Review*, 87.3 (May 1996): 315. The conclusion she draws from this is that courtly love derives from *invidia*: it serves to codify and thereby defuse envy in a culture characterised by a 'growing [visual] fascination with the world' (307). While I agree that envy and courtly love share the same pathology, it seems more likely that they are in fact two expressions of the same basic emotion: desire. As I argue later in this section, physiological explanations of the evil eye often link it to men-struation, which in turn is held responsible for women's insatiable sexual appetite. Envy, if we follow this line of reasoning, was a malevolent form of lust.
35. *Eneas*, 220.
36. J. Cerquiglini, ' "Le Clerc et le Louche": Sociology of an Esthetic', *Poetics Today*, 5.3 (1984): 480, 481 n.6. Andreas Capellanus seems aware of this asso-ciation between blindness and impotence when he notes that the lover who loses his eye inevitably loses his sweetheart. That is, the loss of an eye results in the loss of love. *De amore*, 2.7.15, cited in Cerquiglini, 482.
37. Cerquiglini, 'Le Clerc et le Louche', 481.
38. Albert the Great (c.1200–80), *Questions on Animals*, 15 Q.14, paraphrased and quoted in Jacquart and Thomasset, *Sexuality and Medicine*, 55–6.
39. Jacquart and Thomasset note that in 'the Middle Ages, the deterioration of the eyesight was constantly being mentioned as part of the damage caused by coitus . . .' *Sexuality and Medicine*, 56.
40. 'Queritur quare tanta delectatio sit in coitu?' *Prose Salernitan Questions*, B 16, quoted in Jacquart and Thomasset, *Sexuality and Medicine*, 83. See also J. Baldwin's *Language of Sex* for a discussion of this question and related themes, 129 ff.
41. According to Cline, the troubadour Bernard of Ventadorn was the 'first known poet of the West to make the eye . . . an active agent in the cause of love'. 'Heart and Eyes', 289. On 'the painful vision' and related themes in Western medieval love literature, see: Klassen, *Chaucer on Love, Knowledge and Sight*, especially chapter 3: 'The Hostility of Love and Knowledge', 75–114.
42. Plato, *Timaeus*, 62 (13.45).
43. In keeping with classical Greek tradition, Plato's lovers are both male. Plato, *Phaedrus*, in *Phaedrus and the Seventh and Eighth Letters*, trans. W. Hamilton (Harmondsworth: Penguin, 1973), 57–8 (250–1). For a more detailed treat-ment of Platonic love and its relation to philosophy, see: G. R. F. Ferrari, 'Platonic Love', in *The Cambridge Companion to Plato*, ed. R. Kraut (Cambridge: Cambridge University Press, 1992), 248–76.
44. Plato, *Phaedrus*, 64 (255).
45. L. K. Donaldson-Evans, *Love's Fatal Glance: a study of Eye Imagery in the Poets of the Ecole Lyonnaise* (Mississippi: Romance Monographs, 1980), 11–14.

46. For examples of the mutual, interlocking gaze in medieval literature, see R. Baldwin, ' "Gates Pure and Shining and Serene": Mutual Gazing as an Amatory Motif in Western Literature and Art', *Renaissance and Reformation*, 10 (1986): 23–48. Baldwin argues that the motif of mutual gazing (as distinct from the more violent topos of 'one-sided devastation') is particularly associated with conjugal and Platonic love (23, 27); and as such is found less often in amatory literature than in religious and Neoplatonic texts, as well as in Renaissance conjugal portraiture. The reciprocal gaze of Christ and the soul—identified with the bride and bridegroom of the Song of Songs—is discussed in Chapter 6 of this book.

47. References for these motifs are provided by Cline, 'Heart and Eyes', 267–8, 271–2; and Donaldson-Evans, *Love's Fatal Glance*, 14–16, 18–21.

48. The translation is from A. J. Arberry, *The Seven Odes*, and is quoted in Donaldson-Evans, 26–7.

49. Cline lists the extraordinary range of ocular feats and associated weaponry found in the *Arabian Nights*: the weapon may be 'cast by the eye (1: 177; 2: 1020; 5: 3025), or by the lid (1: 541), or by the lashes (2: 773), or by the eyebrows acting as a bow (4: 2628), and it pierces the bosom (4: 2628; 5: 3025), or heart (1: 568; 2: 782, 1081; 4: 2499, 2628), or core (2: 773, 782), or soul (1: 177), or brain (5: 3025). The eye is powerful, sending the 'dreadful sword-lunge of her look' (2: 864), and has the sharpness of a Yamáni sword (1: 568), or of a thin-ground sword (2: 773), or a keen-edged scymitar (2: 1111; 3: 1615), and it pierces deeper than swords (2: 764). This weapon, however, produces not so much a wound as sickness or death (1: 177, 541; 2: 1135). The vitals are set afire (1: 121; 3: 1615) and the body is weakened (2: 773–6).' Cline, 'Heart and Eyes', 282. All references are to R. F. Burton's translation of *The Book of the Thousand Nights and a Night* (New York: Heritage, 1962).

50. *Arabian Nights*, 2: 200. Quoted in Donaldson-Evans, *Love's Fatal Glance*, 29.

51. Donaldson-Evans, *Love's Fatal Glance*, 21, 29.

52. An introduction to the treatise is provided by D. L. Clark in 'Optics for Preachers: the *De Oculo Morali* by Peter of Limoges', *The Michigan Academician* (Winter 1977). Richard Newhauser discusses its provenance as well as Peter's methods and influences in: 'Nature's Moral Eye: Peter of Limoges' *Tractatus Moralis de Oculo*' in *Man and Nature in the Middle Ages*, ed. S. J. Ridyard and R. G. Benson (Sewanee, TN: University of the South Press, 1995).

53. The basilisk is featured in medieval bestiaries. See, for example, *The Book of Beasts*, ed. White, 168–9. The creature also makes an appearance in the *Etymologies* of Isidore of Seville (c. 560–636) and in the twelfth-century *Prose Salernitan Questions* (B 05–B 08) The earliest known mention of the basilisk is in Pliny's *Natural History* (8.33 and 29.19). Jacquart and Thomasset, *Sexuality and Medicine*, 211 n.81.

54. Peter of Limoges, *De Oculo Morali*, quoted in Clark, 'Optics for Preachers', 342.

55. Heliodorus (fl. 3rd–4th century) confuses the Galenic theory of pneumatic contagion—in which the eyes 'breathe' infected air—with the Platonic idea of libidinous effluxion in which the eyes are the primary organs of transmis-

sion. The relevant passage from the *Ethiopian History* is quoted in Donaldson-Evans (*Love's Fatal Glance*, 22–3) and Cline ('Heart and Eyes', 274). M. W. Dickie argues that Heliodorus's account of the erotic and maleficent potency of the eye is ironic, and is drawn almost entirely from Plutarch (c. 46–120 CE), a notable exception being Heliodorus's reference to the basilisk. Dickie, 'Heliodorus and Plutarch on the Evil Eye', *Classical Philology*, 86.1 (Jan. 1991): 17–29.

56. See: Deut. 15.9; Job 16.9 ('my adversary sharpens his gaze on me'); Ps. 35.19; Prov. 6.12–14, 10.10, 16.30, 28.22.

57. B. Kern-Ulmer points to a similar gender asymmetry with respect to the evil eye in ancient and early medieval Rabbinic Judaism. 'The Power of the Evil Eye and the Good Eye in Midrashic Literature', *Judaism*, 159.40.3 (Summer 1991): 347–51. She also cites a number of midrashic texts in which the phenomenon of the destructive female gaze is likened to the maleficent forces accompanying menstruation (350–1).

58. In *Generation of Animals*, 2.7.747a Aristotle writes: 'For the region about the eyes is, of all the head, the most seminal part . . . The reason is that the nature of the semen is similar to that of the brain, for the material of it is watery (the heat being acquired later).' Aristotle is referring here to the watery humours of the eye rather than an efflux or 'ejaculation' of visual spirit. In *On Dreams* (460a), however, he likens ocular 'menstruation' to seminal discharge, implying that both semen and menstrual blood can be emitted through the eyes.

59. On the 'menstrual' evil eye, see: *Women's Secrets: a Translation of Pseudo-Albertus Magnus's* De Secretis Mulierum *with Commentaries*, trans. H. Rodnite Lemay (New York: State University of New York Press, 1992), 128–31; and for further references: Jacquart and Thomasset, *Sexuality and Medicine*, 74–5, 191, 212 n.82, 83.

60. In *On Dreams* (459b) Aristotle claims that 'when women during their menstrual periods look into the mirror, the surface of the mirror becomes a sort of bloodshot cloud . . . The cause is . . . that the eye is not only affected by the air but also has an effect upon it and moves it . . .' Michael Camille reproduces several thirteenth-century illustrations of this phenomenon in 'The Eye in the Text: Vision in the Illuminated Manuscripts of the Latin Aristotle', *Micrologus VI: La Visione e lo Sguardo nel Medio Evo* (Sismel, Edizioni del Galluzzo, 1998), 133, 142. In *De Secretis Mulierum* the infected (menstrual) eye leaves 'a red mark like a vein' on the mirror. *Women's Secrets*, 131.

61. References are cited in Jacquart and Thomasset, *Sexuality and Medicine*, 74, 212 n.82.

62. In Part 2 of the *Ancrene Wisse*, for example, Dina and Bathsheba are held up as examples of women whose sin was not in looking at a man, but in allowing themselves to be looked at (23–4). Warning his readers that a woman's beauty is like a pit, the author of the *Ancrene Wisse* writes: 'You uncover this pit, you who do anything by which a man is bodily tempted by you, even though you may be unaware of it' (25).

63. Augustine, *On Genesis, Against the Manichees* (2.18): 'we cannot be tempted by the devil except through that animal part, which reveals, so to speak, the image or exemplification of the woman in the one whole man.' Quoted by Aquinas, *Summa Theologiæ*, 2a2æ Q.165.2.

64. In the *Ancrene Wisse* lust, the 'stinking whore, makes war against the lady of chastity, that is, the spouse of God'. Her weapons are the 'glances' she 'shoots . . . from her wanton eyes'. Part 2: 26.

65. *Eneas*, 216–17.

66. *Eneas*, 217.

67. *Eneas*, 216.

68. On the trope of the 'devil's gateway' and similar images of female corporeality, see P. A. Du Bois, ' "The Devil's Gateway": Women's Bodies and the Earthly Paradise', *Women's Studies*, 7 (1980): 43–58.

69. Cline, 'Heart and Eyes', 286.

70. The commentary on Jer. 9.21 provided by Origen (c. 185–c. 254) is particularly explicit in this regard: 'We can take the windows as meaning the bodily senses through which life or death gains entrance to the soul; for this is what the prophet Jeremias means when, speaking of sinners, he says: *Death is come up through your windows*. How does death come up through your windows? If the eyes of a sinner should *look upon a woman to lust after her*, and because he who has thus looked upon a woman has committed adultery in his heart, then death has gained entrance to that soul through the windows of the eyes.' Origen, *The Song of Songs, Commentary and Homilies*, quoted in Cline, 'Heart and Eyes', 286.

71. Bernard of Clairvaux, *On Conversion*, 72–3 (6.8).

72. Bernard of Clairvaux, *On Conversion*, 75 (6.11).

73. Bernard of Clairvaux, *On Conversion*, 72 (5.7).

74. Bernard of Clairvaux, *On Conversion*, 71 (5.6). References cited in text: Deut. 13.17; 1 Cor 7.31; Ezek. 44.2.

75. For a survey of the literature see M. W. Bloomfield, *The Seven Deadly Sins: an Introduction to the History of a Religious Concept, with Special Reference to Medieval English Literature* (Michigan: Michigan State University Press, 1952).

76. Alan of Lille, *Plaint of Nature*, 117–18 (6).

77. Alan of Lille, *Plaint of Nature*, 199 (16).

78. Jocelyn Wogan-Browne remarks that 'the body as figurative edifice [was] an image newly intense and prevalent in late twelfth- and early thirteenth-century culture'. 'Chaste Bodies: Frames and Experiences', *Framing Medieval Bodies*, ed. S. Kay and M. Rubin (Manchester: Manchester University Press, 1994), 28. For a detailed account of this motif, see R. D. Cornelius, *The Figurative Castle: a study in the Medieval Allegory of the Edifice with Special Reference to Religious Writings* (Pennsylvania: Bryn Mawr, 1930).

79. The text was written in Anglo-French and subsequently translated into Middle English. For a synopsis of the *Chateau d'amour*, see: *A Manual of the Writings in Middle English 1050–1500*, ed. A. E. Hartung (New Haven: Connecticut Academy of Arts and Sciences, 1986), 2338–9.

80. Bloomfield, *Seven Deadly Sins*, 141. The Middle English adaptations of Gros-seteste's text are listed in *A Manual of the Writings in Middle English*, 2337–8.

81. The *Roman de la Rose* was begun around 1230 by Guillaume de Lorris and completed some fifty years later by Jean de Meun. I have used the translation by F. Horgan: *The Romance of the Rose* (Oxford: Oxford University Press, 1994).

82. If there is any doubt in the *Rose* that the 'window' in the edifice is really a vagina, it is dispelled in the final, climactic scene. The lover, following Venus's cue, approaches the entrance to the 'sanctuary', and 'full of agility and vigour', proceeds to thrust his 'unshod staff' into the narrow opening. Mind-ful of the delicate nature of the rose therein, he gently palpitates the bud and, 'prob[ing] its very depths', deposits 'a little seed'. *Romance of the Rose*, 332–4.

83. *Romance of the Rose*, 320. As Camille notes, the 'hole in the wall' metaphor comes from The Song of Songs (5.4): 'My beloved put his hand by the hole in the wall and my bowels were moved at his touch.' *Gothic Idol*, 321.

84. Valencia, Biblioteca de la Universidad, MS 1327 (*Roman de la Rose*), fol. 144r: reproduced, with commentary, in Camille, *Gothic Idol*, 321 (Fig. 172).

85. S. Stanbury, 'The Voyeur and the Private Life in *Troilus and Criseyde*', *Studies in the Age of Chaucer*, ed. T. J. Heffernan, 13 (1991): 142.

86. Stanbury, 'Voyeur and the Private Life', 143.

87. *Romance of the Rose*, 26–7.

88. *Romance of the Rose*, 327.

89. This generalised application of the castle metaphor is found, for example, in the *Miserere* of Barthélemy, Recluse of Molliens. Written around 1200, the poem incorporates the five senses, with their respective vices, into the castle metaphor. Bloomfield, *Seven Deadly Sins*, 132.

90. *Ancrene Wisse*, Part 2: 26.

91. *Ancrene Wisse*, Part 2: 26. The following sentences make it clear that the bolts received 'between the eyes' are equivalent to the more conventional wound-ing of the eye itself. In this instance, the devil's weapons 'blind' the heart through the eyes.

92. I have taken these details from the 'General Introduction' to the *Ancrene Riwle: Introduction and Part I*, ed. and trans. R. W. Ackerman and R. Dahood (Binghamton, NY: Medieval and Renaissance Texts and Studies, 1984), 16.

93. *Ancrene Wisse*, Part 2: 27, 40.

94. Georgianna, *Solitary Self*, 59. Wogan-Browne argues along the same lines that 'Much of the *Guide's* account of sense experience focuses on entry and im-permeability, enclosure and leakage, sealing and opening . . . The recluse's bodily experience in the cell is represented as a constant struggle for regula-tion of these permeabilities . . .' 'Chaste Bodies', 28.

95. *Ancrene Wisse*, Part 2: 23.

96. *Ancrene Wisse*, Part 2, quoted in Georgianna, *Solitary Self*, 65.

97. Georgianna, *Solitary Self*, 72–4.

98. Georgianna, *Solitary Self*, 77.

99. E. A. Kaplan, 'Is the Gaze Male?' in *Women and Film: Both Sides of the Camera* (London: Routledge, 1983), quoted in Stanbury, 'Voyeur and the

Private Life', 148. Stanbury's understanding of the 'gaze' is informed by the work of a number of feminist film theorists including (in addition to Kaplan): M. A. Doane, L. Mulvey and K. Silverman.

100. In Lacanian psychoanalysis, the identification of the penis (or clitoris) with the phallus is illusory: one is an organ; the other a signifier. See 'The Meaning of the Phallus' in *Feminine Sexuality: Jacques Lacan and the École Freudienne*, ed. J. Mitchell and J. Rose, trans. J. Rose (New York: Norton, 1982), in particular 79–80. There has, however, been some debate (and not a little confusion) over the supposed arbitrariness of the penis–phallus relationship in recent feminist theory. For two contrasting responses to this question, see: E. Grosz, *Jacques Lacan: a Feminist Introduction* (London: Routledge, 1990), 122–6; and E. Ragland-Sullivan, 'Jacques Lacan: Feminism and the Problem of Gender Identity', *Sub-Stance*, 36 (1982): 6–20.

101. S. Stanbury, 'Feminist Film Theory: Seeing Chrétien's *Enide*', *Literature and Psychology*, 36.4 (1990): 52.

102. Stanbury, 'Feminist Film Theory', 56.

103. *Troilus and Criseyde*, 1.304–5, quoted in Stanbury, 'Voyeur and the Private Life', 145.

104. S. Stanbury, 'The Virgin's Gaze: Spectacle and Transgression in Middle English Lyrics of the Passion', *PMLA*, 106.5 (Oct. 1991), 1084.

105. Although she focuses on fourteenth- and fifteenth-century sources, Stanbury's argument is equally persuasive in the context of earlier devotional literature and visual art, such as the examples discussed in Chapter 6 of this book.

106. Stanbury, 'Virgin's Gaze', 1091.

107. Stanbury defends her use of feminist film theory on the grounds that it provides 'a context within the cultural unconscious for understanding the gaze, and one that can relate the Middle Ages with our own time . . .' 'Feminist Film Theory', 63.

3   Scientific Visions

1. Aristotle, *Metaphysics*, 1.1.980a.

2. David Lindberg discusses the impact and dissemination of Bacon's optical theories in *Theories of Vision from Al-Kindi to Kepler* (Chicago: University of Chicago Press, 1976), 116–22.

3. Bacon, *Opus majus*, 2: 419 (5.1.1.1). The *Perspectiva*, for which this passage serves as in introduction, was disseminated both as Part 5 of Bacon's *Opus majus*, and as a separate text. There are 36 surviving manuscript copies of the text. Lindberg, *Theories of Vision*, 120.

4. See for example Jay, *Downcast Eyes*, 38, 44.

5. Bacon, *Opus majus*, 2: 420 (5.1.1.1).

6. As with any such generalisation, the polarisation of scholastic philosophy into Augustinian and Aristotelian traditions has attracted due criticism. For an overview of the issue, see F. C. Copleston, *A History of Medieval Philosophy* (London: Methuen, 1972), 156–9.

7. H. Blumenberg, *The Legitimacy of the Modern Age*, trans. R. M. Wallace (Cambridge, MA: MIT Press, 1983), 336.

8. Augustine, *Confessions* (Fathers of the Church 21), 311 (10.35.54). The Biblical reference is to 1 John 2.16: 'For all that is in the world—the lust of the flesh, the lust of the eyes, and the pride of life—is not of the Father but is of the world.' The 'lust for experience' is also mentioned by Augustine in *The Trinity*, 357 (12.10.15).

9. Augustine, *The Trinity*, 359 (12.12.17).

10. Madeline Caviness makes a convincing case that the philosophical (specifically Aristotelian) interest in the natural world during this period flowed through into the visual arts in the form of pictorial naturalism, albeit without stylistic consistency. As she points out, Grosseteste's conviction (voiced in his Oxford lectures during the 1230s) that the study of optics could provide insight into the creation and workings of the natural world had significant implications for art as well as science. It effectively 'banished the profane from scientific observation'. M. H. Caviness, ' "The Simple Perception of Matter" and the Representation of Narrative, ca. 1180–1280', *Gesta*, 30.1 (1991): 59.

11. *Omnis scientia bona est* is Thomas Aquinas's rendering of Aristotle's introduction to the *Metaphysics* (1.1.980a). The quotation is from Aquinas, *In Aristotelis librum de anima commentarium*, 1.1.3, cited in full in Blumenberg, *Legitimacy of the Modern Age*, 635 n.15.

12. Augustine's debt to Neoplatonism is evident in his privileging of transcendental Being (visible only to the 'inner' man) over the outward, bodily gaze at a world in perpetual flux: the realm of Becoming.

13. J. Owens, 'Faith, Ideas, Illumination, and Experience', *The Cambridge History of Later Medieval Philosophy: From the Rediscovery of Aristotle to the Disintegration of Scholasticism 1100–1600*, ed. N. Kretzmann, et al. (Cambridge: Cambridge University Press, 1982), 444. It is a testimony to the abiding influence of Augustinian and Neoplatonic thought that most medieval philosophers retained some version of Platonic Ideas and insisted on the necessary role of divine illumination for intellectual knowledge. For a survey of these theories in the later Middle Ages, see Owens.

14. Blumenberg discusses Siger of Brabant's formulation of this principle in *Legitimacy of the Modern Age*, 337–8.

15. Blumenberg illustrates the transition from early to high scholasticism through Albert the Great (c. 1200–80) and Thomas Aquinas (c. 1225–74). It is arguable, however, that Grosseteste is a more appropriate transitional figure, not least of all because his commentary on Aristotle's *Posterior Analytics* predates Blumenberg's examples.

16. Lindberg, *Theories of Vision*, 94.

17. C. Burnett, 'Scientific Speculations', *A History of Twelfth-Century Western Philosophy*, ed. P. Dronke (Cambridge: Cambridge University Press, 1992) 154. C. Riedl identifies Grosseteste with the beginnings of 'a new tradition, characterized by the blending of philosophy with experimental science'. 'Introduction' to Grosseteste's *On Light*, 2. On Grosseteste's contribution to early modern science, see also Southern, *Robert Grosseteste*, 150; A. C.

NOTES   189

Crombie, *Robert Grosseteste and the Origins of Experimental Science 1100–1700*
(Oxford: Clarendon, 1953), 43; and B. Eastwood, 'Medieval Empiricism: the
Case of Grosseteste's Optics', *Speculum*, 43 (1968), 306.

18. On James of Venice see the *Dictionary of Scientific Biography*, ed. C. C. Gillispie
(New York: Scribner, 1973), vol. 7: 65–7.

19. The dating of Grosseteste's commentary on the *Posterior Analytics* is discussed
by Southern; 1220–5 is his assessment. *Robert Grosseteste*, 131–2, 150–5. See
also S. P. Marrone, *William of Auvergne and Robert Grosseteste: New Ideas of Truth
in the Early Thirteenth Century* (Princeton: Princeton University Press, 1983).

20. 'So from perception there comes memory . . . and from memory, experience
. . . And from experience . . . there comes a principle of skill and of understanding . . .' Aristotle, *Posterior Analytics*, 2.19.100a.

21. Grosseteste, *Commentary on the Posterior Analytics*, quoted in Crombie, *Robert
Grosseteste*, 73.

22. Grosseteste, *Commentary on the Posterior Analytics*, quoted in Crombie, *Robert
Grosseteste*, 73.

23. Grosseteste, *Commentary on the Posterior Analytics*, quoted in Crombie, *Robert
Grosseteste*, 73.

24. On the etymological equation of seeing and knowing in Indo-European languages, see S. A. Tyler, 'The Vision Quest in the West, or What the Mind's Eye
Sees', *Journal of Anthropological Research*, 40 (1984): 23–40. Tyler notes that in
Dravidian languages, in contrast to Indo-European, words for thinking and
knowing are not dominated by visual tropes, but employ a range of sensory
metaphors in addition to kinaesthetic, verbal and emotive tropes (the latter
including 'desire', 'intention', 'hope', and 'wish'), 34–5.

25. Whereas thinking as seeing is mimetic, Tyler maintains that an equally ancient
tradition of kinetic tropes configures thinking as 'knowing how'. Examples
of the latter include the English 'can' and 'know' (from IE *gana*, 'be able').
'Vision Quest in the West', 33.

26. See, for example, Crombie, *Robert Grosseteste*, 116; Lindberg, *Theories of Vision*,
99; and S. L. Goldman, 'On the Interpretation of Symbols and the Christian
Origins of Modern Science', *The Journal of Religion*, 62.1 (Jan. 1982): 6.

27. For Evelyn Fox Keller and Christine Grontkowski, Western science and epistemology have developed according to the principle that 'Vision connects us
to truth as it distances us from the corporeal.' 'The Mind's Eye', *Discovering
Reality: Feminist Perspectives on Epistemology, Metaphysics, Methodology, and
Philosophy of Science*, ed. S. Harding and M. B. Hintikka (Dordrecht, Neth.:
Reidel, 1983), 209. While their observation certainly holds true for the
geometrical strand of medieval optics, and the theological polarisation of
sight into carnal and spiritual vision, it is by no means universally applicable.
Chapters 4 and 6 of this book demonstrate an intimate relationship between
'truth' (scientific and divine respectively), and the corporeality of vision.

28. On the Platonic origins of this association, and its implications for modern
science, see Keller and Grontkowski, 'The Mind's Eye', 210–17.

29. There is some controversy over the dating of this text. The date I have given
is proposed by Southern, *Robert Grosseteste*, 137–9.

30. Grosseteste, *On Light*, 10–11. On Grosseteste's Platonic and Neoplatonic sources see Lindberg, *Theories of Vision*, 95–8.

31. Crombie, *Robert Grosseteste*, 106. This point is clarified in Grosseteste's *De motu corporali et luce*, quoted by Crombie (107): 'I hold that the first form of a body is the first corporeal mover . . . when light generates itself in one direction drawing matter with it, it produces local motion (*motus localis*); and when the light within matter is sent out and what is outside is sent in, it produces qualitative change (*alteratio*).' In other words, light effects movement (as a force external to bodies), and change (when light is incorporated with matter).

32. Lindberg identifies four strands in Grosseteste's philosophy of light: an epistemology of light, a metaphysics (or cosmogony) of light, a physics of light, and a theology of light. *Theories of Vision*, 95–8.

33. In his *Hexaemeron*, Grosseteste develops the theological significance of the 'first corporeal form' by differentiating between the first light of Genesis (1.3) and the secondary creation (three days later) of the sun and stars (1.14–15). As Riedl explains, the same distinction seems to be denoted, in Grosseteste's *On Light* by the terms *lux* and *lumen*, where '*lux* is light in its source', and '*lumen* is reflected or radiated light'. Riedl, 'Introduction' to *On Light*, 5. It should be noted, however, that the terms *lux* and *lumen* were not used consistently by medieval writers, and that a further distinction was often made between God *as light* (*lux*), and corporeal light (rendered either as *lux* or *lumen*). See Crombie, *Robert Grosseteste*, 104–16, 131.

34. D. C. Lindberg, *Studies in the History of Medieval Optics* (London: Variorum Reprints, 1983) 338–9, 349–54. Pecham's *Perspectiva Communis* (probably written between 1277 and 1279) is available in a critical edition and English translation by Lindberg, *John Pecham and the Science of Optics* (Madison, Wis.: University of Wisconsin Press, 1970). Witelo's *Perspectiva* was written some time after 1270. Although the text was printed several times in the sixteenth century (as well as surviving in 19 mss copies), there is no complete modern edition. See the entry in the *Dictionary of Scientific Biography* for a bibliography of commentaries.

35. Lindberg, *Studies in the History of Medieval Optics*, 354.

36. Lindberg, *Theories of Vision*, 99.

37. Grosseteste, *De lineis, angulis, et figuris*, quoted in Crombie, *Robert Grosseteste*, 110.

38. Goldman, 'Interpretation of Symbols', 1. Goldman points out that the equation of mathematical models with natural phenomena remained largely unchallenged until the scientific relativism associated with quantum mechanics.

39. P. A. Heelan, *Space-Perception and the Philosophy of Science* (Berkeley: University of California Press, 1983), 157. In applying Heelan's schema to Grosseteste's philosophy of light, I am tacitly disagreeing with his assessment that modern science has its origins in fifteenth-century perspectivism (158).

40. Barthes claims that the 'reality effect' is pervasive in contemporary Western culture, citing as examples: the realist novel, the diary, the documentary, news

media, historical discourse and photography. The effect, he explains, is based on a confusion of meaning or interpretation (the signified) and the referent, so that the signifier seems to be a direct representation of the Real. R. Barthes, 'Historical Discourse' (1967) in *Introduction to Structuralism*, ed. M. Lane (New York: Basic, 1970), 154. Although he is concerned here with verbal and pictorial signifiers, Barthes's analysis of the reality principle is equally applicable to mathematical languages.

41. Barthes, 'Historical Discourse', 154.

42. See, for example, Bacon, *Opus majus*, 1: 232 (4.4.16).

43. Goldman contrasts this tendency to interpret metaphors and symbols ontologically with the 'intensely aniconic, deliberately nonpictorial, and consequently positivistic attitude toward metaphors and symbols in the contemporary [medieval and Renaissance] Judaic thought'. 'Interpretation of Symbols', 2.

44. Goldman, 'Interpretation of Symbols', 10.

45. Goldman notes the correlation between Panofsky's reading of Renaissance perspective as 'symbolic form' and the mathematical 'symbolism' of medieval optics. 'Interpretation of Symbols', 9.

46. Lindberg, *Theories of Vision*, 94.

47. *De lineis, angulis, et figuris*, quoted in Crombie, *Robert Grosseteste*, 110.

48. Crombie, *Robert Grosseteste*, 115.

49. For standard formulations of the nobility of sight (and a critique of Vasco Ronchi's contention that vision was regarded with deep suspicion in the Middle Ages), see: D. Lindberg and N. H. Steneck, 'The Sense of Vision and the Origins of Modern Science', *Studies in the History of Medieval Optics*, 29–45. Pouchelle discusses the nobility of the eye (and other 'noble' organs, including the lips and penis) in relation to the social metaphor of the body's 'offices'. *Body and Surgery*, 119.

50. Augustine, *The Trinity*, 316 (11.1.1). Augustine is not referring to the scientific value of sight, but rather to the fact that the Creator is visible (by analogy) in the creation. Note, however, that the expression 'spiritual vision' in this passage is synonymous with 'intellectual' vision or the sight of the mind.

51. Grosseteste, *On Light*, 10.

52. Grosseteste, *On Light*, 16.

53. D. E. Sharp, *Franciscan Philosophy at Oxford in the Thirteenth Century* (New York: Russell, 1964), 28. Sharp likens this mediating function of *lux* in Grosseteste's work to the modern concept of ether (22–3); as well as the *pneuma* (fiery 'breath' or spirit) of the Neoplatonists, and the medical theory of 'animal spirits' (28).

54. Aristotle uses the sailor-ship analogy in *On the Soul*, 2.1.413a to illustrate the relationship between the soul (the sailor) and the body.

55. Grosseteste, *De iride*, quoted in Lindberg, *Theories of Vision*, 100. In the same text Grosseteste repeats Aristotle's analogy of water issuing from a pipe to describe the operation of vision, hearing and smell (101). However, as Lindberg points out, Grosseteste's appeal to Aristotle in defence of the theory of extramission is based on a mistranslation (250, n.79).

56. Lindberg includes Grosseteste's subsequent remarks on the extramission–intromission controversy, observing that while Grosseteste defends the Platonic theory of fiery 'visual species', he does not reject the doctrine of intromission which he regards as incomplete rather than wrong. *Theories of Vision*, 100–1.

57. *Sollertia* generally refers to intellectual dexterity: cleverness, acumen, skill, ingenuity. Interestingly, the term is synonymous with *subtilitas*, one of the gifts Grosseteste ascribed to the bodies of the blessed (see Chapter 1).

58. Grosseteste, *Commentary on the Posterior Analytics*, quoted in Southern, *Robert Grosseteste*, 168.

59. John Wyclif (c.1328–84), *Sermones*, quoted in H. Phillips, 'John Wyclif and the Optics of the Eucharist', *From Ockham to Wyclif*, ed. A. Hudson and M. Wilks (Oxford: Blackwell, 1987), 247. Wyclif would have been familiar with the optical writings of Alhazen and Witelo from his studies at Oxford; and Phillips considers Roger Bacon a likely source for the text I have quoted from.

60. M. J. Carruthers, *The Book of Memory: a Study of Memory in Medieval Culture*, Cambridge Studies in Medieval Literature (Cambridge: Cambridge University Press, 1990), 27.

61. Carruthers, *Book of Memory*, 78, 94.

62. Thomas Bradwardine (d. 1349, shortly after becoming Archbishop of Canterbury). 'De Memoria Artificiali', trans. and quoted by Carruthers, *Book of Memory*, Appendix C, 281.

63. K. H. Tachau, *Vision and Certitude in the Age of Ockham: Optics, Epistemology and the Foundations of Semantics 1250–1345* (Leiden: Brill, 1988), 25–6.

64. As Lindberg observes, Bacon 'lifts Grosseteste's physics of light . . . out of its metaphysical and cosmogonical context and develops it into a comprehensive doctrine of physical causation'. D. C. Lindberg, *Roger Bacon's Philosophy of Nature: a Critical Edition, with English Translation, Introduction, and Notes, of* De multiplicatione specierum *and* De speculis comburentibus (Oxford: Clarendon, 1983), liv.

65. Like Grosseteste, Bacon studied at Oxford and Paris, and joined the Franciscan Order upon returning to Oxford, probably in 1257. Unlike his predecessor, whose career was furthered by his religious association, Bacon suffered censorship by the Order, and may eventually have been imprisoned on the grounds of propagating 'suspected novelties'. Lindberg, *Roger Bacon's Philosophy of Nature*, xvi–xxvi.

66. On thirteenth-century optical sources generally, and their incorporation into the Baconian synthesis, see Lindberg, 'The Optical Synthesis of the Thirteenth Century', *Theories of Vision*, 104–21.

67. On Alhazen's life, works and extensive influence on the development of optics in the West, see: Lindberg, 'Alhazen and the New Intromission Theory of Vision', *Theories of Vision*, 58–86. Bacon's debt to Alhazen is covered in Chapter 6 of the same volume, pages 109–16.

68. Epicurus, 'Letter to Herodotus' in Diogenes Laertius, *Lives of Eminent Philosophers,* trans. R. D. Hicks, 2 vols (Cambridge, MA: Harvard University Press, 1991), 2: 577–9 (10.48–9).

69. Lindberg, *Studies in the History of Medieval Optics*, 340. For Aristotle's theory of vision, see: *On the Soul*, 2.5.418a-2.7.419a; and *Sense and Sensibilia*, 1.437a–3.439b.

70. Lindberg, *Studies in the History of Medieval Optics*, 340.

71. On Bacon's sources, see: Lindberg, *Theories of Vision*, 104–16; and Lindberg, *Roger Bacon's Philosophy of Nature*, xxxv–liv.

72. Aristotle, *Posterior Analytics*, 2.19.99b.

73. Lindberg (citing Pierre Michaud-Quantin), *Roger Bacon's Philosophy of Nature*, liv.

74. 'For the species of the body, which is perceived, produces the species which arises in the sense of the percipient; this latter gives rise to the species in the memory; finally, the species in the memory produces the species which arises in the gaze of thought.' Augustine, *The Trinity*, 11.9.16, quoted in Lindberg, *Roger Bacon's Philosophy of Nature*, lv. Lindberg observes, however, that Augustine's understanding of species is primarily psychological: there is no attempt to account for sensation and thought in terms of physical causation.

75. Augustine, *Literal Meaning of Genesis*, 2: 199 (12.16).

76. Lindberg, *Roger Bacon's Philosophy of Nature*, lv.

77. The synonyms omitted from my list are: 'intention', 'passion' (discussed in Chapter 4), and the 'shadow of the philosophers'. The latter refers to the fact that species are not generally visible in the medium; thus although species conform to the properties of light, they are figurative 'shadows' whose operation can be discerned only by 'skilful philosophers'. Bacon, *De multiplicatione specierum*, 3–5 (1.1).

78. As Heelan notes, perspectivism (artistic or scientific) rests on precisely this premise that 'reality is *pictorial*'. *Space-Perception*, 102.

79. Bacon, *De multiplicatione specierum,* 179 (3.1).

80. See *On the Soul*, 2.5.418a–2.7.419a; *Sense and Sensibilia*, 2.438b.

81. Bacon, *Opus majus*, 2: 490 (5.1.9.4).

82. Bacon, *De multiplicatione specierum*, 45 (1.3). On the seal and wax metaphor, see Carruthers, *Book of Memory*, 16–32, 55–7.

83. Bacon, *De signis*, quoted in T. S. Maloney, 'The Semiotics of Roger Bacon', *Mediaeval Studies*, 45 (1983): 142. Bacon makes a further basic distinction between natural signs that signify by rational inference, connotation or analogy, and signs that so resemble their significates that they are immediately recognised. The latter group include 'images, pictures, likenesses, things that are similar, and the species of colors, tastes, sounds, and all substances and accidents' (Bacon, quoted in Maloney, 134). While words are generally natural signs by *inference*, because their meaning is inferred from the species of things, the species themselves are signs by *resemblance*. This applies not only to sense impressions but to concepts derived from extramental objects (130–6).

84. Tachau, *Vision and Certitude*, 18.

85. 'Mathematics is an abstractive science considering things [forms] existing in matter, but without the matter.' Domingo Gundisalvo (or Gundissalinus)

194   SIGHT AND EMBODIMENT IN THE MIDDLE AGES

(fl. 1140), 'Classification of the Sciences', trans. M. Clagett and E. Grant, in *A Source Book in Medieval Science*, ed. E. Grant (Cambridge, MA: Harvard University Press, 1974), 65. Hugh of St Victor (d. 1141) writes similarly that mathematics 'is the branch of theoretical knowledge "which considers abstract quantity. Now quantity is called abstract when, intellectually separating it from matter or from other accidents, we treat of it as equal, unequal, and the like, in our reasoning alone"—a separation which it receives only in the domain of mathematics and not in nature.' He is quoting here from Cassiodorus's *Introduction to Divine and Human Readings*. Hugh of St Victor's 'Classification of the Sciences', trans. J. Taylor, in *A Source Book in Medieval Science*, 55.

86. Gundisalvo, 'Classification of the Sciences', 66.
87. Gundisalvo, 'Classification of the Sciences', 65.
88. Bacon, *De multiplicatione specierum*, 93 (2.1).
89. Bacon, *De multiplicatione specierum*, 93–5 (2.1). A full account of these 'paths' is given on pages 97–103 (2.2). That species are able to deviate from these principles of direct radiation, reflection and refraction according to the 'soul's needs' refers to the transmission of species along the 'twisting path' of the nervous system. 103 (2.2); Bacon, *Opus majus*, 1: 136 (4.2.2).
90. Bacon, *Opus majus*, 1: 136–8 (4.2.3).
91. Bacon, *Opus majus*, 2: 454–5 (5.1.6.1).
92. Bacon, *Opus majus*, 2: 454 (5.1.6.1).
93. Magnitude, Bacon explains, is discerned from the angle of the visual pyramid at its apex, in addition to a judgement of the pyramid's depth from the scale of intervening objects. The perception of distance is thus aided by memory and association. *Opus majus*, 2: 530–2 (5.2.3.5). Peter of John Olivi, who probably met Bacon in Paris in the late 1260s, rejected this account of distance perception. His critique of Bacon's perspectivism is discussed in Tachau, *Vision and Certitude*, 39ff. On the infinite divisibility of quantity, and hence the eye's ability to apprehend very large objects, see *Opus majus*, 2: 455–6 (5.1.6.1).
94. Bacon, *Opus majus*, 2: 456–8 (5.1.6.2).
95. Bacon, *Opus majus*, 2: 471 (5.1.7.4).
96. Bacon, *Opus majus*, 2: 471 (5.1.7.4).
97. Bacon, *Opus majus*, 2: 471 (5.1.7.4).
98. Bacon, *Opus majus*, 2: 471 (5.1.7.4).
99. Tachau, *Vision and Certitude*, 130.
100. William of Ockham, *Opera Theologica*, 5, quoted in Tachau, *Vision and Certitude*, 130.
101. The continuing currency of causal, physical models of sight is evidenced in Bartholomæus Anglicus's Latin encyclopedia, *De proprietatibus rerum* (On the Properties of Things), compiled in c.1230–c.1240. By the end of the fourteenth century the text had been translated into French and English. John Trevisa's translation (extant in eight manuscripts) has been edited by M. C. Seymour et al. (Oxford: Clarendon, 1975). See Book 3.17: '*De sensu visus*', 108–13.

102. K. H. Tachau, 'The Problem of the *Species in Medio* at Oxford in the Generation after Ockham', *Mediaeval Studies*, 44 (1982): 395.

103. Bacon, *De multiplicatione specierum*, 103 (2.2).

104. In his effort to synthesise a number of sources, Bacon's description is not particularly clear. Immediately after this account he notes that some authors differentiate between six coats (posterior and anterior of three membranes), then settles on tripartite division consisting of the consolidativa, the cornea, and the uvea, thus treating the retina merely as the other side of the uvea and not as a separate membrane. *Opus majus*, 2: 434 (5.1.2.2). I have used his initial schema because it is closer to the modern anatomy of the eye.

105. Bacon, *Opus majus*, 2: 432–5 (5.1.2.2–3).

106. Bacon, *Opus majus*, 2: 436 (5.1.3.1).

107. Bacon, *Opus majus*, 2: 440–1 (5.1.3.3).

108. Bacon, *De multiplicatione specierum*, 103 (2.2).

109. Bacon, *De multiplicatione specierum*, 103 (2.2).

110. On the significance of this conception of space, see E. Grant, *Much Ado About Nothing: Theories of Space and Vacuum from the Middle Ages to the Scientific Revolution* (Cambridge: Cambridge University Press, 1981), especially chapter 4: 'Nature's Abhorrence of a Vacuum', 67–100.

111. Bacon qualifies this point, insisting that the 'marrow-like substance of the brain' is only 'the container and storehouse of the sensitive faculties, containing slender nerves in which sense and sensible forms are located'. *Opus majus*, 2: 428 (5.1.1.5). While this would seem to be an attempt to minimise the materiality of the internal senses, Bacon's use of humoral theory to account for the receptive and retentive functions of these senses suggests that the brain was not merely a series of hollow cavities, but a potent receptacle. It will be argued in the next chapter that this conception of the brain as a receptacle is analogous to the medieval understanding of the womb as both the container and material substance for the foetus.

112. In assigning cognitive functions to the internal senses as well as to the intellect, Bacon is following a precedent set by Aristotle and Avicenna. Tachau, *Vision and Certitude*, 10.

113. Bacon, *Opus majus*, 2: 421 (5.1.1.2).

114. Bacon, *Opus majus*, 2: 422 (5.1.1.2).

115. Bacon, *Opus majus*, 2: 422 (5.1.1.2).

116. Bacon lists the following general properties in addition to the 'special properties' perceived by the individual senses: distance, position, figure, magnitude, continuity, discreetness or separation, number, motion, rest, roughness, smoothness, transparency, thickness, shadow, darkness, beauty, ugliness, similarity and difference. *Opus majus*, 2: 423 (5.1.1.3).

117. Bacon, *Opus majus*, 2: 425 (5.1.1.3).

118. Thomas Aquinas, *Commentary on Aristotle's De anima*, trans. K. Foster and S. Humphries (London: Routledge, 1951), Lectio 14 on Bk II, par. 417.

119. Bacon, *Opus majus*, 2: 426 (5.1.1.3).

120. Bacon, *Opus majus*, 2: 426 (5.1.1.3).

121. Bacon, *Opus majus*, 2: 426 (5.1.1.3).

122. Tachau, *Vision and Certitude*, 34, n.20. On the historical specificity of the mind–body question, see also: W. I. Matson, 'Why Isn't the Mind-Body Problem Ancient?' *Mind, Matter and Method: Essays in Philosophy and Science in Honor of Herbert Feigl*, ed. P. K. Feyerabend and G. Maxwell (Minneapolis: University of Minnesota Press, 1966) 92–102; and H. Putnam, 'How Old is the Mind?' *Words and Life*, ed. J. Conant (Cambridge, MA: Harvard University Press, 1994), 3–21.

123. Bacon, *Opus majus*, 1: 43–5 (2.5). Z. Kuksewicz outlines the major positions on this issue, including the variations within Bacon's writings, in 'The Potential and the Agent Intellect', *The Cambridge History of Later Medieval Philosophy: From the Rediscovery of Aristotle to the Disintegration of Scholasticism 1100–1600*, ed. N. Kretzmann et al. (Cambridge: Cambridge University Press, 1982), 595–601.

124. '. . . species causes every action in this world; for it acts on sense, on intellect, and all the matter in the world for the production of things, because one and the same thing is done by a natural agent on whatsoever it acts, because it has no freedom of choice . . .' Bacon, *Opus majus*, 1: 130 (4.2.1).

125. Olivi raised this issue of free will in his critique of perspectivism. Tachau, *Vision and Certitude*, 40.

126. Kuksewicz notes that Bacon's treatment of the intellect can be divided into three distinct phases. The last, of which the *Opus majus* is representative, forms the basis of this discussion. 'Potential and Agent Intellect', 599–600.

127. Bacon, *Opus majus*, 1: 45 (2.5).

128. Bacon comments that the active intellect 'knows all things'. *Opus majus*, 1: 44 (2.5).

129. Owens, 'Faith, Ideas, Illumination and Experience', 449.

4 The Optical Body

1. Plotinus, *Enneads*, 4.3.8, quoted in M. Miles, 'Vision: the Eye of the Body and the Eye of the Mind in Saint Augustine's *De Trinitate* and *Confessions*', *The Journal of Religion*, 63.2 (Apr. 1983),129 n.14.

2. I am using the term 'objective' here in the sense that both extramental objects and their sensory and mental simulacra were assumed to have real (and material) existence independent of the operations of an immaterial intellect.

3. Bacon, *Opus majus*, 2: 468 (5.1.7.2): 'It is clear . . . that a species is produced by vision just as by other things, because accidental qualities and substances inferior to vision are able to produce their own forces; much more therefore has vision this power.'

4. Bacon also describes this visual force as the 'species of the eye', and in more Platonic language, as 'visual rays'. *Opus majus*, 2: 468 (5.1.7.2).

5. Bacon, *Opus majus*, 2: 470 (5.1.7.3).

6. Much of Merleau-Ponty's argument in the *Phenomenology of Perception* takes the form of a dialectical interrogation of intellectualism and empiricism. His version of a synthesis is most fully worked out in *The Visible and the Invisible*.

7. Merleau-Ponty, *The Visible and the Invisible*, 15.

8. Merleau-Ponty, *Phenomenology of Perception*, 40.
9. Merleau-Ponty, *The Visible and the Invisible*, 29. Lacan comments similarly on the 'disconcerting' awareness that '. . . I see outside, that perception is not in me, that it is on the objects that it apprehends'. Yet at the same time, 'as soon as I perceive, my representations belong to me'. 'Anamorphosis', *Four Fundamental Concepts*, 80–1.
10. 'Perceptual faith' is Merleau-Ponty's expression. See *The Visible and the Invisible*, especially pages 3–14.
11. Bacon, *Opus majus*, 2: 468, 470 (5.1.7.2–3); *De multiplicatione specierum*, 33 (1.2).
12. Bacon, *Opus majus*, 2: 470 (5.1.7.4). For Plato's theory of vision, see: Plato, *The Republic*, trans. H. D. P. Lee (Harmondsworth: Penguin, 1955), 272–3 (7.5.508–9); and *Timaeus*, 62–4 (13).
13. Bacon, *Opus majus*, 2: 471 (5.1.7.4).
14. Bacon, *Opus majus*, 2: 471 (5.1.7.4). He adds that 'the species of the eye is the species of an animate substance, in which the force of the soul holds sway, and therefore it bears no comparison to the species of an inanimate thing . . .' (472). Presumably when one sees a reflected image of one's own eyes, their visible species (light and colour) are of the same inanimate category as any other object. In contrast, the species of *vision*, which passes *through* the pupil and not from the eye as a whole, is not itself visible.
15. Jay, *Downcast Eyes*, 30. Gadamer's comments refer specifically to the Greek concept of *theoria*. Jay suggests that 'Residues of such reciprocity in the notion of theory may well in fact have persisted until the late Middle Ages, when belief in extramission was finally laid to rest.' *Downcast Eyes*, 31.
16. For Lacan, the incident with the sardine can ('*You see that can? Do you see it? Well, it doesn't see you.*') suggested an impersonal, disembodied power of vision, entirely external to the subject: what he calls the 'gaze'. 'The Line and the Light', *Four Fundamental Concepts*, 95–6.
17. Brennan, 'Contexts of Vision', 219.
18. Brennan, 'Contexts of Vision', 219–24. It is important to stress, however, that the dominant late medieval understanding of vision—represented here by Bacon—held (however contradictorily) that sight was both active and passive, and both in a physical sense. I would therefore disagree with Brennan's claim that the proponents of extramission regarded sight as purely active (223). Certainly, the eye is both vulnerable/receptive and aggressive/penetrating in the literature of courtly love.
19. Brennan, 'Contexts of Vision', 219. A notable exception is Merleau-Ponty's attempt re-think this division through the 'elemental' (as opposed to psychical or physical) medium of 'flesh'. The result is a carnal/perceptual 'intertwining' of self and world that resists resolution into the traditional binaries of active and passive, subject and object, mind (or intellect) and body. *The Visible and the Invisible*, in particular Chapter 4: 'The Intertwining—the Chiasm', 130–55.
20. Crombie, *Robert Grosseteste*, 152.

21. I noted in Chapter 3 that the 'mind–body' problem is a modern one. For Bacon and his contemporaries the mind and soul were embodied, a point I will return to later in this chapter.

22. For another critique of this widespread assumption, see Margaret Miles's commentary on Augustine's theory of vision in 'Vision'. She points out that for Augustine, physical contact and emotional engagement were standard features of vision: 'The ray theory of vision specifically insisted on the connection and essential continuity of viewer and object in the act of vision' (127).

23. Grosz, *Jacques Lacan*, 38. Grosz makes this observation in the context of a discussion of Lacan's 'mirror stage'. The recurrence of this theme in contemporary French thought is treated at length by Martin Jay in *Downcast Eyes*.

24. Jay discusses a number of such interpretations of perspectivism in *Downcast Eyes*, 53ff.

25. To cite just one example, in 'Mind's Eye' (221) Keller and Grontkowski speculate about forms of knowledge based on auditory or tactile metaphors rather than visual ones. In order to underscore the need to re-think the metaphorical foundations of modern epistemology, they quote G. N. A. Vesey's definition of 'vision' from *The Encyclopedia of Philosophy* (8: 252): 'We can imagine a disembodied mind having visual experiences but not tactile ones. Sight does not require our being part of the material world in the way in which feeling by touching does.' Bacon would surely disagree, as I argue later in this chapter.

26. Bacon, *Opus majus*, 2: 471 (5.1.7.4).

27. Bacon, *Opus majus*, 2: 474 (5.1.8.1).

28. Bacon, *Opus majus*, 2: 474 (5.1.8.1). Bacon's source here is Aristotle's *On the Soul*, 2.11.423a–424a.

29. Such a distinction between sight and touch leads Irigaray to argue that Western ocularcentrism and phallocentrism are inter-implicated, and as such that 'the predominance of the visual, and of the discrimination and individualization of form, is particularly foreign to female eroticism'. 'Woman', she concludes, 'takes pleasure more from touching than from looking . . .' L. Irigaray, *This Sex Which Is Not One*, trans. C. Porter and C. Burke (Ithaca, NY: Cornell University Press, 1985), 25–6.

30. Roger Caillois, for example, described psychosis as an inability to remain comfortably 'inside' one's skin: 'the body separates itself from thought, the individual breaks the boundary of his skin and occupies the other side of his senses.' Quoted in E. Grosz, *Volatile Bodies: Toward a Corporeal Feminism* (Sydney: Allen, 1994), 47. Grosz also discusses more familiar blurrings of the body's borders on pages 79ff. Julia Kristeva's treatment of the skin as 'the essential if not initial boundary of biological and psychic individuation' similarly emphasises permeability rather than the delineation of a fixed and impregnable border. *Powers of Horror: an Essay on Abjection*, trans. L. S. Roudiez (New York: Columbia University Press, 1982), 101. See also pages 69–70.

31. G. Didi-Huberman, 'The Figurative Incarnation of the Sentence (Notes on the "Autographic" Skin)', *Journal*, The Los Angeles Institute of Contemporary Art (Spring 1987), 68.

32. Bacon, *Opus majus*, 2: 474 (5.1.8.1).

33. Aristotle, *On the Soul*, 2.11.423a. Aristotle does go on to say that touch and taste are peculiar in that the organ of sense and the medium are not clearly delineated, whereas in vision, hearing and smell they are distinct. His comparison of tactility and sight, however, suggests that the distinction is not so clear after all. For our purposes, Bacon's separation of the senses retains this ambiguity.

34. Galen, *On the Doctrines of Hippocrates and Plato*, ed. and trans. P. de Lacy, 2nd ed., 2 vols (Berlin: Akademie-Verlag, 1984), 2: 461 (7.5.32–41). For a commentary on Galen's theory of sight, see R. E. Siegel, *Galen on Sense Perception* (Basel: Karger, 1970).

35. Bacon, *Opus majus*, 2: 471 (5.1.7.4). See also 'Moral Philosophy', *Opus majus*, 2: 756 (7.3.18): 'When the mind following its senses has with their aid extended itself to external objects, it should be master of them and of itself.'

36. Bacon, *Opus majus*, 2: 449 (5.1.5.1).

37. Bacon, *Opus majus*, 2: 440 (5.1.3.3); 2: 468 (5.1.7.2).

38. Plotinus (working from an extramissionist position) observes that in 'any perception we attain by sight, the object is grasped there where it lies in the direct line of vision; it is there that we attack it; there, then, that the perception is formed; *the mind looks outward . . .*' (emphasis added). Plotinus, *The Enneads*, trans. Stephen MacKenna, 4th ed. (London: Faber, 1969), 338 (4.6.1).

39. Keller and Grontkowski, 'Mind's Eye', 209.

40. Keller and Grontkowski, 'Mind's Eye', 209.

41. Keller and Grontkowski, 'Mind's Eye', 220.

42. Keller and Grontkowski, 'Mind's Eye', 209–13.

43. Grosseteste, for example, likens the species emitted by the eye to the sun's rays. The relevant passage is quoted and discussed in Chapter 3.

44. Keller and Grontkowski, 'Mind's Eye', 212.

45. Keller and Grontkowski, 'Mind's Eye', 220.

46. Keller and Grontkowski, 'Mind's Eye', 220.

47. Keller and Grontkowski, 'Mind's Eye', 220.

48. 'In Plato's understanding incorporeality and communion were not in conflict.' Keller and Grontkowski, 'Mind's Eye', 213.

49. Keller and Grontkowski, 'Mind's Eye', 213.

50. Vesey, quoted in Keller and Grontkowski, 'Mind's Eye', 221.

51. This chronological leap from Plato to the seventeenth century is made on page 213.

52. For Lacan's account of the mirror stage, see Jacques Lacan, 'The Mirror Stage as Formative of the Function of the *I* as Revealed in Psychoanalytic Experience' (1949), *Écrits: a Selection*, trans. A. Sheridan (London: Tavistock, 1977), 1–7. In addition to this source, my synopsis and discussion draw on: J. Gallop, *Reading Lacan* (Ithaca: Cornell University Press, 1985), especially chapter 3; E. Grosz, *Jacques Lacan*; and M. Jay, *Downcast Eyes* (chapter 6).

53. As Gallop notes, Lacan's mirror stage is not an empirical account of early childhood. It is, rather, a retroactive 'phantasy'. Concurring with Laplanche and Pontalis (*The Language of Psychoanalysis*), she argues: 'What appears to precede the mirror stage is simply a projection or a reflection. There is nothing on the other side of the mirror.' *Reading Lacan*, 80.

54. Lacan, 'Mirror Stage', 1.

55. Lacan, 'Mirror Stage', 2, 4.

56. Thus, 'the specular image is a totalized, complete, external image—a *gestalt*—of the subject, the subject as seen from outside; the visual *gestalt* is in conflict with the child's fragmentary, disorganized felt reality . . .' Grosz, *Jacques Lacan*, 48. See Lacan, 'Mirror Stage', 2.

57. Grosz, *Jacques Lacan*, 37, 42.

58. Grosz, *Jacques Lacan*, 42.

59. Grosz is referring here to Jean-Paul Sartre's comments on vision in *Being and Nothingness*. Grosz, *Jacques Lacan*, 38.

60. Lacan, 'Mirror Stage', 2–3.

61. Similarly, Grosz distinguishes between the child's 'psychic' and 'neurophysiological' images of self, others and world. It is through the internalisation of its *visible* 'self' that the child gains a (psychic) 'self-image' as well as an 'understanding of space, distance, and position'. *Jacques Lacan*, 32. Lacan's comments on the relationship between the gaze, the eye and light are too complicated to go into here. See chapters 6–9 of *Four Fundamental Concepts*; and for a commentary on these seminars: Jay, *Downcast Eyes*, 357–70; and K. Silverman, 'Fassbinder and Lacan: a Reconsideration of Gaze, Look and Image', *Camera Obscura*, 19 (Jan. 1989): 54–85.

62. Tachau, '*Species in Medio*', 443.

63. Bacon, *Opus majus*, 2: 445–6 (5.1.4.2).

64. Bacon, *De multiplicatione specierum*, 7 (1.1).

65. Bacon, *De multiplicatione specierum*, 19–21 (1.1). His source is Aristotle, *On the Soul*, 2.2.413b.

66. Augustine, *The Trinity*, 322 (11.2.5). Augustine claims that 'numerous examples' of this phenomenon can be found in nature, and recalls the story (Gen. 30.37–41) in which Jacob places wooden rods of different hues in his watering troughs so that the offspring of his sheep and goats will be coloured accordingly.

67. Bacon, *De multiplicatione specierum*, 7 (1.1). For Aristotle's explanation of this process, see: *On the Soul*, 2.5.416b, 418a.

68. H. Putnam and M. C. Nussbaum, 'Changing Aristotle's Mind', *Words and Life*, ed. J. Conant (Cambridge, MA: Harvard University Press, 1994), 32–42. For Aristotle's theory of perception and emotion as bodily functions, see: *On the Soul*, 403a25–b27; 427a27.

69. Aristotle, *On the Soul*, 1.1.403a25: 'the affections of the soul are enmattered accounts [or proportions]'. Bacon is working on the same principle when he says 'there must be something more active and productive of change in the sentient body than light and color, because it not only causes apprehension

but also a state of fear or love or flight or delay.' Bacon, *Opus majus*, 2: 425 (5.1.1.4).

70. Aristotle, *On the Soul*, 2.4.415b.

71. Thomas Slakey argues that in *On the Soul* Aristotle presents perception as 'simply the movement which occurs in the sense-organs, not some psychic process in addition to the movement in the organs'. In other words, Aristotle understands perception as a bodily process, not as a mental 'interpretation' of a physiological alteration of the sense organ. 'Aristotle on Sense-perception', *Aristotle's De Anima in Focus*, ed. M. Durrant (London: Routledge, 1993), 77.

72. Aristotle, *On the Soul*, 2.5.418a.

73. Aristotle, *On the Soul*, 2.5.417a.

74. Bacon, *De multiplicatione specierum*, 191 (3.2). See also 47 (1.3) in the same text.

75. Aristotle, *Physics*, 1.9.192a. Klassen mentions this metaphor in relation to Aquinas's theory of understanding. *Chaucer on Love*, 30–4.

76. Plotinus, *Enneads*, 337 (4.5.8).

77. Plotinus rejects Aristotle's claim that the medium performs a necessary, causal function in vision. *Enneads*, 328–38 (4.5). For a commentary on the text, see: E. K. Emilsson, *Plotinus on Sense-Perception: a Philosophical Study* (Cambridge: Cambridge University Press, 1988), especially chapters 3 and 4: 'The relation between the eye and the object of vision' and 'Sensory affection'.

78. This is Emilsson's interpretation of Plotinus's concept of *sympatheia*, *Plotinus on Sense-Perception*, 59.

79. Lacan, 'Mirror Stage', 5.

80. I would therefore disagree with Pouchelle's emphasis on corporeal, architectural and symbolic closure. In her view, 'All "spaces"—the cosmos, Paradise, syllogistic reasoning, the body—were at that time [in the Middle Ages] closed.' *Body and Surgery*, 125 She does, however, mention the symbolic significance of the senses, as 'breaks in the wholeness of the body' (149).

81. Lacan, 'Mirror Stage', 5.

82. Gallop, *Reading Lacan*, 60–1.

83. See the entries for 'Imaginary' and 'Symbolic' in J. Laplanche and J.-B. Pontalis, *The Language of Psycho-Analysis*, trans. D. Nicholson-Smith (London: Hogarth/Institute of Psycho-Analysis, 1973), 210, 439–40.

84. Chapters 5 and 6 will elaborate on the redemptive role of bodily sight as the conduit between humanity and divinity; and the flesh of Christ as the focus of redemptive vision.

85. Olivi, commentary on Peter Lombard's *Sentences* (written 1287–8), quoted in Tachau, *Vision and Certitude*, 50.

86. Olivi, quoted in Tachau, *Vision and Certitude*, 50.

87. Olivi (b. 1247/8) was a student in Paris from 1266–8, and probably met Bacon and Pecham there. His critique of perspectivism is discussed by Tachau, *Vision and Certitude*, 39–54.

88. Putnam and Nussbaum, 'Changing Aristotle's Mind', 24–5.

89. Putnam and Nussbaum, 'Changing Aristotle's Mind', 25.

90. Aristotle, *Metaphysics*, 6.10.1035b32.

91. Bacon, *Opus majus*, 2: 432 (5.1.2.2).

92. Bacon, *Opus majus*, 2: 433–5 (5.1.2.2–3).

93. Bacon, *Opus majus*, 2: 433 (5.1.2.2). Of relevance here is a comment made by Leo Steinberg in relation to Filippo Lippi's London *Annunciation* (painted in c.1449–60). Steinberg argues that the painting depicts 'Mary's womb . . . impregnated by light as the eye is by sights received . . . [reflecting] a theory, widely held in medieval and Renaissance speculation, concerning the nature of visual perception'. Steinberg, "How Shall This Be?" Reflections on Filippo Lippi's *Annunciation* in London, Part 1', *Artibus et historiae*, 8.16 (1987): 39.

94. Bacon, *Opus majus*, 2: 434–5 (5.1.2.3).

95. Meister Eckhart (c.1260–1327) uses Gen. 2.24—'They were two in one flesh'—to elucidate the relationship between matter and form, or 'the sense faculty and the sense object'. Meister Eckhart, 'Latin Works' in *Meister Eckhart: the Essential Sermons, Commentaries, Treatises, and Defence*, trans. E. Colledge and B. McGinn (New York: Paulist, 1981), 105.

96. T. Laqueur, *Making Sex: Body and Gender from the Greeks to Freud* (Cambridge, MA: Harvard University Press, 1990), 35, 59.

97. The idea of perceptual transformation (and its associated 'passion') is exploited in medieval devotional practices, most notably as a means of identifying *bodily* with Christ's suffering. I expand on this theme in Chapter 6.

98. Merleau-Ponty, *The Visible and the Invisible*, 32. The context of this statement is a critique of objective science and philosophical reflection, but Merleau-Ponty's reproductive metaphors serve more generally to confound binary thinking.

99. Bacon, *Opus majus*, 2: 419 (5.1.1.1), quoted in full in Chapter 3 of this book.

100. Bacon, 'Moral Philosophy', *Opus majus*, 2: 680 (7.3.5).

101. See Aristotle, *On the Soul*, 3.13.435a–b; *Sense and Sensibilia*, 1.436b–437a.

102. Bacon, 'The Application of Mathematics to Sacred Subjects', *Opus majus*, 1: 241.

103. Bacon, *Opus majus*, 1: 241. Here too, however, Bacon's example pertains to sight and hearing more than touch or taste. When receiving the confession of a woman, he says, it is crucial to avoid 'short pyramids' and direct, perpendicular angles of reception so as to minimise the effect of her species (242).

104. Bacon, *Opus majus*, 1: 234.

105. Aristotle, *On the Soul*, 2.2.413b.

106. Aristotle, *Metaphysics*, 1.1.980a.

107. Plato, *Phaedo*, ed. and trans. David Gallop (Oxford: Oxford University Press, 1993), 36 (83d).

108. Augustine, *The Trinity*, 318 (11.2.2), emphasis added.

109. Augustine, *The Trinity*, 316 (11.2.2).

110. Miles, 'Vision'.

111. Augustine, *The Trinity*, 322 (11.3.6).
112. Bacon, *Opus majus*, 1: 232.
113. Bacon, 'Moral Philosophy', *Opus majus*, 2: 654 (7.1).

5 The Custody of the Eyes

1. Bernard of Clairvaux, *On the Song of Songs* (28.10), quoted in B. McGinn, *The Growth of Mysticism*, vol. 2 of *The Presence of God: a History of Western Christian Mysticism*, 4 vols (New York: Crossroad, 1994), 187.

2. Boethius (c. 480–c. 525), *De institutione arithmetica*, quoted in Winthrop Wetherbee, 'Philosophy, Cosmology, and the Twelfth-Century Renaissance', *A History of Twelfth-Century Western Philosophy*, ed. Dronke, 30. Wetherbee notes that the passage was 'much quoted in the twelfth century'.

3. Blindness is one of the most widely exploited metaphors for the postlapsarian corruption of the bodily senses by the flesh. To give just a few examples: Roger Bacon remarks that sensual pleasure 'blindfolds the eyes of the mind' in 'Moral Philosophy', *Opus majus*, 2: 679 (7.3.5). The same logic lies behind Augustine's erotically charged image of the mind paralysed by sensation; Alan of Lille's description of the flesh as a 'fog' or 'shadow' clouding the eye of the mind like a cataract; and Richard of St Victor's reference to the 'fog of error' and 'cloud of sin' that dulls the eye of reason with the 'darkness of ignorance'. See Chapter 1 for details.

4. Plato, for example, had condemned the body as contagion, asserting that knowledge is 'achieved most purely by one who approaches each object with his intellect alone . . . neither applying sight in his thinking, nor dragging in any other sense to accompany his reasoning . . .' *Phaedo*, 11. Similarly, painting and poetry are condemned in *The Republic* as appealing to 'a low element in the mind', namely that concerned with sensation and emotion. He who 'stirs up and encourages and strengthens' these inferior faculties, does so 'at the expense of reason'. 382 (10.2).

5. G. E. R. Lloyd, *Polarity and Analogy: Two Types of Argumentation in Early Greek Thought* (Bristol: Bristol Classics, 1987), 436.

6. Jon Whitman argues this point from the Neoplatonic perspective of Bernard Silvestris (c. 1100–c. 1160). Because the material world is conceived as a divergence from the One, the awareness of humanity's 'otherness' is coupled with the desire for reunion. As Whitman says of Bernard's use of allegory: 'for all the evil he associates with the material world . . . he seeks to resolve its ambiguous condition not by escaping it, but by engaging it . . . In the end, he suggests that the very process of exploiting the diversities of a divided world and a divided language leads toward an integrity beyond them.' *Allegory: the Dynamics of an Ancient and Medieval Technique* (Cambridge, MA: Harvard University Press, 1987), 249–50.

7. For example, citing 'the exploitation of eroticisation from sun-tan products to pornographic films', Foucault argues that corporeal control and surveillance function paradoxically to *stimulate* one's 'desire, for, in and over [one's]

body'. M. Foucault, 'Body/Power', *Power/Knowledge*, trans. C. Gordon, et al. (Brighton: Harvester, 1980), 57. The relationship between power, desire and its repression is explored in greater detail by Foucault in *The History of Sexuality, Volume 1: An Introduction*, trans. R. Hurley (Harmondsworth: Penguin, 1978).

8. Bernard of Clairvaux, *On Conversion*, 85 (13.25).

9. Coleman, *Ancient and Medieval Memories*, 195.

10. Coleman, *Ancient and Medieval Memories*, 198.

11. G. R. Evans notes that the 'term *conversio* at this date had, most commonly, the sense of "deciding to enter a religious order" ', although Bernard was also referring to a conversion of the heart. Introduction to Bernard of Clairvaux, *On Conversion*, 65.

12. Quoted in J. F. Hamburger, 'Art, Enclosure and the *Cura Monialium*: Prolegomena in the Guise of a Postscript', *Gesta*, 31.2 (1992): 109.

13. *Ancrene Wisse*, Part 2: 27, 40.

14. Peter of Celle (d. 1183), *Selected Works*, trans. H. Feiss (Kalamazoo: Cistercian Publications, 1987), 79, quoted in M. Camille, *Image on the Edge: the Margins of Medieval Art* (London: Reaktion, 1992), 56.

15. In the *Ancrene Wisse*, for example, the anchoress's heightened spiritual sense is not achieved by mortifying the flesh, by dulling her sensations and desires; rather, her enclosure and identification with Christ ensure that her flesh is 'more living', more 'sensitive' than that of ordinary people. *Ancrene Wisse*, Part 2: 50–1.

16. Hence Guillaume Durand's observation: 'by the windows the senses of the body are signified . . .' *The Symbolism of Churches and Church Ornaments*, trans. J. M. Neale and B. Webb (Leeds: Green, 1843), 29 (1.24). See Chapter 2 for further examples.

17. S. F. Kruger's reading of *Piers Plowman* traces a similar narrative and redemptive trajectory 'inward . . . outward and upward'. 'Mirrors and the Trajectory of Vision in *Piers Plowman*', *Speculum*, 66.1 (1991): 74–95.

18. Bernard of Clairvaux, *On Conversion*, 66 (1.1).

19. Bernard of Clairvaux, *On Conversion*, 67 (1.2).

20. Bernard of Clairvaux, *On Conversion*, 68 (2.35).

21. Bernard of Clairvaux, *On Conversion*, 68 (2.35).

22. Bernard of Clairvaux, *On Conversion*, 68 (2.35). References cited in text: Ps. 49.21; Rom. 2.15.

23. Bernard of Clairvaux, *On Conversion*, 69 (3.4). It hardly needs pointing out that the memory and its contents were conceived in bodily terms by Bernard and his contemporaries. On the neuropsychology of memory from a medieval point of view, see Carruthers, *Book of Memory*, 46–56.

24. Bernard of Clairvaux, *On Conversion*, 71 (5.6). References cited in text: Deut. 13.17.

25. Bernard of Clairvaux, *On Conversion*, 73 (6.8).

26. Bernard of Clairvaux, *On Conversion*, 73 (6.8).

27. Bernard of Clairvaux, *On Conversion*, 74 (6.10).

28. Bernard of Clairvaux, *On Conversion*, 75 (6.11). References cited in text: Jer. 9.21.
29. Bernard of Clairvaux, *On Conversion*, 80 (9.18). References cited in text: Heb. 4.12.
30. This reference to the flesh as a 'corruptible garment' is just one of many metaphors used by Bernard in *On Conversion*, 69 (3.4).
31. This is the section heading for Part 9. Bernard of Clairvaux, *On Conversion*, 80 (9.18).
32. Bernard of Clairvaux, *On Conversion*, 83 (9.23). References cited in text: Ps. 118.136; Prov. 6.4; Acts 22.11.
33. Bernard of Clairvaux, *On Conversion*, 84 (12.24). Durand similarly uses the figure of windows in this double sense: 'by the windows', he writes, 'the senses of the body are signified: which ought to be shut to the vanities of this world, and open to receive with all freedom spiritual gifts. *Symbolism of Churches*, 29 (1.24). References cited in text: Song 2.9; Matt. 2.1.
34. Part 12 is entitled: 'After Grief Comes Comfort and the Kindling of the Desire to Contemplate Heavenly Things.' Bernard of Clairvaux, *On Conversion*, 84 (12.24).
35. Bernard of Clairvaux, *On Conversion*, 84 (12.24). References cited in text: Matt. 28.6; John 20.4–8; 14.23.
36. Bernard describes this inner paradise as 'an enclosed garden', invoking the lovers' garden of Canticles (Song 4.12). *On Conversion*, 85 (13.25).
37. Bernard of Clairvaux, *On Conversion*, 84 (13.25). References cited in text: Gen. 2.8. Bernard's sermons on the Song of Songs similarly emphasise the non-corporeal nature of the bride's delights in the garden of love. Commenting on the verse 'Your cheeks are beautiful as the turtle-dove's', he cautions: 'You must not give an earth bound meaning to this coloring of the corruptible flesh, to this gathering of blood-red liquid that spreads evenly beneath the surface of her pearly skin, quietly mingling with it to enhance her physical beauty by the pink and white loveliness of her cheeks. For the substance of the soul is incorporeal and invisible . . .' Bernard of Clairvaux, *On the Song of Songs*, trans. J. Leclerq and K. Walsh, Cistercian Fathers Series 40, 4 vols (Kalamazoo: Cistercian Publications, 1976), 2: 199 (Sermon 40).
38. Bernard of Clairvaux, *On Conversion*, 87 (15.28).
39. Bernard of Clairvaux, *On Conversion*, 85 (13.25). References cited in text: Eph. 1.18; Ps. 50.10; Gen. 27.27; Song 2.14.
40. Bernard wrote 86 sermons on the Song of Songs between 1135 and his death in 1153.
41. A. W. Astell, *The Song of Songs in the Middle Ages* (Ithaca: Cornell University Press, 1990), 17.
42. I have borrowed Janet Coleman's translation here because it lends greater resonance to the more familiar terms 'purged', 'cleansed' or 'purified'. *Ancient and Medieval Memories*, 185.
43. Augustine (whose discourse on memory in the *Confessions* pervades much of Bernard's writing on the same subject) uses a great many metaphors for this

faculty. It is like 'a great field or a spacious palace'. Each sensation is 'retained in the great storehouse of the memory, which in some indescribable way secretes them in its folds'. In 'the vast cloisters of my memory . . . are the sky, the earth, and the sea . . .' *Confessions*, 214–15 (10.8). The memory is also 'a sort of stomach for the mind', 220 (10.14), and the 'wide plains' of the memory contain 'innumerable caverns and hollows . . . full beyond compute of countless things . . .' *Confessions*, 224 (10.17).

44. Coleman, *Ancient and Medieval Memories*, 176, 191. On the medieval *ars memorativa*, see also: M. J. Carruthers, *The Book of Memory: a Study of Memory in Medieval Culture* (Cambridge: Cambridge University Press, 1990); Lewis, *Reading Images*, 242–59; and F. A. Yates, *The Art of Memory* (Harmondsworth: Penguin, 1969), 63–113 (chapters 3 and 4).

45. Bernard of Clairvaux, *On Conversion*, 87 (15.28).

46. Bernard of Clairvaux, *On Conversion*, 87 (15.28). Carruthers notes that the idea of memory as a surface that is written on or imprinted (and then read as a text) is 'so ancient and so persistent in all Western cultures' that it functions as a 'cognitive archetype'. *Book of Memory*, 16.

47. Bernard of Clairvaux, *On Conversion*, 87 (15.28).

48. Bernard of Clairvaux, *On Conversion*, 87 (15.28).

49. Bernard of Clairvaux, *On Conversion*, 87 (15.28).

50. Bernard of Clairvaux, *On Conversion*, 88 (15.28).

51. Bernard of Clairvaux, *On Conversion*, 88 (15.28).

52. Alan of Lille's remark that the five senses 'guard' the body like sentries is consistent with this idea. *Plaint of Nature*, 117 (6).

53. Augustine, *Confessions*, 243 (10.35).

54. Augustine, *The Trinity*, 318 (11.2.3).

55. 'For before the vision arose there already was a will which directed the sense to the body in order that it might be formed by seeing it . . .' Augustine, *The Trinity*, 328 (11.5.9).

56. Augustine, *The Trinity*, 318 (11.2.2–3).

57. Augustine, *The Trinity*, 336 (11.8.15).

58. Margaret Miles also makes this point, arguing that 'Augustine does not advocate that the bodily eye be "cleansed" of sensible objects'. He is concerned, instead, with the 'cleansing' and 'strengthening' of the eye of the mind. Miles, 'Vision', 131–2.

59. Augustine, *The Trinity*, 322 (11.3.6).

60. Augustine, *The Trinity*, 325 (11.4.7).

61. In *The Literal Meaning of Genesis*, 199 (12.15), Augustine remarks that 'Chaste people while awake curb and restrain these [sexual] motions, though in their sleep they are unable to do so because they cannot control the appearance of those corporeal images that are indistinguishable from bodies.'

62. Augustine, *The Trinity*, 336 (11.8.15).

63. Bernard of Clairvaux, *Song of Songs*, 1: 150 (Sermon 20.3).

64. Bernard's source is Augustine's definition of lust (in its generic sense) as a fault in the 'soul which *perversely* delights in sensual pleasures' (my emphasis). St Augustine, *City of God*, 481 (12.8). Sin, in other words, results when one's

attention and desire are oriented towards the world, rather than towards the ultimate—and 'far more beautiful'—realities of the spirit (481).

65. Peter of Limoges, *De Oculo Morali*, quoted in Clark, 'Optics for Preachers', 333.

66. Peter of Limoges, *De Oculo Morali*, quoted in Clark, 'Optics for Preachers', 333.

67. It is evident that Peter has consulted contemporary works on optics such as Bacon's *Perspectiva*. According to Clark (330), he would probably have met Roger Bacon, a fellow Franciscan, at the University of Paris during the 1260s. On Peter's sources, see: Clark, 'Optics for Preachers'; and Newhauser, 'Nature's Moral Eye', 127–8, 133.

68. Newhauser, 'Nature's Moral Eye', 131.

69. Paraphrasing Peter of Limoges, Clark writes that 'the brain contains an internal sense that can censor sensory stimuli being received through the eye, filter out immoral stimulation, and enable desirable sensations to effect the will'. 'Optics for Preachers', 333.

70. Clark, 'Optics for Preachers', 334. See also H. A. Wolfson, 'The Internal Senses in Latin, Arabic, and Hebrew Philosophical Texts', *Studies in the History of Philosophy and Religion*, 2 vols (Cambridge, MA: Harvard University Press, 1973), 1: 250–314.

71. The work's popularity is attested by the large number of surviving manuscripts: see M. W. Bloomfield et al., *Incipits of Latin Works on the Virtues and Vices, 1100–1500 AD* (Cambridge, MA: Harvard University Press, 1979), 475–6, no. 5332, where 103 mss are listed. Clark comments on the popularity of the text through to the fifteenth century. 'Optics for Preachers', 329–30.

72. Peter of Limoges, *De Oculo Morali*, quoted in Clark, 'Optics for Preachers', 339–40.

73. Clark, 'Optics for Preachers', 338.

74. Bacon, 'Moral Philosophy', *Opus majus*, 2: 654 (7.1).

75. Peter of Limoges, *De Oculo Morali*, quoted in Clark, 'Optics for Preachers', 338.

76. Bacon's use of the term *passio* (passion) to denote the alteration of the sense organ in perception is discussed in Chapter 4.

77. Aquinas, *Summa Theologiæ*, 1a Q.35.1. For Augustine's formulation of the same idea, see *The Trinity*, 6.2.

78. William of Auxerre, *Summa Aurea*, ed. J. Ribailler, 4 vols in 7 parts, Spicilegium Bonaventurianum 16–20 (Paris and Grottaferrata, 1980–7). Cited in Phillips, 'John Wyclif', 251–2.

79. John Wyclif, *De Benedicta Incarnacione* (c. 1371), quoted in Phillips, 'John Wyclif', 251. Phillips thinks it likely that Bacon's *Opus majus* provided Wyclif with a model for the allegorical interpretation of optics (249). Given the dissemination of Peter of Limoges's *Tractatus* as a preaching aid, Wyclif's exposure to the theological and moral application of optics may have been broader still.

80. John Scotus Eriugena (c. 810–c. 877), *De Divisione Naturae* (5.3), quoted in Eco, *Thomas Aquinas*, 139.

81. It has been argued that 'the whole structure of language and the whole utility of signs, marks, symbols, pictures, and representations of various kinds, rest upon analogy'. W. S. Jevons, quoted in Lloyd, *Polarity and Analogy*, 172. For the purposes of this chapter, however, I will focus on the relationship between visible signifiers and spiritual, moral or intellectual signifieds; that is, between material things and immaterial ideas.

82. Coleman sees both strategies as an attempt to negotiate the rift between reason and sensation produced by dualistic habits of thought. *Ancient and Medieval Memories*, 218–19. Bonaventure (1221–74), for example, writes of 'this universe of things' as 'a ladder whereby we may ascend to God'. *The Journey of the Mind to God*, in *Late Medieval Mysticism*, ed. R. C. Petry, Library of Christian Classics, 13 (London: SCM, 1957), 133 (1.2). Elsewhere in the same work mirror and ladder images are integrated, the 'sensible world' as mirror forming the 'first step' of Jacob's ladder: 135 (1.9).

83. On Thomas Aquinas's analysis of these interpretive modes, and their application to religious art, see Eco, *Thomas Aquinas*, 148–58. For a reconsideration of later medieval attitudes towards pictorial naturalism in relation to these levels of perception, see Caviness, 'Simple Perception of Matter'.

84. Durand is referring specifically to the interpretation of Scripture. *Symbolism of Churches*, 8 (Proeme 9–10).

85. Durand, *Symbolism of Churches*, 9 (Proeme 10).

86. Durand, *Symbolism of Churches*, 10 (Proeme 12). 'Et dicitur allegoria ab ἄλλο, Graece quod est alienum, et γορο, quod est sensus, quasi alienus sensus . . . Αυαγογή, dicitur ab ἁυο, quod est sursum et ἁγω, quod est duco, quasi sursum ductio. Unde sensus anagogicus dicitur, qui a visibilibus ad invisibilia ducit, ut lux prima die.' G. Durand, *Rationale Divinorum Officiorum*, Proemium (Venice, 1589), fol. 2r.

87. On Suger, abbot of St Denis from 1122 until his death in 1151, see: E. Panofsky, *Abbot Suger on the Abbey Church of St-Denis and its Art Treasures* (Princeton: Princeton University Press, 1946); and *Meaning in the Visual Arts*, Chapter 3: 'Abbot Suger of St-Denis', 139–80.

88. Suger, quoted in Panofsky, *Meaning in the Visual Arts*, 162.

89. Both Eco and Panofsky contrast Suger's attitude towards ecclesiastical decoration to Bernard of Clairvaux's more austere, iconophobic stance. Eco, *Thomas Aquinas*, 13–15; Panofsky, *Meaning in the Visual Arts*, 149 ff.

90. *Integumenta* is translated as 'figurative language' by Wetherbee, who observes that the term usually referred to classical or mythological texts which were read for their hidden, Christian meaning. Less frequently, the same metaphor was used in relation to the etymological investigation of particular words. Wetherbee, 'Philosophy, Cosmology, and the Twelfth-Century Renaissance', 36. See also T. Gregory, 'The Platonic Inheritance', *A History of Twelfth-Century Western Philosophy*, ed. P. Dronke, 58 n.13, 59.

91. Peter Abelard, *Theologia 'Summi boni'*, paraphrased in Luscombe, 'Peter Abelard', 297.

92. Abelard uses the term *translationes*, as cited in Luscombe, 'Peter Abelard', 297. 'Transposition' (Luscombe's rendering)—from the Latin *ponere*, 'put'—

conveys an idea of movement in keeping with the 'transports' of analogy and the notion of 'ascending' a perceptual hierarchy. For a discussion of this principle in the work of Fra Angelico, see G. Didi-Huberman, *Fra Angelico: Dissemblance and Figuration*, trans. J. M. Todd (Chicago: University of Chicago Press, 1995); especially 'The Four Senses of Scripture' and 'The Dialectic of Dissemblance', 34–60.

93. M. de Certeau, 'Mysticism', *Diacritics*, 22.2 (Summer 1992): 16–17. The article was first published in 1968, as an entry in the *Encyclopaedia Universalis*.

94. de Certeau, 'Mysticism', 16.

95. 'Allegoria enim animae longe e deo positae quasi quandam machinam facit, ut per illam leuetur ad deum', Gregory the Great (c. 540–604), *Expositio in Canticum Canticorum*, quoted in E. A. Matter, *The Voice of My Beloved: the Song of Songs in Western Medieval Christianity* (Philadelphia: University of Pennsylvania Press, 1990), 55, 79 n.26. Astell also refers to Gregory's machine metaphor, and its reiteration by Pseudo-Richard of St Victor: *Song of Songs*, 20.

96. On Bonaventure's concept of analogy, see E. Gilson, *The Philosophy of St Bonaventure*, trans. I. Trethowan and F. J. Sheed (London: Sheed, 1938), chapter 7: 'Universal Analogy', 204–37.

97. Bonaventure, *Journey of the Mind to God*, 138–9 (7.1).

98. Bonaventure, *Journey of the Mind to God*, 133 (1.4).

99. Bonaventure, *Journey of the Mind to God*, 133 (1.4).

100. Richard of St Victor, *The Twelve Patriarchs*, in *The Twelve Patriarchs, The Mystical Ark, Book Three of the Trinity*, trans. G. A. Zinn (London: SPCK, 1979), 131 (74); and *Mystical Ark*, 156 (1.3).

101. Astell, *Song of Songs*, 89, 92–4.

102. Astell, *Song of Songs*, 94–9.

103. Astell does not, however, define 'sublimation', and her use of the term is somewhat ambiguous. The comment quoted above follows a comparison of Bernard and Origen in which she maintains that while ' . . . Origen sought to sublimate eros by suppressing the carnality of the Song, the twelfth-century exegetes, impressed by the unitary nature of love, aimed at an organic transference of the *affectus* by joining the literal image of the Bridegroom to its Christological tenor . . .' Astell, *Song of Songs*, 19.

104. Astell, *Song of Songs*, 19.

105. According to Laplanche and Pontalis, the 'lack of a coherent theory of sublimation remains one of the lacunae in psycho-analytic thought'. 'Sublimation', *Language of Psycho-Analysis*, 433. Attempts to address this lacuna include: H. W. Loewald, *Sublimation: Inquiries into Theoretical Psychoanalysis* (New Haven: Yale University Press, 1988); and J. Whitebook, 'Sublimation: a Frontier Concept' in *Perversion and Utopia: a Study in Psychoanalysis and Critical Theory* (Cambridge, MA: MIT Press, 1995), 217–46.

106. S. Freud, 'Anxiety and Instinctual Life', *New Introductory Lectures on Psychoanalysis*, trans. and ed. J. Strachey (New York: Norton, 1965), 86.

107. Freud, 'Anxiety and Instinctual Life', 86.

108. Laplanche and Pontalis make the point that the 'domain of sublimated activities is badly demarcated' in Freud's discussions of the subject. It is unclear, for instance, whether all thought is the product of sublimated, 'desexualised' energy, or 'merely certain types of intellectual production'. *Language of Psycho-Analysis*, 432.

109. 'Sublimation of instinct', writes Freud, 'is an especially conspicuous feature of cultural development; it is what makes it possible for higher psychical activities, scientific, artistic or ideological, to play such an important part in civilized life'. From *Civilization and its Discontents*, quoted in Loewald, *Sublimation*, 6.

110. W. W. Skeat notes that the Latin term *sublimis* probably comes from *sub* and *limen*: literally 'up to the lintel', an etymology that sheds some light on the vertical mobility associated with sublimation, as well as the connection between the terms liminal and sublime, designating experiences that occur at the threshold (lintel) or margins of ordinary perception. *A Concise Etymological Dictionary of the English Language* (New York: Capricorn, 1963), 527.

111. Loewald, quoting the *Oxford English Dictionary* definition of 'sublimation', *Sublimation*, 12.

112. Chaucer, 'The Canon's Yeoman's Tale', cited in Loewald, *Sublimation*, 12.

113. Bonaventure, *Journey of the Mind to God*, 140 (7.4–5). Richard of St Victor also describes the apex of human understanding as 'sublime with regard to sublime things'. *Mystical Ark*, 323 (5.9).

114. This emphasis on de-materialisation extends to chemical sublimation: the conversion of 'a substance from the solid state directly to its vapour by heat'. *Concise Oxford Dictionary*.

115. 'Carnal overflow' is Kristeva's description. *Powers of Horror*, 124.

116. 'We may call it a border; abjection is above all ambiguity.' Kristeva, *Powers of Horror*, 9.

117. Kristeva, *Powers of Horror*, 8.

118. Loewald makes the point that, through sublimation, the '"lowest" and "highest" are enveloped as one within an original unitary experience; one *is* the other', and further: 'in sublimation the experience of unity is restored, or at least evoked, in the form of symbolic language'. *Sublimation*, 13, 45.

119. Kristeva, *Powers of Horror*, 8–9.

120. Kristeva does not tease out the paradoxical nature of this relationship between sublimation and sublime, instead running the two together almost without pause: 'In the symptom [disgust, nausea] the abject permeates me, I become abject. Through sublimation, I keep it under control. The abject is edged with the sublime.' *Powers of Horror*, 11.

121. Kristeva, *Powers of Horror*, 9.

122. Richard of St Victor, *Mystical Ark*, 323 (5.9). The same spatialised image of mind is evoked in Kristeva's observation that 'As soon as I perceive it, as soon as I name it, the sublime triggers—it has always already triggered—a spree of perceptions and words *that expands memory boundlessly*' (my emphasis). *Powers of Horror*, 11.

123. Kristeva, *Powers of Horror*, 9.

124. Augustine observes that in a state of ecstasy, 'the attention of the mind is completely carried off and turned away from the senses of the body' as is the case when the 'whole soul is intent upon images of bodies present to spiritual vision or upon incorporeal realities present to intellectual vision . . .' *Literal Meaning of Genesis*, 194 (12.25). Medieval discussions of ecstasy and rapture tend to follow this basic idea of a displacement or transferral of attention from outer, corporeal to inner, spiritual senses. Thus, Meister Eckhart maintains that a 'man is called senseless and rapt' when 'the soul draws to itself all its powers it had loaned to the five senses'. *On Detachment* in *Meister Eckhart: the Essential Sermons, Commentaries, Treatises, and Defence*, trans. E. Colledge and B. McGinn (New York: Paulist, 1981), 290.

125. Bonaventure, *Journey of the Mind to God*, 140 (7.4).

126. Bonaventure, *Journey of the Mind to God*, 141 (7.4).

127. For Kristeva, the sublime transcends neither perception nor language: it is, she writes, 'Not at all short of but always with and through perception and words . . .' *Powers of Horror*, 12.

128. Richard of St Victor, *Twelve Patriarchs*, 130 (72).

129. Richard of St Victor, *Twelve Patriarchs*, 130 (72).

130. Richard also exploits extramissionist metaphors. The gaze of meditation strives to 'grasp any lofty things . . . to break through obstructions, to penetrate into hidden things'. Richard of St Victor, *Mystical Ark*, 157 (1.4). The mutuality of redemptive vision will be discussed at length in the next chapter.

6   Ocular Communion

1. The observation is made by (amongst others): H. Belting, *The Image and its Public in the Middle Ages: Form and Function of Early Paintings of the Passion*, trans. M. Bartusis and R. Meyer (New Rochelle, NY: Caratzas, 1990), 7; M. Camille, *Gothic Art*, 12, and *Gothic Idol*, 203–20; Caviness, 'Simple Perception of Matter', Lewis, *Reading Images*, 264; and M. R. Miles, *Image as Insight: Visual Understanding in Western Christianity and Secular Culture* (Boston: Beacon, 1985), 65–6 (on fourteenth-century visual culture).

2. Belting, *Image and its Public*, 80. Although Belting notes that this 'need to see' has been 'much discussed', he does not pursue the point any further, remarking only that the phenomenon 'has not yet been sufficiently elucidated sociologically'.

3. Belting, *Image and its Public*, 82.

4. I am paraphrasing Belting here. *Image and its Public*, 82.

5. Belting, *Image and its Public*, 16, 83.

6. Belting, *Image and its Public*, 3, 58.

7. Richard of St Victor, *Mystical Ark*, 323 (5.9). The passage is quoted in full in Chapter 5.

8. Belting, *Image and its Public*, 58.

9. A. Neumeyer, quoted in Belting, *Image and its Public*, 57.

10. Belting's paradigm is one of verbal and affective 'communication'. *Devotio*, for example, is defined as a 'religious dialogue' (*Image and its Public*, 3, 58, 65); the new images have a 'communicative quality' (16); they 'speak' (80); and exhibit the same 'rhetorical' features as the relic ostensory (83).

11. The 'body of optics' is the subject of Chapter 4.

12. A number of excellent historical and iconographic studies have focused on this particular representation of Christ, and I do not propose to add to these accounts. The seminal iconographic study is Erwin Panofsky's ' "Imago Pietatis": Ein Beitrag zur Typengeschichte des "Schmerzensmanns" und der "Maria Mediatrix" ', *Festschrift für Max J. Friedländer zum 60. Geburtstag* (Leipzig: Seemann, 1927): 261–308. Major studies of the Man of Sorrows include: H. Belting, *Image and its Public*; L. M. La Favia, *The Man of Sorrows: Its Origin and Development in Trecento Florentine Painting* (Rome: 'Sanguis', 1980); and S. Ringbom, *Icon to Narrative: the Rise of the Dramatic Close-up in Fifteenth-Century Devotional Painting*, 2nd ed. (Doornspijk, Neth.: Davaco, 1984). The iconographic development and regional variations of the Man of Sorrows are documented in G. Schiller, *Iconography of Christian Art*, trans. J. Seligman, 2 vols (London: Humphries, 1972), 2: 197–229.

13. While consistent with this general trend, the concept of the 'period eye' goes some of the way towards reconciling art history with the historical permutations of vision. See, for example: M. Baxandall, *Painting and Experience in Fifteenth-Century Italy*, 2nd ed. (Oxford: Oxford University Press, 1988), 'The Period Eye', 29–108; and Michael Camille, who approaches 'Gothic art as the embodiment of medieval visual experience' (*Gothic Art*, 12). Because Camille's use of thirteenth-century optics is limited to the intromissionist, perspectivist model, the conclusions he draws about 'visual experience' differ substantially from those proposed in this book.

14. Julian of Norwich, *Showings*, trans. E. Colledge and J. Walsh, Classics of Western Spirituality Series (New York: Paulist, 1978), 178 (ch. 2, long text).

15. Julian of Norwich, *Showings*, 180 (ch. 3, long text).

16. Gal. 2.20.

17. For example, in Chapter 5 'spiritual sight' comes after Julian's corporeal vision of the Passion. She makes it clear that this secondary, interior 'sight'—seen by 'the eye of my understanding'—is a received interpretation ('understanding') of the preceding, 'real' vision. In other words, her bodily revelation is followed by 'insight' into it. Julian of Norwich, *Showings*, 183.

18. It is argued in Chapter 1 that both body and flesh are feminised, each performing a different discursive function in relation to the masculine soul or mind.

19. In his study of Florentine religious life during the Renaissance, Richard Trexler points out that sacred images were addressed as persons (for example, '*Nostra Donna*' rather than 'the image of Our Lady') and worshipped—or violated—accordingly. The holy person's presence in their likeness is further evinced by the attribution of sensitive faculties to images (one image of the Virgin was said to have closed her eyes when confronted with an offensive scene in the street below). R. C. Trexler, *Church and Community 1200–1600*:

Studies in the History of Florence and New Spain (Rome: Storia e Letteratura, 1987), 50–1; and Public Life in Renaissance Florence (New York: Academic Press, 1980), 68–9.

20. Trexler, Church and Community, 39 ff.

21. Surveys of medieval attitudes to images include: Camille, Gothic Idol, 203–20; T. A. Heslop, 'Attitudes to the Visual Arts: the Evidence of Written Sources', The Age of Chivalry: Art in Plantagenet England 1200–1400, ed. J. Alexander and P. Binski (London: Weidenfeld with Royal Academy of Arts, 1987), 26–32; W. R. Jones, 'Art and Christian Piety: Iconoclasm in Medieval Europe', The Image and the Word: Confrontations in Judaism, Christianity and Islam, ed. J. Gutmann (Missoula: Scholars, 1977); and Ringbom, 'Devotional Images'. For primary sources, see: C. Davis-Weyer, Early Medieval Art 300–1150: Sources and Documents (Englewood Cliffs, NJ: Prentice-Hall, 1971); and in the same series, T. G. Frisch, Gothic Art 1140–c.1450 (Englewood Cliffs, NJ: Prentice-Hall, 1971).

22. Trexler, Church and Community, 40. Hamburger approaches the convergence of bodily and spiritual vision from a rather different perspective in his work on devotional images and their female viewers. In his most recent study he argues that bodily sight can be 'both the means and the end of the devotional act', for 'to look is to love, and to love is to look'. Hamburger, Nuns as Artists, 129.

23. These sources, which were disseminated by mendicant preachers, include Peter the Venerable's De mira-miraculis (1135–44), Herbert of Clairvaux's De miraculis (1178), Gerald of Wales's Gemma Ecclesiastica (c.1215) and Caesarius of Heisterbach's Dialogus miraculorum (c.1220). Other examples are provided by Ringbom, 'Devotional Images', 160.

24. Miles, Image as Insight, 64–5.

25. Miles, quoting R. Fawtier, Image as Insight, 65. It has been observed by a number of commentators that female saints outnumbered their male contemporaries in accounts of visionary experiences involving image devotion. Women were also more often associated with somatic phenomena like stigmatisation and mysterious illnesses: female stigmatics, for example, outnumber men by roughly eight to one according to The Catholic Encyclopedia, ed. C. G. Herbermann et al., 15 vols (New York: The Encyclopedia Press, 1913), 14: 295. On the possible reasons for this gender asymmetry, see: Bynum, Fragmentation and Redemption: Essays on Gender and the Human Body in Medieval Religion (New York: Zone, 1991).

26. J. F. Hamburger, The Rothschild Canticles (New Haven: Yale University Press, 1990), 165.

27. Angela of Foligno's Memorial, ed. C. Mazzoni, trans. J. Cirignano, Library of Medieval Women series (Cambridge: Brewer, 1999), 32. Christine Mazzoni notes that 'Inordinately powerful effects of holy images on one's physical constitution were . . . common among women mystics of Angela's time', 35 n.25.

28. Angela of Foligno's Memorial, 43.

29. Angela of Foligno's Memorial, 44.

30. D. L. Jeffrey, 'Franciscan Spirituality and the Growth of Vernacular Culture' in *By Things Seen: Reference and Recognition in Medieval Thought*, ed. D. L. Jeffrey (Ottawa: University of Ottawa Press, 1979), 151.

31. See for example: Hamburger, 'Art, Enclosure and the *Cura Monialium*', 120 ff., and *Rothschild Canticles*, 162–7; Miles, *Image as Insight*, 65; Ringbom, 'Devotional Images', 160–2.

32. Julian of Norwich, *Showings*, 193 (ch. 10, long text).

33. Bacon, *De multiplicatione specierum*, 7 (1.1). The relevant passage is quoted in Chapter 4.

34. This process is discussed in detail by D. Despres in *Ghostly Sights: Visual Meditation in Late-Medieval Literature* (Norman, OK: Pilgrim, 1989). See in particular Chapter 2: 'Franciscan Meditation: Historical and Literary Contexts', 19–54.

35. I have used *Nicholas Love's Mirror of the Blessed Life of Jesus Christ*, ed. M. G. Sargent (New York: Garland, 1992), an early fifteenth-century English translation of the *Meditationes Vitae Christi*. Quotes are cross-referenced with Isa Ragusa's widely available modern translation: *Meditations on the Life of Christ* (Princeton, NJ: Princeton University Press, 1961).

36. *Nicholas Love's Mirror*, 176.10. *Meditations on the Life of Christ*, 333.

37. *Nicholas Love's Mirror*, 162.16. *Meditations on the Life of Christ*, 317.

38. Angela of Foligno's *Memorial*, 27, 29, 60.

39. Belting, *Image and its Public*, 83.

40. Sicard of Cremona (d. 1215), *Mitrale Liber III*, quoted in Belting, *Image and its Public*, 6.

41. See Chapter 4 for a more extensive discussion of this idea.

42. Bacon, *De multiplicatione specierum*, 45 (1.3): discussed in Chapter 3.

43. Bacon, *De multiplicatione specierum*, 191 (3.2).

44. Jacopone da Todi (d. 1307), *Laudi, trattato e detti*, cited in N. J. Perella, *The Kiss Sacred and Profane: an Interpretative History of Kiss Symbolism and Related Religio-Erotic Themes* (Berkeley: University of California Press, 1969), 68.

45. I am thinking in particular of Giotto's paintings of St Francis receiving the stigmata, including the Louvre panel (*Stigmatisation of St Francis, with Three Scenes from his Life*, tempera, c.1310–15), and the slightly earlier fresco in the upper church of San Francesco in Assisi.

46. Camille reproduces a stained glass image of the Stigmatisation of St Francis (1235–45) from Barfüsser-kirche, Erfurt, commenting that the medium itself conveys the 'idea of the transforming power of light'. *Gothic Art*, 108, Fig. 75.

47. I have used the translation by E. Gurney Salter: *The Life of Saint Francis by Saint Bonaventura* (London: J. M. Dent, 1904), Chapter 13: 'Of the Sacred Stigmata'.

48. *The Life of Saint Francis*, 142.

49. *The Life of Saint Francis*, 139–40.

50. *The Life of Saint Francis*, 155.

51. *The Life of Saint Francis*, 141.

52. Carruthers discusses both models of representation, but argues that medieval writers understood memory 'images' as signifiers that were more like words

(written and read) than pictures. *Book of Memory*, 22–3. I am not entirely convinced by her emphasis on the verbal paradigm, given the pictorial logic of medieval optics and the mimetic desire expressed in image devotion. It seems likely, rather, that these metaphors—and practices inflected by them—coexisted in the later Middle Ages.

53. Jill Bennett has shown that bodily memory was central to late medieval (specifically Franciscan) image devotion: see her article on 'Stigmata and Sense Memory: St Francis and the Affective Image', *Art History*, 24.1 (Feb. 2001): 1–17.

54. Miri Rubin points out that the regulations surrounding the eucharist functioned as a means of social control. Communion could be received only in the parish in which the communicant resided; it required the appropriate payment of tithes; it was to be taken in a 'state of purity' (thereby excluding menstruating women and imposing restrictions on sexual intercourse). Finally, communicants were required to be in a 'state of charity'—the concept of reconciliation being extended to one's neighbours. M. Rubin, *Corpus Christi: the Eucharist in Late Medieval Culture* (Cambridge: Cambridge University Press, 1991), 148–50.

55. Rubin, *Corpus Christi*, 148.

56. Rubin describes the practice as 'sacramental viewing', *Corpus Christi*, 63. The importance of vision in eucharistic devotion is also noted by J. Ash, 'The Discursive Construction of Christ's Body in the Later Middle Ages: Resistance and Autonomy', *Feminine, Masculine and Representation*, ed. T. Threadgold and A. Cranny-Francis (Sydney: Allen, 1990), 81; Bynum, *Fragmentation and Redemption*, 45; Camille, *Gothic Idol*, 217; Lewis, *Reading Images*, 263–5; and Trexler, *Church and Community*, 67.

57. This interpretation of the fall is discussed in Chapter 2.

58. John 6.54–5.

59. Rubin, *Corpus Christi*, 12.

60. Unlike the sacraments of baptism, marriage and extreme unction, the eucharist could only be administered by a priest. Rubin, *Corpus Christi*, 36.

61. Rubin, *Corpus Christi*, 13.

62. Rubin speaks of an 'economy of the sacred' within which the eucharist served as 'sacramental currency'. *Corpus Christi*, 14.

63. Bishop Quivil of Exeter (writing in 1287), quoted in Rubin, *Corpus Christi*, 57.

64. Unlike the earlier antependium, which was located below the altar, the altarpiece or retable was placed on or behind it (as shown in Fig. 6.1). Henk van Os describes the altarpiece as 'a physical framework for the ritual', observing that it serves to focus the congregation's attention, and to demarcate the sacred space of the host's consecration and elevation. *Sienese Altarpieces 1215–1460*, vol. 1: *Form, Content, Function 1215–1344*, 2 vols (Groningen, Neth.: Forsten, 1988), 13.

65. van Os, *Sienese Altarpieces*, 1: 12–13.

66. William of Auxerre, writing of the heightened visual appeal of the eucharist in his *Summa Aurea*, quoted in Camille, *Gothic Idol*, 217.

67. This is Rubin's description, *Corpus Christi*, 63.
68. Cited in Rubin, *Corpus Christi*, 152.
69. Rubin, *Corpus Christi*, 152.
70. Rubin, *Corpus Christi*, 64.
71. Alexander of Hales, *Sentences*, quoted in Rubin, *Corpus Christi*, 64.
72. By the fourteenth century the consecrated host was available for viewing outside of the mass. Belting, *Image and its Public*, 81–2.
73. Belting, *Image and its Public*, 81.
74. Belting, *Image and its Public*, 82.
75. Schiller, *Iconography*, 2: 9–10.
76. Belting makes a general distinction between Mediterranean paintings of the *Imago Pietatis*, in which the figure is consistently corpse-like, though upright; and the more 'lively' transalpine type, often depicting Christ gesturing towards his side wound. Whereas the former tend to provoke pity and remorse, the transalpine type emphasises reciprocity and dialogue. *Image and its Public*, 32–3.
77. L. Steinberg, 'Animadversions: Michelangelo's Florentine *Pietà*: the Missing Leg Twenty Years After', *The Art Bulletin*, 71 (1989): 489.
78. Belting, *Image and its Public*, 36, 72. The legend of St Gregory's mass is also discussed by Schiller, *Iconography*, 2: 199–200.
79. Belting, *Image and its Public*, 36, 38.
80. This is Belting's date, *Image and its Public*, 3. Schiller argues for a slightly earlier introduction of the image, *Iconography*, 2: 199.
81. Belting, *Image and its Public*, 41 ff.
82. Belting, *Image and its Public*, 53–4.
83. Belting, *Image and its Public*, 54.
84. Belting, *Image and its Public*, 53–4.
85. Hamburger makes a similar point with regard to the late medieval drawings produced in the convent of St Walburg. 'Anything but naturalistic in manner', he argues, 'the drawings nevertheless cultivate an aggressive immediacy of affect closely geared to their devotional context.' *Nuns as Artists*, 215.
86. Panofsky, *Meaning in the Visual Arts*, 321.
87. Panofsky, *Meaning in the Visual Arts*, 321.
88. See for example J. Marrow's 'Symbol and Meaning in Northern European Art of the Late Middle Ages and the Early Renaissance', *Simiolus*, 16 (1986): 150–69. Marrow contends that thirteenth- and fourteenth-century devotional images 'espoused compassion only conceptually or by inference' (157). Fifteenth-century naturalism, in contrast, is seen as heralding a new role for the work of art: that of 'stimulating and directing viewers' emotional responses . . .' (158). This change, for Marrow, marks the transition from a medieval outlook to 'a modern or at least a post-medieval representation of the world' (158). In *Icon to Narrative*, Ringbom similarly construes fifteenth-century naturalism (specifically the 'expressive close-up') as the perfection of earlier 'conceptual' or 'symbolic' modes of painting. See, for example, *Icon to Narrative*, 57–8, 141. Belting's position (which is closer to my own) allows for

the coexistence of symbolic/cultic, didactic/conceptual and affective functions.

89. Paradoxically, this opposition undermines the equally common identification of Renaissance classicism with reason and other manly virtues. It does so by placing naturalism on the side of emotion and sensuality, in opposition to the more 'conceptual' or 'abstract' art of the Middle Ages. It is interesting to note that Michael Camille effectively reverses these terms, describing the transition from the 'dynamic and interactive' Gothic image to Renaissance illusionism as a shift from the 'seen' to the 'scene'. *Gothic Art*, 183. See also Hamburger's response to Norman Bryson's comments on the 'textual' function of medieval art: *Nuns as Artists*, 217.

90. Hamburger's analysis of devotional imagery also turns on the 'reciprocal presence' of Christ and the viewer; their 'mutual regard' and (in the context of nuptial mysticism) the 'reciprocal penetration of lover and beloved'. *Nuns as Artists*, 117, 215.

91. To illustrate this visual dynamic, Belting quotes a passage from a History of Dominicans written before 1269: 'In their cells they had before their eyes images of her [the Virgin] and of her crucified Son so that while reading, praying, and sleeping, *they could look upon them and be looked upon by them [the images], with the eyes of compassion*' (my emphasis). *Image and its Public*, 57.

92. Schiller, *Iconography*, 2: 197.

93. Belting, *Image and its Public*, 173. The German term for the Man of Sorrows—'*Erbärmdebild*' ('image of pity')—is similarly reciprocal. Schiller, *Iconography*, 2: 197.

94. Belting, *Image and its Public*, 58.

95. Bernard of Clairvaux, *On the Song of Songs*, 2: 12 (2.6).

96. The question of *how* Christ could be born into humanity, yet remain untainted by sin was raised by Anselm, archbishop of Canterbury (d. 1109) in his treatise *On the Virginal Conception and on Original Sin*. Cited in J. Pelikan, *The Growth of Medieval Theology (600–1300)*, vol. 3 of *The Christian Tradition: a History of the Development of Doctrine*, 5 vols (Chicago: University of Chicago Press, 1978), 160. The question was not settled until 1854, when the immaculate conception of Mary became dogma, confirming that the Virgin's flesh (and therefore Christ's) was without the hereditary stain of original sin (3: 171–2).

97. See Chapter 1 for a more detailed discussion of the Augustinian origins of medieval flesh, and Bernard's treatment of flesh in *On Conversion*.

98. Peter Damian (d. 1072), *Hymns (Carmina)*, quoted in Pelikan, *Growth of Medieval Theology*, 136.

99. Pelikan, *Growth of Medieval Theology*, 138.

100. Pelikan is quoting here from Peter Damian's *Sermons*, *Growth of Medieval Theology*, 138.

101. V. W. Turner, 'Betwixt and Between: the Liminal Period in *Rites de Passage*' (originally published in 1964), *Reader in Comparative Religion: an Anthropological Approach*, ed. W. A. Lessa and E. Z. Vogt, 4th ed. (New York: Harper,

1979), 234–43; Kristeva, *Powers of Horror.* The potent combination of the holy and the transgressive in medieval religious life has featured in a number of recent studies. Lochrie's work on female mystics locates both sin and redemption in the flesh (*Margery Kempe*, 37–47; *Language of Transgression*, 128–40); while Rubin notes that the eucharist brought together 'the most holy with the most aberrant/abhorrent': cannibalism (*Corpus Christi*, 360).

102.   Bynum has argued that Turner's concept of liminality is an accurate description of the religious experiences of men, but does not account for the spirituality of medieval women. 'Women', she argues, 'are fully liminal only to men.' Bynum, 'Women's Stories, Women's Symbols: a Critique of Victor Turner's Theory of Liminality', *Fragmentation and Redemption*, 49. While it has been beyond the scope of this chapter to look at redemptive vision as a gendered practice, Bynum's observation that femininity functioned (albeit predominantly for men) as a space of liminality has some bearing on the feminisation of Christ as Man of Sorrows. I explore this association further via Kristeva.

103.   Turner, 'Betwixt and Between', 236–7.

104.   Turner, 'Betwixt and Between', 236.

105.   This type of *Pietà* was popular in the Low Countries during the late fourteenth and early fifteenth centuries. J. E. Ziegler, *Sculpture of Compassion: the Pietà and the Beguines in the Southern Low Countries c.1300–c.1600* (Brussels: Institut Historique Belge de Rome, 1992), 141.

106.   Turner, 'Betwixt and Between', 237.

107.   Turner, 'Betwixt and Between', 237.

108.   In her discussion of the Biblical taboo on corpses, Kristeva contends that 'the corpse represents fundamental pollution . . . if the corpse is waste, transitional matter, mixture, it is above all the opposite of the spiritual, of the symbolic, and of divine law.' *Powers of Horror*, 109. See also pages 3–4.

109.   Guerric, abbot of Igny (d. c.1157), quoted in Bynum, *Fragmentation and Redemption*, 159.

110.   L. Steinberg, *The Sexuality of Christ in Renaissance Art and in Modern Oblivion* (New York: October/Pantheon, 1983), 1.

111.   Steinberg, *Sexuality of Christ*, 23.

112.   Steinberg, *Sexuality of Christ*, 13, 45 ff. The link between original sin, concupiscence and death is central to Augustine's understanding of the fall, discussed in Chapter 1.

113.   Hildegard of Bingen (1098–1179), quoted in Bynum, 'The Body of Christ in the Later Middle Ages: a Reply to Leo Steinberg', *Fragmentation and Redemption*, 98.

114.   Bynum, *Fragmentation and Redemption*, 82.

115.   Bynum presents textual and iconographic evidence for widespread devotion to Jesus as Mother in her critique of Steinberg. Her written sources date from the twelfth century, while the earliest visual example cited is an illumination in a French Moralized Bible of c.1240, in which a crucified but 'lively' Christ is shown giving birth to the Church (in anthropomorphic form). *Fragmentation and Redemption*, 93–108 (Fig. 3.6).

116. See Bynum, *Fragmentation and Redemption*, 108–9, 114, 218–22. Laqueur maintains that prior to the Enlightenment, 'Culture . . . suffused and changed the body that to the modern sensibility seems so closed, autarchic, and outside the realm of meaning.' *Making Sex*, 7.

117. Laqueur, *Making Sex*, 25. Bynum draws on Laqueur, amongst others, in her critique of Steinberg (*Fragmentation and Redemption*, 109).

118. Laqueur, *Making Sex*, 29, 43.

119. Laqueur, *Making Sex*, 25–8. Galen implies that the female reproductive organs remain as they were *in utero*, just like the partially formed eyes of the mole. Quoted in Laqueur, 28.

120. Blood, semen, milk, fat and sweat were more or less interchangeable (depending on the amount of heat in one's body) within 'a physiology of fungible fluids and corporeal flux'. Laqueur, *Making Sex*, 35.

121. Laqueur, *Making Sex*, 36–8.

122. Laqueur, *Making Sex*, 123–8.

123. On male lactation and pregnancy see Laqueur, *Making Sex*, 106. Both lactation and pregnancy are ascribed to the maternal Christ. For late medieval visual and textual sources, see Bynum, *Fragmentation and Redemption*, 93–7, 106–8, 205–6.

124. Gaspard Bauhin, *Theatrum anatomicum* (1605), quoted in Laqueur, *Making Sex*, 127. Although this is a seventeenth-century work, Laqueur points out (128) that accounts of female to male sex change had been in circulation at least since Pliny.

125. Laqueur, *Making Sex*, 106.

126. Laqueur, *Making Sex*, 8.

127. Albertus Magnus, *Quaestiones de animalibus*, book XV, q.II, quoted in Cadden, *Meanings of Sex Difference*, 185.

128. Cadden makes this point in *Meanings of Sex Difference*, 209.

129. White, *Book of Beasts*, 31–2.

130. For Laqueur, the one-sex body serves either as 'the microcosmic screen for a macrocosmic, hierarchic order', or 'the more or less stable sign for an intensely gendered social order'. *Making Sex*, 115.

131. This passage (from Vision 7) is quoted in Bynum, *Holy Feast and Holy Fast*, 156. Bynum dates Hadewijch's poetry to the period between 1220 and 1240. Her writings have been translated into English by C. Hart: *Hadewijch: the Complete Works* (New York: Paulist, 1980).

132. I am thinking in particular of Augustine's distinction between the passive, subordinate body and the insubordinate, transgressive flesh: both models of femininity are discussed in Chapter 1.

133. J. Kristeva, 'Stabat Mater', *The Female Body in Western Culture: Contemporary Perspectives*, ed. S. R. Suleiman (Cambridge, MA: Harvard University Press, 1985), 108.

134. On the doctrine of the virgin birth, see Pelikan, *Growth of Medieval Theology*, 163–7.

135. Guibert of Nogent (d. 1124), *On Virginity*, quoted in Pelikan, *Growth of Medieval Theology*, 164.

136. Marguerite of Oingt, quoted in Bynum, *Fragmentation and Redemption*, 162–3. In the same volume (99, Fig. 3.6), Bynum reproduces an image of Christ giving birth from a mid thirteenth-century French Moralized Bible (MS 270b, fol. 6r, Bodleian Library, Oxford). The notion of spiritual 'pregnancy' also occurs in reverse, in the sense that God is enclosed in the individual heart/womb. See Hamburger, *Nuns as Artists*, 171; and on the phenomenon of 'mystical pregnancy', see Bynum, *Fragmentation and Redemption*, 146, 187, 354 n.108.

137. Both Steinberg and Bynum evade this question of eroticism. While Steinberg does not discuss the distinction between sexuality and eroticism, he clearly does not regard the exhibition of Christ's genitals as having been of erotic interest to the Renaissance artist or viewer. Bynum (who misreads Steinberg on this point) argues more explicitly that we (in the twentieth century) 'tend to eroticise the body', medieval people did not. It is notable, however, that her comments are confined to 'breasts and penises' (*Fragmentation and Redemption*, 85). My reading of the crucified body as erotic departs significantly from both accounts. If vision can be an articulation of love or lust, and if one can be aroused or seduced by another's gaze, then 'eroticism' surely cannot be tied to the visible markers of biological sex.

138. Mechtild of Hackeborn (1240–c.1298), cited in Hamburger, *Rothschild Canticles*, 76. On Mechtild and her contemporaries at Helfta, see Bynum, 'Women Mystics in the Thirteenth Century: the Case of the Nuns of Helfta', *Jesus as Mother*, 170–262.

139. Hamburger's work has focused on the role of images in the female monastic context. In addition to his study of the *Rothschild Canticles* and his recent book on the visual culture of a late medieval Benedictine convent, *Nuns as Artists*, the following essays have informed my discussion of image devotion: 'Art, Enclosure and the *Cura Monialium*'; 'The Use of Images in the Pastoral Care of Nuns: the Case of Heinrich Suso and the Dominicans', *The Art Bulletin*, 71.1 (Mar. 1989): 20–46; and 'The Visual and the Visionary: the Image in Late Medieval Monastic Devotions', *Viator*, 20 (1989): 161–82.

140. Hamburger, *Rothschild Canticles*, 3, 8.

141. Hamburger argues that the verbal and visual images comprising the manuscript are neither prescriptive nor descriptive. Rather, they 'occupy a middle ground between theory and practice, example and experience'. *Rothschild Canticles*, 2.

142. Hamburger, *Rothschild Canticles*, 87. Not all the illuminations function in this way. Hamburger makes a distinction between Part I of the original manuscript, in which texts and full-page miniatures form a series of diptychs, and the layout of the text is often determined by the images; and the continuous, visually embellished text of Part II. *Rothschild Canticles*, 9.

143. The *Arma Christi* include: the cross, crown of thorns, lance, scourge, rod with sponge, nails and hammer. For a more detailed inventory and further discussion, see Schiller, *Iconography*, 2: 184–97.

144. Hamburger argues similarly that the 'gap between the figures heightens rather than diminishes the drama'. *Rothschild Canticles*, 72.

145. Bernard of Clairvaux, *On Conversion*, 84 (12.24). Bernard's use of the imagery of the Song of Songs is discussed in Chapter 5.

146. Hamburger, *Rothschild Canticles*, 75–6, 84, 85–6. The Ovidian version of this theme—in which Amor inflicts the wounds of love with his arrows—is represented in devotional handbooks of the period, as well as in secular literature and ivories. See Camille, *Gothic Idol*, 315–16 (Fig. 169). Further iconographic examples of Christ wounded by Caritas or the Virtues are reproduced in Schiller, *Iconography*, 2: figs 446–54.

147. Although this version of the text falls well beyond our period, it is thought that an earlier manuscript provided the model. These verses are quoted in Hamburger, *Rothschild Canticles*, 84.

148. I have used the Vulgate term 'wounded' here, rather than 'ravished'—the expression used in the Septuagint. On the wounding eye topos in the Song of Songs, see Cline, 'Heart and Eyes', 273. Bernard McGinn notes that Song 4.9 was 'a favourite text' amongst Cistercians, including Bernard of Clairvaux, William of St Thierry and Gilbert of Hoyland, as well as appearing in the work of Bernard's contemporary, Peter of Celle. *The Growth of Mysticism*, vol. 2 of *The Presence of God: a History of Western Christian Mysticism* (New York: Crossroad, 1994), 180, 233, 303, 345.

149. Hamburger comments briefly on the correspondence between Canticles 4.9 (quoted on folio 17v of the *Rothschild Canticles*) and the scene discussed here (folio 18v). *Rothschild Canticles*, 72. He does not, however, make any connection between the theme of the wounding eye and its widespread occurrence in amatory literature from the twelfth century onwards.

150. See, for example, 'The Medieval Love Lyric' in Perella, *Kiss*, 84–123.

151. Hamburger, *Rothschild Canticles*, 76.

152. Bonaventure, *De perfectione vitae ad sorores*, quoted in Hamburger, *Rothschild Canticles*, 72–3. Other examples of reciprocal wounding are discussed by Hamburger in *Nuns as Artists*, 117–18; and by McGinn, *Growth of Mysticism*, 303, 306.

153. This is Hamburger's translation, *Rothschild Canticles*, 72.

154. Hamburger, *Rothschild Canticles*, 72.

155. Elsewhere in the *Rothschild Canticles* (75) the same gesture appears as an illustration of Psalm 26, 'The Lord is my light.'

156. Peter of Limoges, *De Oculo Morali*, quoted in Clark, 'Optics for Preachers', 343.

157. Examples of this motif are given in Chapter 2.

158. For example, an indulgenced prayer of 1330—intended for use during communion—reads: 'Hide me between your wounds / And do not let me be separated from you.' Quoted in Rubin, *Corpus Christi*, 157.

159. The text is based on the writings of John of Fécamp, as quoted in Hamburger, *Rothschild Canticles*, 74.

160. '[T]ransfix my heart with the dart of your love . . . so much that from this wound would flow the most copious tears, night and day.' From the *Liber meditationum*, quoted in Hamburger, *Rothschild Canticles*, 74.

161. *Oculus cordis* is the term used by Peter of Limoges for the 'eye of the heart': the fourth and ultimate stage of moral perception. Clark 'Optics for Preachers', 338.

162. St Gertrude (the Great) of Helfta (1241–c.1300), *Revelations* (also known as *The Herald of Divine Love*), 2.5, from E. Petroff, *Medieval Women's Visionary Literature* (Oxford: Oxford University Press, 1986), 226. On Gertrude's life and writings, see Bynum, *Jesus as Mother*, 186–209. Angela of Foligno reports a similar vision in which Love appears in the form of a sickle (a variation on theme of Love's arrow or lance), leaving her 'languishing with the desire to feel and see God'. Angela of Foligno's *Memorial*, 60.

163. Grosseteste, *On Light*, 16. Grosseteste's theory of light is covered in Chapter 3.

164. Gertrude, *Revelations*, 227 (2.6).

BIBLIOGRAPHY

Historical sources

Alan of Lille. *The Plaint of Nature*. Trans. J. J. Sheridan. Toronto: Pontifical Institute of Mediaeval Studies, 1980.

The Ancrene Riwle (*The Corpus MS*: Ancrene Wisse). Trans. M. B. Salu. London: Burns, 1963.

Ancrene Riwle: Introduction and Part I. Ed. and trans. R. W. Ackerman and R. Dahood. Binghamton, NY: Medieval and Renaissance Texts and Studies, 1984.

Andreas Capellanus. *The Art of Courtly Love*. Trans. J. J. Parry. New York: Ungar, 1959.

[Angela of Foligno]. Angela of Foligno's *Memorial*. Ed. C. Mazzoni. Trans. J. Cirignano. Library of Medieval Women series. Cambridge: Brewer, 1999.

Aquinas, St Thomas. *Commentary on Aristotle's De anima*. Trans. K. Foster and S. Humphries. London: Routledge, 1951.

—*Summa Theologiæ*. Latin text and English translation. 61 vols. London: Blackfriars, 1964–81.

[Aristotle]. *The Complete Works of Aristotle: the Revised Oxford Translation*. Ed. J. Barnes. Bollingen Series. 2 vols. Princeton: Princeton University Press, 1984.

Augustine, St. *Concerning the City of God, Against the Pagans*. Trans. H. Bettenson. Harmondsworth: Penguin, 1984.

—*Confessions*. Trans. V. J. Bourke. Fathers of the Church 21. New York: Fathers of the Church, 1953.

—*Confessions*. Trans. R. S. Pine-Coffin. Harmondsworth: Penguin, 1961.

—*Eighty-three Different Questions*. Trans. D. L. Mosher. Fathers of the Church 70. Washington, DC: Catholic University of America Press, 1982.

—*The Literal Meaning of Genesis*. Trans. J. H. Taylor. 2 vols. New York: Newman Press, 1982.

—*On Genesis: Two Books on Genesis Against the Manichees and On the Literal Interpretation of Genesis: an Unfinished Book*. Trans. R. J. Teske. Fathers of the Church 84. Washington, DC: Catholic University of America Press, 1991.

—*Soliloquies and Immortality of the Soul*. Trans. G. Watson. Classical Texts Series. Warminster, Eng.: Aris, 1990.

—*St Augustine on Marriage and Sexuality*. Ed. and trans. E. A. Clark. Selections from the Fathers of the Church 1. Washington, DC: Catholic University of America Press, 1996.

— *The Trinity*. Trans. S. McKenna. Fathers of the Church 45. Washington, DC: Catholic University of America Press, 1963.

Bacon, Roger. *The Opus Majus of Roger Bacon*. Trans. R. B. Burke. 2 vols. New York: Russell, 1962.

[—] D. C. Lindberg. *Roger Bacon's Philosophy of Nature: a Critical Edition with English Translation, Introduction, and Notes, of* De multiplicatione specierum *and* De speculis comburentibus. Oxford: Clarendon, 1983.

[Bartholomæus Anglicus]. *On the Properties of Things: John Trevisa's Translation of Bartholomæus Anglicus* De Proprietatibus Rerum: *a Critical Text*. Ed. M. C. Seymour et al. Oxford: Clarendon, 1975.

Bernard of Clairvaux. *On Conversion. Bernard of Clairvaux, Selected Works*. Trans. G. R. Evans. Classics of Western Spirituality Series. New York: Paulist, 1987. 65–97.

— *On the Song of Songs*. Trans. J. Leclercq and K. Walsh. Cistercian Fathers Series. 4 vols. Shannon: Irish University Press and Kalamazoo: Cistercian, 1971–80.

Bonaventure. *The Journey of the Mind to God. Late Medieval Mysticism*. Ed. R. C. Petry. Library of Christian Classics 13. London: SCM, 1957. 132–41.

— *The Life of Saint Francis by Saint Bonaventura*. Trans. E. Gurney Salter. London: J. M. Dent, 1904.

The Book of Beasts: Being a Translation from a Latin Bestiary of the Twelfth Century. Ed. and trans. T. H. White. New York: Dover, 1984.

The Book of the Thousand Nights and a Night. Trans. R. F. Burton. New York: Heritage, 1962.

Davis-Weyer, C. *Early Medieval Art 300–1150: Sources and Documents*. Sources and Documents in the History of Art Series. Englewood Cliffs, NJ: Prentice-Hall, 1971.

Diogenes Laertius. *Lives of Eminent Philosophers*. Trans. R. D. Hicks. 2 vols. Cambridge, MA: Harvard University Press, 1991.

Durandus, William. *The Symbolism of Churches and Church Ornaments*. Trans. J. M. Neale and B. Webb. Leeds: Green, 1843.

[Eckhart, Johannes, called Meister Eckhart]. *Meister Eckhart: the Essential Sermons, Commentaries, Treatises, and Defence*. Trans. E. Colledge and B. McGinn. Classics of Western Spirituality Series. New York: Paulist, 1981.

Eneas: a Twelfth-Century French Romance. Trans. J. A. Yunck. New York: Columbia University Press, 1974.

Frisch, T. G. *Gothic Art 1140–c. 1450*. Sources and Documents in the History of Art Series. Englewood Cliffs, NJ: Prentice-Hall, 1971.

Galen. *On the Doctrines of Hippocrates and Plato*. Ed. and trans. P. de Lacy. 2nd ed. 2 vols. Berlin: Akademie-Verlag, 1984.

Gerald of Wales. *The Jewel of the Church: a Translation of Gemma Ecclesiastica by Giraldus Cambrensis*. Trans. J. J. Hagen. 2 vols. Leiden: Brill, 1979.

Grosseteste, Robert. *On Light*. Trans. C. C. Riedl. Milwaukee, WI: Marquette University Press, 1978.

Guillaume de Lorris and Jean de Meun. *The Romance of the Rose*. Trans. F. Horgan. Oxford: Oxford University Press, 1994.

Gundisalvo, Domingo. 'Classification of the Sciences'. Trans. M. Clagett and E. Grant. *A Source Book in Medieval Science*. Ed. E. Grant. Cambridge, MA: Harvard University Press, 1974. 59–76.

Hadewijch: the Complete Works. Trans. C. Hart. Classics of Western Spirituality Series. New York: Paulist, 1980.

Hartung, A. E., ed. *A Manual of the Writings in Middle English 1050–1500*. New Haven: Connecticut Academy of Arts and Sciences, 1986.

Hugh of St Victor. 'Classification of the Sciences'. Trans. J. Taylor. *A Source Book in Medieval Science*. Ed. E. Grant. Cambridge, MA: Harvard University Press, 1974. 54–9.

[John Pecham]. *John Pecham and the Science of Optics. Perspectiva Communis*. Ed. and trans. D. C. Lindberg. Madison, Wis.: University of Wisconsin Press, 1970.

Julian of Norwich. *Showings*. Trans. E. Colledge and J. Walsh. Classics of Western Spirituality Series. New York: Paulist, 1978.

Meditations on the Life of Christ. Paris, Bibliothèque Nationale, MS Ital. 115. Trans. I. Ragusa. Princeton: Princeton University Press, 1961.

Meister Eckhart. *Meister Eckhart: the Essential Sermons, Commentaries, Treatises, and Defence*. Trans. E. Colledge and B. McGinn. Classics of Western Spirituality Series. New York: Paulist, 1981.

Nicholas Love's Mirror of the Blessed Life of Jesus Christ: a Critical Edition Based on Cambridge University Library Add. MSS 6578 and 6686. Ed. M. G. Sargent. Garland Medieval Texts 18. New York: Garland, 1992.

Ovid. *The Art of Love. The Erotic Poems*. Trans. P. Green. Harmondsworth: Penguin, 1982.

—— *Metamorphoses*. Trans. M. M. Innes. Harmondsworth: Penguin, 1955.

Peter of Celle. *Selected Works*. Trans H. Feiss. Cistercian Studies Series 100. Kalamazoo: Cistercian, 1987.

Petroff, E. *Medieval Women's Visionary Literature*. Oxford: Oxford University Press, 1986.

Plato. *Phaedo*. Ed. and trans. D. Gallop. Oxford: Oxford University Press, 1993.

—— *Phaedrus and The Seventh and Eighth Letters*. Trans. W. Hamilton. Harmondsworth: Penguin, 1973.

—— *The Republic*. Trans. H. D. P. Lee. Harmondsworth: Penguin, 1955.

—— *Timaeus and Critias*. Trans. D. Lee. Harmondsworth: Penguin, 1971.

Pliny. *Natural History*. Ed. T. E. Page, et al. Trans. H. Rackham. Loeb Classical Library. 10 vols. London: Heinemann, 1942.

Plotinus. *The Enneads*. Trans. S. MacKenna. 4th ed. London: Faber, 1969.

[Pseudo-Albertus Magnus]. *Women's Secrets: a Translation of Pseudo-Albertus Magnus's De Secretis Mulierum with Commentaries*. Trans. H. R. Lemay. Albany: State University of New York Press, 1992.

Pseudo-Dionysius. *Pseudo-Dionysius: the Complete Works*. Trans. C. Luibheid. Classics of Western Spirituality Series. New York: Paulist, 1987.

Richard of St Victor. *The Twelve Patriarchs, The Mystical Ark, Book Three of the Trinity*. Trans. G. A. Zinn. Classics of Western Spirituality Series. London: SPCK, 1979.

[Suger, Abbot of St-Denis]. *Abbot Suger on the Abbey Church of St-Denis and its Art Treasures*. Ed. and trans. E. Panofsky. 2nd ed. Princeton: Princeton University Press, 1979.

William of Auxerre. *Summa Aurea*. Ed. J. Ribailler. 4 vols in 7 parts. Spicilegium Bonaventurianum 16–20. Paris and Grottaferrata, 1980–7.

General sources

Ackerman, R. W. 'The Debate of the Body and Soul and Parochial Christianity'. *Speculum*, 37 (Oct. 1962): 541–65.

Allert, B., ed. *Languages of Visuality: Crossings between Science, Art, Politics and Literature*. Detroit: Wayne State University Press, 1996.

Amos, T. L., E. A. Green and B. M. Kienzle, eds. *De Ore Domini: Preacher and Word in the Middle Ages*. Kalamazoo: Medieval Institute, 1989.

Ash, J. 'The Discursive Construction of Christ's Body in the Later Middle Ages: Resistance and Autonomy'. *Feminine, Masculine and Representation*. Ed. T. Threadgold and A. Cranny-Francis. Sydney: Allen, 1990. 75–105.

Astell, A. W. *The Song of Songs in the Middle Ages*. Ithaca, NY: Cornell University Press, 1990.

Baldwin, J. W. 'Five Discourses on Desire: Sexuality and Gender in Northern France around 1200'. *Speculum*, 66.4 (Oct. 1991): 797–819.

—— *The Language of Sex: Five Voices from Northern France around 1200*. Chicago: University of Chicago Press, 1994.

—— *Masters, Princes, and Merchants: the Social Views of Peter the Chanter and His Circle*. 2 vols. Princeton: Princeton University Press, 1970.

Baldwin, R. '"Gates Pure and Shining and Serene": Mutual Gazing as an Amatory Motif in Western Literature and Art'. *Renaissance and Reformation*, 10 (1986): 23–48.

Bardoel, A. A. 'The Psychology of Vision in Hadewijch'. *Mystics Quarterly*, 17.2 (June 1991): 79–93.

Barratt, A. 'The Five Wits and their Structural Significance in Part II of *Ancrene Wisse*'. *Medium Aevum*, 56.1 (1987): 12–24.

Barthes, R. 'Historical Discourse'. *Introduction to Structuralism*. Ed. M. Lane. New York: Basic, 1970. 145–55.

Bartlett, R. *Gerald of Wales, 1145–1223*. Oxford Historical Monographs. Oxford: Clarendon, 1982.

Baxandall, M. *Painting and Experience in Fifteenth-Century Italy*. 2nd ed. Oxford: Oxford University Press, 1988.

Beckwith, S. *Christ's Body: Identity, Culture and Society in Late Medieval Writings*. London: Routledge, 1993.

—— 'A Very Material Mysticism: the Medieval Mysticism of Margery Kempe'. *Medieval Literature: Criticism, Ideology and History*. Ed. D. Aers. New York: St Martin's, 1986. 34–57.

Belting, H. *The Image and its Public in the Middle Ages: Form and Function of Early Paintings of the Passion*. Trans. M. Bartusis and R. Meyer. New Rochelle, NY: Caratzas, 1990.

Bennett, J. 'Stigmata and Sense Memory: St Francis and the Affective Image'. *Art History*, 24.1 (Feb. 2001): 1–17.

Bensimon, M. 'The Significance of Eye Imagery in the Renaissance from Bosch to Montaigne'. *Image and Symbol in the Renaissance*. Special issue of *Yale French Studies*, 47 (1972): 266–90.

Benson, R. L. and G. Constable, eds. *Renaissance and Renewal in the Twelfth Century*. Cambridge, MA: Harvard University Press, 1982.

Best, S. 'Sexualising Space'. *Sexy Bodies: the Strange Carnalities of Feminism*. Ed. E. Grosz and Elspeth Probyn. London: Routledge, 1995. 181–94.

Bloomfield, M. W. et al. *Incipits of Latin Works on the Virtues and Vices, 1100–1500 AD*. Cambridge, MA: Harvard University Press, 1979.

Bloomfield, M. W. *The Seven Deadly Sins: an Introduction to the History of a Religious Concept, with Special Reference to Medieval English Literature*. Michigan: Michigan State University Press, 1952.

Blumenberg, H. *The Legitimacy of the Modern Age*. Trans. R. M. Wallace. Cambridge, MA: MIT Press, 1983.

—'Light as a Metaphor for Truth: At the Preliminary Stage of Philosophical Concept Formation'. *Modernity and the Hegemony of Vision*. Ed. D. M. Levin. Berkeley: University of California Press, 1993. 30–62.

Blumenfeld-Kosinski, R. and T. Szell, eds. *Images of Sainthood in Medieval Europe*. Ithaca, NY: Cornell University Press, 1991.

Bornkamm, G. *Paul*. Trans. D. M. G. Stalker. London: Hodder, 1975.

Børresen, K. E. *Subordination and Equivalence: the Nature and Role of Woman in Augustine and Thomas Aquinas*. Trans. C. H. Talbot. Washington, DC: University Press of America, 1981.

Boureau, A. 'The Sacrality of One's Own Body in the Middle Ages'. Trans. B. Semple. *Corps Mystique, Corps Sacré: Textual Transfigurations of the Body from the Middle Ages to the Seventeenth Century*. Special issue of *Yale French Studies*, 86 (1994): 5–17.

Boyarin, D. 'The Eye in the Torah: Ocular Desire in Midrashic Hermeneutic'. *Critical Inquiry*, 16 (Spring 1990): 532–50.

Brennan, T. '"The Contexts of Vision" from a Specific Standpoint'. *Vision in Context: Historical and Contemporary Perspectives on Sight*. Ed. T. Brennan and M. Jay. New York: Routledge, 1996. 219–30.

Brennan, T. and M. Jay, eds. *Vision in Context: Historical and Contemporary Perspectives on Sight*. New York: Routledge, 1996.

Brown, C., ed. *The New International Dictionary of New Testament Theology*. 3 vols. Exeter: Paternoster, 1975.

Brown, J. V. 'Abstraction and the Object of the Human Intellect According to Henry of Ghent'. *Vivarium*, 11 (1973): 80–104.

Brown, P. *The Body and Society: Men, Women and Sexual Renunciation in Early Christianity*. London: Faber, 1991.

Bryson, N. *Vision and Painting: the Logic of the Gaze*. New Haven: Yale University Press, 1983.

Bunim, M. S. *Space in Medieval Painting and the Forerunners of Perspective*. New York: Columbia University Press, 1940.

Burnett, C. 'Scientific Speculations'. *A History of Twelfth-Century Western Philosophy*. Ed. P. Dronke. Cambridge: Cambridge University Press, 1988. 151–76.

Butler, J. *Bodies That Matter: On the Discursive Limits of 'Sex'*. New York: Routledge, 1993.

Bynum, C. W. *Fragmentation and Redemption: Essays on Gender and the Human Body in Medieval Religion*. New York: Zone, 1991.

—*Holy Feast and Holy Fast: the Religious Significance of Food to Medieval Women*. Berkeley: University of California Press, 1987.

—*The Resurrection of the Body in Western Christianity 200–1336*. New York: Columbia University Press, 1995.

⩗ —'Why All the Fuss About the Body? A Medievalist's Perspective'. *Critical Inquiry*, 22.1 (Autumn 1995): 1–33.

Cadden, J. *Meanings of Sex Difference in the Middle Ages: Medicine, Science, and Culture*. Cambridge: Cambridge University Press, 1993.

Camille, M. 'The Eye in the Text: Vision in the Illuminated Manuscripts of the Latin Aristotle'. *Micrologus VI: La Visione e lo Sguardo nel Medio Evo*. Sismel: Edizioni del Galluzzo, 1998. 129–45.

—*Gothic Art: Visions and Revelations of the Medieval World*. The Everyman Art Library. London: Orion, 1996.

—*The Gothic Idol: Ideology and Image-making in Medieval Art*. Cambridge: Cambridge University Press, 1989.

—*Image on the Edge: the Margins of Medieval Art*. London: Reaktion, 1992.

—'The Image and the Self: Unwriting Late Medieval Bodies'. *Framing Medieval Bodies*. Ed. S. Kay and M. Rubin. Manchester: Manchester University Press, 1994. 62–99.

—'Seeing and Reading: Some Visual Implications of Medieval Literacy and Illiteracy'. *Art History*, 8.1 (Mar. 1985): 26–49.

Carruthers, M. J. *The Book of Memory: a Study of Memory in Medieval Culture*. Cambridge: Cambridge University Press, 1990.

The Catholic Encyclopedia. Ed. C. G. Herbermann et al. 15 vols. New York: Encyclopedia, 1913.

Caviness, M. H. 'Images of Divine Order and the Third Mode of Seeing'. *Gesta*, 22 (1983): 99–120.

—'"The Simple Perception of Matter" and the Representation of Narrative, ca. 1180–1280'. *Gesta*, 30.1 (1991): 48–64.

Cerquiglini, J. '"Le Clerc et le Louche": Sociology of an Esthetic'. *Poetics Today*, 5.3 (1984): 479–91.

Chidester, D. *Word and Light: Seeing, Hearing, and Religious Discourse*. Urbana: University of Illinois Press, 1992.

Cixous, H. 'Sorties'. Trans. A. Liddle. *New French Feminisms: an Anthology*. Ed. E. Marks and I. de Courtivron. New York: Schocken, 1981. 90–8.

Clark, D. L. 'Optics for Preachers: the *De Oculo Morali* by Peter of Limoges'. *The Michigan Academician* (Winter 1977): 329–43.

Classen, C. 'Engendering Perception: Gender Ideologies and Sensory Hierarchies in Western History'. *Body and Society*, 3.2 (1997): 1–19.

Cline, R. H. 'Heart and Eyes'. *Romance Philology*, 25.2 (Nov. 1971): 263–97.

Coleman, J. *Ancient and Medieval Memories: Studies in the Reconstruction of the Past.* Cambridge: Cambridge University Press, 1992.

Copleston, F. C. *A History of Medieval Philosophy.* London: Methuen, 1972.

Cornelius, R. D. *The Figurative Castle: a Study in the Medieval Allegory of the Edifice with Special Reference to Religious Writings.* Pennsylvania: Bryn Mawr, 1930.

Crary, J. *Techniques of the Observer: On Vision and Modernity in the Nineteenth Century.* Cambridge, MA: MIT Press, 1990.

Crombie, A. C. *Robert Grosseteste and the Origins of Experimental Science 1100–1700.* Oxford: Clarendon, 1953.

—*Science, Art and Nature in Medieval and Modern Thought.* London: Hambledon, 1996.

Damisch, H. *The Origin of Perspective.* Trans. J. Goodman. Cambridge, MA: MIT Press, 1994.

Davies, O. *God Within: the Mystical Tradition of Northern Europe.* Classics of Western Spirituality Series. New York: Paulist, 1988.

d'Avray, D. L. 'Some Franciscan Ideas about the Body'. *Modern Questions about Medieval Sermons: Essays on Marriage, Death, History and Sanctity.* Ed. N. Bériou and D. L. d'Avray et al. Spoleto: Centro Italiano di Studi Sull'Alto Medioevo, 1994. 155–74.

de Bolla, P. 'The Visibility of Visuality'. *Vision in Context: Historical and Contemporary Perspectives on Sight.* Ed. T. Brennan and M. Jay. New York: Routledge, 1996. 65–81.

Despres, D. *Ghostly Sights: Visual Meditation in Late-Medieval Literature.* Norman, OK: Pilgrim, 1989.

Deutscher, P. 'The Evanescence of Masculinity: Deferral in Saint Augustine's *Confessions* and Some Thoughts on its Bearing on the Sex/Gender Debate'. *Australian Feminist Studies*, 15 (Autumn 1992): 41–56.

Dickie, M. W. 'Heliodorus and Plutarch on the Evil Eye'. *Classical Philology*, 86.1 (Jan. 1991): 17–29.

Didi-Huberman, G. 'The Figurative Incarnation of the Sentence (Notes on the "Autographic" Skin)'. *Journal.* The Los Angeles Institute of Contemporary Art (Spring 1987): 67–70.

Doane, M. A. 'Film and the Masquerade: Theorising the Female Spectator'. *Screen*, 23.3–4 (Sep./Oct. 1982): 74–87.

Donaldson-Evans, L. K. *Love's Fatal Glance: a Study of Eye Imagery in the Poets of the École Lyonnaise.* Mississippi: Romance Monographs, 1980.

Douglas, M. 'The Two Bodies'. *Natural Symbols: Explorations in Cosmology.* London: Barrie, 1970. 93–112.

Du Bois, P. A. '"The Devil's Gateway": Women's Bodies and the Earthly Paradise'. *Women's Studies*, 7 (1980): 43–58.

Dunning, W. V. *Changing Images of Pictorial Space: a History of Spatial Illusion in Painting.* Syracuse, NY: Syracuse University Press, 1991.

Eastwood, B. 'Medieval Empiricism: the Case of Grosseteste's Optics'. *Speculum*, 43 (1968): 306–21.

Eco, U. *The Aesthetics of Thomas Aquinas.* Trans. H. Bredin. Cambridge, MA: Harvard University Press, 1988.

——*Art and Beauty in the Middle Ages*. Trans. H. Bredin. New Haven: Yale University Press, 1986.

——'Living in the New Middle Ages'. *Travels in Hyperreality*. Trans. W. Weaver. London: Picador, 1987. 73–85.

Edgerton, S. Y., Jr. 'Observations on Art and Science'. *Art and Science*. Special issue of *Daedalus*, 115.3 (Summer 1986): 182–6.

——*The Renaissance Rediscovery of Linear Perspective*. New York: Basic, 1975.

Emilsson, E. K. *Plotinus on Sense-Perception: a Philosophical Study*. Cambridge: Cambridge University Press, 1988.

Erickson, C. *The Medieval Vision: Essays in History and Perception*. New York: Oxford University Press, 1976.

Febvre, L. *The Problem of Unbelief in the Sixteenth Century: the Religion of Rabelais*. Trans. B. Gottlieb. Cambridge, MA: Harvard University Press, 1982.

Ferrari, G. R. F. 'Platonic Love'. *The Cambridge Companion to Plato*. Ed. R. Kraut. Cambridge: Cambridge University Press, 1992. 248–76.

Foster, H. *Vision and Visuality*. DIA Art Foundation Discussions in Contemporary Culture 2. Seattle: Bay, 1988.

Foucault, M. 'Body/Power'. *Power/Knowledge*. Trans. C. Gordon et al. Brighton: Harvester, 1980. 55–62.

——*The History of Sexuality, Volume 1: an Introduction*. Trans. R. Hurley. Harmondsworth: Penguin, 1978.

Freedberg, D. *The Power of Images: Studies in the History and Theory of Response*. Chicago: University of Chicago Press, 1989.

Freud, S. 'Anxiety and Instinctual Life'. *New Introductory Lectures on Psychoanalysis*. Trans. and ed. J. Strachey. New York: Norton, 1965. 72–98.

——*Civilization and its Discontents*. Trans. J. Riviere. Revised and ed. J. Strachey. International Psycho-Analytical Library 17. London: Hogarth/Institute of Psycho-Analysis, 1973.

——'Instincts and their Vicissitudes'. *The Standard Edition of the Complete Psychological Works of Sigmund Freud*. Ed. J. Strachey. Trans. J. Strachey et al. 24 vols. London: Hogarth, 1957. 14: 109–40.

Friedman, J. B. *The Monstrous Races in Medieval Art and Thought*. Cambridge, MA: Harvard University Press, 1981.

Funkenstein, A. *Theology and the Scientific Imagination from the Middle Ages to the Seventeenth Century*. Princeton: Princeton University Press, 1986.

Gallop, J. *Reading Lacan*. Ithaca, NY: Cornell University Press, 1985.

Gatens, M. 'A Critique of the Sex/Gender Distinction'. *Beyond Marxism? Interventions After Marx*. Ed. P. Patton and J. Allen. Sydney: Intervention, 1983. 143–61.

Georgianna, L. *The Solitary Self: Individuality in the Ancrene Wisse*. Cambridge, MA: Harvard University Press, 1981.

Gillispie, C. C., ed. *Dictionary of Scientific Biography*. New York: Scribner, 1970–.

Gilson, E. *The Philosophy of St Bonaventure*. Trans. I. Trethowan and F. J. Sheed. London: Sheed, 1938.

Goering, J. 'The *De Dotibus* of Robert Grosseteste'. *Mediaeval Studies*, 44 (1982): 83–109.

Gold, B. K., P. A. Miller and C. Platter, eds. *Sex and Gender in Medieval and Renaissance Latin Texts: the Latin Tradition*. Albany: State University of New York Press, 1997.

Goldman, S. L. 'On the Interpretation of Symbols and the Christian Origins of Modern Science'. *The Journal of Religion*, 62.1 (Jan. 1982): 1–20.

Gombrich, E. H. 'Achievement in Mediaeval Art'. 1937. Trans. M. Podro. *Meditations on a Hobby Horse and Other Essays on the Theory of Art*. London: Phaidon, 1963. 70–7.

— 'The "What" and the "How": Perspective Representation and the Phenomenal World'. *Logic and Art: Essays in Honour of Nelson Goodman*. Ed. R. Rudner and I. Scheffler. Indianapolis: Bobbs-Merrill, 1972. 129–49.

Gombrich, E. H. and R. L. Gregory, eds. *Illusion in Nature and Art*. London: Duckworth, 1973.

Grant, E. 'The Condemnation of 1277, God's Absolute Power, and Physical Thought in the Late Middle Ages'. *Viator*, 10 (1979): 211–44.

— *Much Ado About Nothing: Theories of Space and Vacuum from the Middle Ages to the Scientific Revolution*. Cambridge: Cambridge University Press, 1981.

Grayson, J. *Structure and Imagery in the Ancrene Wisse*. Hanover: published for the University of New Hampshire by the University Press of New England, 1974.

Gregory, T. 'The Platonic Inheritance'. *A History of Twelfth-Century Western Philosophy*. Ed. P. Dronke. Cambridge: Cambridge University Press, 1988. 54–80.

Grosz, E. *Jacques Lacan: a Feminist Introduction*. London: Routledge, 1990.

— 'Notes Towards a Corporeal Feminism'. *Australian Feminist Studies*, 5 (Summer 1987): 1–15.

— *Volatile Bodies: Toward a Corporeal Feminism*. Sydney: Allen, 1994.

Hahn, C. 'Purification, Sacred Action and the Vision of God: Viewing Medieval Narratives'. *Word and Image*, 5.1 (Jan.–Mar. 1989): 71–84.

Hamburger, J. F. 'Art, Enclosure and the *Cura Monialium*: Prolegomena in the Guise of a Postscript'. *Gesta*, 31.2 (1992): 108–34.

— *Nuns as Artists: the Visual Culture of a Medieval Convent*. Berkeley: University of California Press, 1997.

— *The Rothschild Canticles*. New Haven: Yale University Press, 1990.

— 'The Use of Images in the Pastoral Care of Nuns: the Case of Heinrich Suso and the Dominicans'. *The Art Bulletin*, 71.1 (Mar. 1989): 20–46.

— 'The Visual and the Visionary: the Image in Late Medieval Monastic Devotions'. *Viator*, 20 (1989): 161–82.

Harbison, C. 'Visions and Meditations in Early Flemish Painting'. *Simiolus*, 15 (1985): 87–118.

Heelan, P. A. *Space-Perception and the Philosophy of Science*. Berkeley: University of California Press, 1983.

Heidegger, M. 'The Age of the World Picture'. *The Question Concerning Technology and Other Essays*. Trans. W. Lovitt. New York: Harper, 1977. 115–54.

Heslop, T. A. 'Attitudes to the Visual Arts: the Evidence of Written Sources'. *The Age of Chivalry: Art in Plantagenet England 1200–1400*. Ed. J. Alexander and P. Binski. London: Weidenfeld with Royal Academy of Arts, 1987. 26–32.

Holly, M. A. 'Past Looking'. *Critical Inquiry*, 16 (Winter 1990): 371–95.

— 'Vision and Revision in the History of Art'. *Theory Between the Disciplines: Authority/Vision/Politics*. Ed. M. Kreiswirth and M. A. Cheetham. Ann Arbor: University of Michigan Press, 1990. 151–65.

Hubel, D. H. *Eye, Brain and Vision*. New York: Scientific American Library, 1988.

Huizinga, J. *The Autumn of the Middle Ages*. Trans. R. J. Payton and U. Mammitzsch. Chicago: University of Chicago Press, 1996.

Irigaray, L. *Speculum of the Other Woman*. Trans. G. C. Gill. Ithaca, NY: Cornell University Press, 1985.

— *This Sex Which Is Not One*. Trans. C. Porter and C. Burke. Ithaca, NY: Cornell University Press, 1985.

Ivins, W. M., Jr. *Art and Geometry: a Study in Space Intuitions*. New York: Dover, 1946.

— *On the Rationalization of Sight, with an Examination of Three Renaissance Texts on Perspective*. New York: Metropolitan Museum of Art, 1938.

Jacquart, D. and C. Thomasset. *Sexuality and Medicine in the Middle Ages*. Trans. M. Adamson. Princeton: Princeton University Press, 1988.

Jager, E. 'The Book of the Heart: Reading and Writing the Medieval Subject'. *Speculum*, 71.1 (Jan. 1996): 1–26.

Jay, M. 'Disciplinary Prisms: Responding to My Critics'. *Comparative Studies in Society and History*, 38.2 (Apr. 1996): 370–94.

— *Downcast Eyes*. Berkeley: University of California Press, 1994.

— 'Vision in Context: Reflections and Refractions'. *Vision in Context: Historical and Contemporary Perspectives on Sight*. Ed. T. Brennan and M. Jay. New York: Routledge, 1996. 3–12.

Jeffrey, D. L. 'Franciscan Spirituality and the Growth of Vernacular Culture'. *By Things Seen: Reference and Recognition in Medieval Thought*. Ed. D. L. Jeffrey. Ottawa: University of Ottawa Press, 1979. 143–60.

Jencks, C., ed. *Visual Culture*. London: Routledge, 1995.

Jonas, H. 'The Nobility of Sight: a Study in the Phenomenology of the Senses'. *The Phenomenon of Life: Towards a Philosophical Biology*. New York: Harper, 1966. 135–56.

Jones, W. R. 'Art and Christian Piety: Iconoclasm in Medieval Europe'. *The Image and the Word: Confrontations in Judaism, Christianity and Islam*. Ed. J. Gutmann. Missoula, MT: Scholars, 1977. 75–105.

Kaplan, E. A. 'Is the Gaze Male?' *Women and Film: Both Sides of the Camera*. London: Routledge, 1983. 23–35.

Kay, S. 'Women's Body of Knowledge: Epistemology and Misogyny in the *Romance of the Rose*'. *Framing Medieval Bodies*. Ed. S. Kay and M. Rubin. Manchester: Manchester University Press, 1994. 211–35.

Keller, E. F. and C. R. Grontkowski. 'The Mind's Eye'. *Discovering Reality: Feminist Perspectives on Epistemology, Metaphysics, Methodology, and Philosophy of Science*. Ed. S. Harding and M. B. Hintikka. Dordrecht, Neth.: Reidel, 1983. 207–24.

Kelly, H. A. 'The Metamorphoses of the Eden Serpent During the Middle Ages and Renaissance'. *Viator*, 2 (1971): 301–27.

Kern-Ulmer, B. 'The Power of the Evil Eye and the Good Eye in Midrashic Literature'. *Judaism*, 159.40.3 (Summer 1991): 344–53.

Kessler, H. L. ' "Facies Bibliothecae Revelata": Carolingian Art as Spiritual Seeing'. *Testo e Immagine nell'Alto Medioevo*. Settimane di Studio del Centro Italiano di Studi sull'Alto Medioevo 41 (15–21 Apr. 1993). 2 vols. Spoleto: Presso la Sede del Centro, 1994. 2: 534–94.

Kieckhefer, R. *Unquiet Souls: Fourteenth-Century Saints and their Religious Milieu*. Chicago: University of Chicago Press, 1984.

Klassen, N. *Chaucer on Love, Knowledge and Sight*. Chaucer Studies 21. Cambridge: Brewer, 1995.

Krauss, R. E. *The Optical Unconscious*. Cambridge, MA: MIT Press, 1993.

Kretzmann, N. et al. eds. *The Cambridge History of Later Medieval Philosophy: From the Rediscovery of Aristotle to the Disintegration of Scholasticism 1100–1600*. Cambridge: Cambridge University Press, 1982.

Krieger, M. 'The Ambiguities of Representation and Illusion: an E. H. Gombrich Retrospective'. *Critical Inquiry*, 11.2 (Dec. 1984): 181–94.

Kristeva, J. *Powers of Horror: an Essay on Abjection*. Trans. L. S. Roudiez. New York: Columbia University Press, 1982.

—'Stabat Mater'. *The Female Body in Western Culture: Contemporary Perspectives*. Ed. S. R. Suleiman. Cambridge, MA: Harvard University Press, 1985. 99–118.

Kruger, S. F. 'Mirrors and the Trajectory of Vision in *Piers Plowman*'. *Speculum*, 66.1 (1991): 74–95.

Kubovy, M. *The Psychology of Perspective and Renaissance Art*. Cambridge: Cambridge University Press, 1986.

Kuksewicz, Z. 'The Potential and the Agent Intellect'. *The Cambridge History of Later Medieval Philosophy: From the Rediscovery of Aristotle to the Disintegration of Scholasticism 1100–1600*. Ed. N. Kretzmann et al. Cambridge: Cambridge University Press, 1982. 595–601.

Lacan, J. *The Four Fundamental Concepts of Psycho-Analysis*. Ed. J.-A. Miller. Trans. A. Sheridan. New York: Norton, 1978.

—'The Meaning of the Phallus'. *Feminine Sexuality: Jacques Lacan and the École Freudienne*. Ed. J. Mitchell and J. Rose. Trans. J. Rose. New York: Norton, 1982. 74–85.

—'The Mirror Stage as Formative of the Function of the *I* as Revealed in Psychoanalytic Experience'. *Écrits: a Selection*. Trans. A. Sheridan. London: Tavistock, 1977. 1–7.

La Favia, L. M. *The Man of Sorrows: Its Origin and Development in Trecento Florentine Painting*. Rome: 'Sanguis', 1980.

Lapidge, M. 'The Stoic Inheritance'. *A History of Twelfth-Century Western Philosophy*. Ed. P. Dronke. Cambridge: Cambridge University Press, 1988. 81–112.

Laplanche, J. and J.-B. Pontalis. *The Language of Psycho-Analysis*. Trans. D. Nicholson-Smith. London: Hogarth/Institute of Psycho-Analysis, 1973.

Laqueur, T. *Making Sex: Body and Gender from the Greeks to Freud*. Cambridge, MA: Harvard University Press, 1992.

Latham, R. E. *Dictionary of Medieval Latin from British Sources*. London: Oxford University Press, 1975.

Leclercq, J. *Monks and Love in Twelfth-Century France: Psycho-Historical Essays*. Oxford: Clarendon, 1979.

Leclercq, J., F. Vanderbroucke and L. Bouyer. *The Spirituality of the Middle Ages.* Tunbridge Wells: Burns, 1968.

Le Goff, J. 'Head or Heart: the Political Use of Body Metaphors in the Middle Ages'. Trans. P. Ranum. *Fragments for a History of the Human Body, Part III.* Ed. M. Feher, R. Naddaff and N. Tazi. 3 vols. New York: Zone, 1989. 13–27.

—— *The Medieval Imagination.* Trans. A. Goldhammer. Chicago: University of Chicago Press, 1992.

Lewis, S. *Reading Images: Narrative Discourse and Reception in the Thirteenth-Century Illuminated Apocalypse.* Cambridge: Cambridge University Press, 1995.

Levin, D. M. *The Opening of Vision: Nihilism and the Postmodern Situation.* New York: Routledge, 1988.

Levin, D. M., ed. *Modernity and the Hegemony of Vision.* Berkeley: University of California Press, 1993.

—— *Sites of Vision: the Discursive Construction of Sight in the History of Philosophy.* Cambridge, MA: MIT Press, 1997.

Lindberg, D. C. *Roger Bacon's Philosophy of Nature: a Critical Edition with English Translation, Introduction, and Notes, of* De multiplicatione specierum *and* De speculis comburentibus. Oxford: Clarendon, 1983.

—— *Studies in the History of Medieval Optics.* London: Variorum Reprints, 1983.

—— *Theories of Vision from Al-Kindi to Kepler.* Chicago: University of Chicago Press, 1976.

Lindberg, D. C. and N. H. Steneck. 'The Sense of Vision and the Origins of Modern Science'. *Studies in the History of Medieval Optics.* London: Variorum Reprints, 1983. 29–45.

Lloyd, G. *The Man of Reason: 'Male' and 'Female' in Western Philosophy.* London: Methuen, 1984.

Lloyd, G. E. R. *Polarity and Analogy: Two Types of Argumentation in Early Greek Thought.* Bristol: Bristol Classics, 1987.

Lochrie, K. 'Desiring Foucault'. *Journal of Medieval and Early Modern Studies,* 27.1 (Winter 1997): 3–16.

—— 'The Language of Transgression: Body, Flesh, and Word in Mystical Discourse'. *Speaking Two Languages: Traditional Disciplines and Contemporary Theory in Medieval Studies.* Ed. A. J. Frantzen. Albany: State University of New York Press, 1991. 115–40.

—— *Margery Kempe and Translations of the Flesh.* Philadelphia: University of Pennsylvania Press, 1991.

Loewald, H. W. *Sublimation: Inquiries into Theoretical Psychoanalysis.* New Haven: Yale University Press, 1988.

Lomperis, L. and S. Stanbury, eds. *Feminist Approaches to the Body in Medieval Literature.* Philadelphia: University of Pennsylvania Press, 1993.

Luscombe, D. E. 'Peter Abelard'. *A History of Twelfth-Century Western Philosophy.* Ed. P. Dronke. Cambridge: Cambridge University Press, 1988. 279–307.

Maloney, T. S. 'The Semiotics of Roger Bacon'. *Mediaeval Studies,* 45 (1983): 120–54.

Marrone, S. P. *William of Auvergne and Robert Grosseteste: New Ideas of Truth in the Early Thirteenth Century.* Princeton: Princeton University Press, 1983.

Marrow, J. H. *Passion Iconography in Northern European Art of the Late Middle Ages and Early Renaissance: a Study of the Transformation of Sacred Metaphor into Descriptive Narrative*. Kortrijk, Belg.: Van Ghemmert, 1979.

— 'Symbol and Meaning in Northern European Art of the Late Middle Ages and the Early Renaissance'. *Simiolus*, 16 (1986): 150–69.

Matson, W. I. 'Why Isn't the Mind-Body Problem Ancient?' *Mind, Matter and Method: Essays in Philosophy and Science in Honor of Herbert Feigl*. Ed. P. K. Feyerabend and G. Maxwell. Minneapolis: University of Minnesota Press, 1966. 92–102.

Matter, E. A. *The Voice of My Beloved: the Song of Songs in Western Medieval Christianity*. Philadelphia: University of Pennsylvania Press, 1990.

McEvoy, J. *The Philosophy of Robert Grosseteste*. Oxford: Clarendon, 1982.

McGinn, B. 'The Changing Shape of Late Medieval Mysticism'. *Church History*, 65.2 (Jun. 1996): 197–219.

— *The Growth of Mysticism*. Vol. 2 of *The Presence of God: a History of Western Christian Mysticism*. 4 vols. New York: Crossroad, 1994.

McLaughlin, E. C. 'Equality of Souls, Inequality of Sexes: Woman in Medieval Theology'. *Religion and Sexism: Images of Woman in the Jewish and Christian Traditions*. Ed. R. R. Ruether. New York: Simon, 1974. 213–65.

McMullin, E., ed. *The Concept of Matter in Greek and Medieval Philosophy*. Notre Dame, IN: University of Notre Dame Press, 1963.

Merleau-Ponty, M. *Phenomenology of Perception*. Trans. C. Smith. London: Routledge, 1962.

— *The Visible and the Invisible*. Ed. C. Lefort. Trans. A. Lingis. Evanston: Northwestern University Press, 1968.

Meskimmon, M. 'Visuality: the New, New Art History?' Review article. *Art History*, 20.2 (Jun. 1997): 331–3.

Miles, M. *Augustine on the Body*. American Academy of Religion Dissertation Series 31. Missoula: Scholars, 1979.

— *Image as Insight: Visual Understanding in Western Christianity and Secular Culture*. Boston: Beacon, 1985.

— 'Vision: the Eye of the Body and the Eye of the Mind in Saint Augustine's *De Trinitate and Confessions*'. *The Journal of Religion*, 63.2 (April 1983): 125–42.

Mitchell, W. J. T. *Picture Theory: Essays on Verbal and Visual Representation*. Chicago: University of Chicago Press, 1995.

Morrison, K. F. *'I Am You': the Hermeneutics of Empathy in Western Literature, Theology, and Art*. Princeton: Princeton University Press, 1988.

Mulvey, L. 'Visual Pleasure and Narrative Cinema'. *Screen*, 16.3 (1975): 6–18.

Newhauser, R. 'Nature's Moral Eye: Peter of Limoges' *Tractatus Moralis de Oculo*'. *Man and Nature in the Middle Ages*. Ed. S. J. Ridyard and R. G. Benson. Sewanee, TN: University of the South Press, 1995. 125–36.

Niermeyer, J. F. *Mediae Latinitatis Lexicon Minus*. Leiden: Brill, 1976.

Nolan, B. *The Gothic Visionary Perspective*. Princeton: Princeton University Press, 1977.

— 'The *Vita Nuova* and Richard of St Victor's Phenomenology of Vision'. *Dante Studies*. Ed. A. L. Pellegrini. 92 (1974): 35–52.

Owens, J. 'Faith, Ideas, Illumination, and Experience'. *The Cambridge History of Later Medieval Philosophy: From the Rediscovery of Aristotle to the Disintegration of Scholasticism 1100–1600*. Ed. N. Kretzmann et al. Cambridge: Cambridge University Press, 1982. 440–59.

Panofsky, E. *Gothic Architecture and Scholasticism*. New York: Meridian, 1957.

—'"Imago Pietatis": Ein Beitrag zur Typengeschichte des "Schmerzensmanns" und der "Maria Mediatrix."' *Festschrift für Max J. Friedländer zum 60. Geburtstag*. Leipzig: Seemann, 1927. 261–308.

—*Meaning in the Visual Arts*. Harmondsworth: Penguin, 1970.

—*Perspective as Symbolic Form*. Trans. C. S. Wood. New York: Zone, 1991.

—*Renaissance and Renascences in Western Art*. London: Paladin, 1970.

Paris, J. *Painting and Linguistics*. Pittsburgh: Carnegie-Mellon University, 1975.

Pavlis-Baig, B. 'Vision and Visualization: Optics and Light Metaphysics in the Imagery and Poetic Form of Twelfth and Thirteenth Century Secular Allegory, with Special Attention to the *Roman de la Rose*'. Diss. University of California, Berkeley, 1982.

Pelikan, J. *The Growth of Medieval Theology (600–1300)*. Vol. 3 of *The Christian Tradition: a History of the Development of Doctrine*. 5 vols. Chicago: University of Chicago Press, 1978.

Perella, N. J. *The Kiss Sacred and Profane: an Interpretative History of Kiss Symbolism and Related Religio-Erotic Themes*. Berkeley: University of California Press, 1969.

Phillips, H. 'John Wyclif and the Optics of the Eucharist'. *From Ockham to Wyclif*. Ed. A. Hudson and M. Wilks. Studies in Church History 5. Oxford: Blackwell, 1987. 245–58.

Phillips, J. A. *Eve: the History of an Idea*. San Francisco: Harper, 1984.

Pouchelle, M. C. *The Body and Surgery in the Middle Ages*. Trans. R. Morris. Cambridge: Polity, 1990.

Putnam, H. 'How Old is the Mind?' *Words and Life*. Ed. J. Conant. Cambridge, MA: Harvard University Press, 1994. 3–21.

Putnam, H. and M. C. Nussbaum. 'Changing Aristotle's Mind'. *Words and Life*. Ed. J. Conant. Cambridge, MA: Harvard University Press, 1994. 22–61

Ragland-Sullivan, E. 'Jacques Lacan: Feminism and the Problem of Gender Identity'. *Sub-Stance*, 36 (1982): 6–20.

Riehle, W. 'The Experience of God as a Spiritual Sense Perception'. *The Middle English Mystics*. Trans. B. Standring. London: Routledge, 1977. 104–27.

Ringbom, S. 'Devotional Images and Imaginative Devotions: Notes on the Place of Art in Late Medieval Private Piety'. *Gazette des Beaux-Arts*, 73 (1969): 159–70.

—*Icon to Narrative: the Rise of the Dramatic Close-up in Fifteenth-Century Devotional Painting*. 2nd ed. Doornspijk, Neth.: Davaco, 1984.

Robertson, E. 'Medieval Medical Views of Women and Female Spirituality in the *Ancrene Wisse* and Julian of Norwich's *Showings*'. *Feminist Approaches to the Body in Medieval Literature*. Ed. L. Lomperis and S. Stanbury. Philadelphia: University of Pennsylvania Press, 1993. 142–67.

Ronchi, V. *Optics: the Science of Vision*. Trans. E. Rosen. New York: New York University Press, 1957.

Rubin, M. *Corpus Christi: the Eucharist in Late Medieval Culture*. Cambridge: Cambridge University Press, 1991.

— 'Medieval Bodies: Why Now, and How?' *The Work of Jacques Le Goff and the Challenges of Medieval History*. Ed. M. Rubin. Woodbridge: Boydell, 1997. 209–19.

Salisbury, J. E. *Medieval Sexuality: a Research Guide*. New York: Garland, 1990.

Schiller, G. *Iconography of Christian Art*. Trans. J. Seligman. 2 vols. London: Humphries, 1972.

Sharp, D. E. *Franciscan Philosophy at Oxford in the Thirteenth Century*. New York: Russell, 1964.

Siegel, R. E. *Galen on Sense Perception*. Basel: Karger, 1970.

Silverman, K. 'Fassbinder and Lacan: a Reconsideration of Gaze, Look and Image'. *Camera Obscura*, 19 (Jan. 1989): 54–85.

Simons, P. 'Women in Frames: the Gaze, the Eye, the Profile in Renaissance Portraiture'. *The Expanding Discourse: Feminism and Art History*. Ed. N. Broude and M. D. Garrard. New York: Icon, 1992. 39–57.

Siraisi, N. G. *Medieval and Early Renaissance Medicine*. Chicago: University of Chicago Press, 1990.

Skeat, W. W. *A Concise Etymological Dictionary of the English Language*. New York: Capricorn, 1963.

Slakey, T. J. 'Aristotle on Sense-perception'. *Aristotle's De Anima in Focus*. Ed. M. Durrant. London: Routledge, 1993. 75–89.

Sobchack, V. *The Address of the Eye: a Phenomenology of Film Experience*. Princeton: Princeton University Press, 1992.

Soskice, J. M. 'Sight and Vision in Medieval Christian Thought'. *Vision in Context: Historical and Contemporary Perspectives on Sight*. Ed. T. Brennan and M. Jay. New York: Routledge, 1996. 31–43.

Souter, A. *A Glossary of Later Latin to 600 AD*. Oxford: Clarendon, 1949.

Southern, R. W. *Robert Grosseteste: the Growth of an English Mind in Medieval Europe*. 2nd ed. Oxford: Clarendon, 1992.

Spearing, A. C. *The Medieval Poet as Voyeur: Looking and Listening in Medieval Love-Narratives*. Cambridge: Cambridge University Press, 1993.

Spence, S. '"Lo Cop Mortal": the Evil Eye and the Origins of Courtly Love'. *The Romantic Review*, 87.3 (May 1996): 307–18.

Stanbury, S. 'Feminist Film Theory: Seeing Chrétien's Enide'. *Literature and Psychology*, 36.4 (1990): 47–66.

— 'In God's Sight: Vision and Sacred History in *Purity*'. *Text and Matter: New Critical Perspectives of the Pearl-Poet*. Ed. R. J. Blanch, M. Y. Miller and J. N. Wasserman. Troy, NY: Whitston, 1991. 105–16.

— 'The Virgin's Gaze: Spectacle and Transgression in Middle English Lyrics of the Passion'. *PMLA*, 106.5 (Oct. 1991): 1083–93.

— 'The Voyeur and the Private Life in *Troilus and Criseyde*'. *Studies in the Age of Chaucer*. Ed. T. J. Heffernan. 13 (1991): 141–58.

Stefaniak, R. 'Corregio's *Camera di San Paolo*: an Archaeology of the Gaze'. *Art History*, 16.2 (June 1993): 203–38.

— 'Replicating Mysteries of the Passion: Rosso's *Dead Christ with Angels*'. *Renaissance Quarterly*, 45.4 (Winter 1992): 677–738.

Steinberg, L. 'Animadversions: Michelangelo's Florentine *Pietà*: the Missing Leg Twenty Years After'. *The Art Bulletin*, 71 (1989): 480–505.

— ' "How Shall This Be?" Reflections on Filippo Lippi's *Annunciation* in London, Part 1'. *Artibus et historiae*, 8.16 (1987): 25–43.

— *The Sexuality of Christ in Renaissance Art and in Modern Oblivion*. New York: October/Pantheon, 1983.

Stock, B. *Augustine the Reader: Meditation, Self-Knowledge, and the Ethics of Interpretation*. Cambridge, MA: Harvard University Press, 1996.

Tachau, K. H. 'The Problem of the *Species in Medio* at Oxford in the Generation after Ockham'. *Mediaeval Studies*, 44 (1982): 394–443.

— *Vision and Certitude in the Age of Ockham: Optics, Epistemology and the Foundations of Semantics 1250–1345*. Leiden: Brill, 1988.

Trexler, R. C. *Church and Community 1200–1600: Studies in the History of Florence and New Spain*. Rome: Storia e Letteratura, 1987.

— *Public Life in Renaissance Florence*. New York: Academic, 1980.

Tuana, N. *The Less Noble Sex: Scientific, Religious, and Philosophical Conceptions of Woman's Nature*. Bloomington: Indiana University Press, 1993.

Turner, V. W. 'Betwixt and Between: the Liminal Period in *Rites de Passage*'. *Reader in Comparative Religion: an Anthropological Approach*. Ed. W. A. Lessa and E. Z. Vogt. 4th ed. New York: Harper, 1979. 234–43.

Tyler, S. A. 'The Vision Quest in the West, or What the Mind's Eye Sees'. *Journal of Anthropological Research*, 40 (1984): 23–40.

van Os, H. *Sienese Altarpieces 1215–1460*. Vol. 1: *Form, Content, Function 1215–1344*. 2 vols. Groningen, Neth.: Forsten, 1988.

Vauchez, A. *The Laity in the Middle Ages: Religious Beliefs and Devotional Practices*. Trans. M. J. Schneider. Notre Dame: University of Notre Dame Press, 1993.

Vesey, G. N. A. 'Vision'. *The Encyclopedia of Philosophy*. Ed. P. Edwards. 8 vols. New York: Macmillan, 1967. 8: 252–3.

von Simson, O. *The Gothic Cathedral: Origins of Gothic Architecture and the Medieval Concept of Order*. Bollingen Series 48. 2nd ed. New York: Pantheon, 1962.

Wartofsky, M. W. 'The Paradox of Painting: Pictorial Representation and the Dimensionality of Visual Space'. *Representation*. Special issue of *Social Research*, 51.4 (Winter 1984): 863–83.

— 'Picturing and Representing'. *Perception and Pictorial Representation*. Ed. C. F. Nodine and D. F. Fisher. New York: Praeger, 1979.

Welton, D. 'Biblical Bodies'. *Body and Flesh: a Philosophical Reader*. Ed. D. Welton. Oxford: Blackwell, 1998. 229–58.

Wetherbee, W. 'Philosophy, Cosmology, and the Twelfth-Century Renaissance'. *A History of Twelfth-Century Western Philosophy*. Ed. P. Dronke. Cambridge: Cambridge University Press, 1988. 21–53.

White, J. *The Birth and Rebirth of Pictorial Space*. 3rd ed. Cambridge, MA: Belknap, 1987.

Whitebook, J. 'Sublimation: a Frontier Concept'. *Perversion and Utopia: a Study in Psychoanalysis and Critical Theory.* Cambridge, MA: MIT Press, 1995. 217–46.

Whitman, J. *Allegory: the Dynamics of an Ancient and Medieval Technique.* Cambridge, MA: Harvard University Press, 1987.

Wippel, J. F. 'The Condemnations of 1270 and 1277 at Paris'. *Journal of Medieval and Renaissance Studies*, 7.2 (Fall 1977): 169–201.

Wogan-Browne, J. 'Chaste Bodies: Frames and Experiences'. *Framing Medieval Bodies.* Ed. S. Kay and M. Rubin. Manchester: Manchester University Press, 1994. 24–42.

Wolfson, H. A. 'The Internal Senses in Latin, Arabic, and Hebrew Philosophical Texts'. *Studies in the History of Philosophy and Religion.* 2 vols. Cambridge, MA: Harvard University Press, 1973. 1: 250–314.

Yates, F. A. *The Art of Memory.* Harmondsworth: Penguin, 1969.

Young, I. M. *Throwing Like a Girl and Other Essays in Feminist Philosophy and Social Theory.* Bloomington: Indiana University Press, 1990.

Ziegler, J. E. *Sculpture of Compassion: the Pietà and the Beguines in the Southern Low Countries c.1300–c.1600.* Brussels: Institut Historique Belge de Rome, 1992.

INDEX

Abelard, Peter, 46–7, 127, 181 n24, 208–9 n92

abjection, Julia Kristeva's theory of, 130–1, 151, 155, 198 n30, 210 n116–n120

Adam and Eve, 23, 29–31, 42–5, 104, 117, 150, 175 n80, 181 n24

affect or emotion, 5–6, 21, 30–1, 36, 51, 63–4, 82–3, 92, 95–7, 102–6, 111, 118–20, 131, 134–8, 145–7, 160, 170 n43, 182 n34, 198 n22, 200 n68–n69, 203 n4, 216 n88, 217 n89. *See also* passion

ageing, as attribute of the body, 36, 38, 100, 150

Alan of Lille, 17–18, 36–8, 54, 171 n12, 203 n3, 206 n52

Albertus Magnus, 49, 64, 153–4, 188 n15

alchemy, 129

Alexander of Hales, 143

Alhazen, 70, 73, 76, 192 n59, n67

Al-Kindi, 69

altarpiece, 3, 6, 143, 215 n64

analogy, medieval theories of, 111–14, 119, 122, 125–30, 162, 193 n83, 208 n81, n92, 209 n96. *See also* polarity

anatomy: of the body, 153; of the eye, 68, 76, 100–1, 172 n20, 195 n104

Ancrene Wisse, 37, 42, 56–8, 98, 115, 180 n9, n11, 184 n62, 185 n64, 186 n91, n94, 204 n15

Angela of Foligno, 136–7, 213 n27, 222 n162

animal, compared to human nature, 18, 21, 27, 103, 185 n63

appetites, 12, 21–2, 29–30, 33–6, 41, 45, 47–8, 53–4, 58–9, 65, 114, 117, 121–2, 149, 175 n80, 177 n96, 182 n34

Aquinas, St Thomas, 45, 53, 64, 82, 124, 179 n124, 181 n29, 208 n83

Arabian Nights, 51, 183 n49

Arabic theories of vision, 50, 65, 69, 73–4

architecture, 56, 167 n21

Aristotle, 32, 63–6, 69, 71, 73–4, 82–3, 87, 91, 93, 97–8, 100, 103, 105–6, 139, 177 n92, 184 n58, n60, 191 n54, n55, 195 n112, 199 n33, 200 n68–n69, 201 n71, n75, n77

art: *see* image devotion; Man of Sorrows; naturalism; symbolism

art history, 3–4, 8, 134–5, 212 n13

atomistic theory of vision, 73–4

attention, theories of, 100, 104–6, 120–2, 127, 131, 173 n46, 206–7 n64, 211 n124

Augustine, St, 18, 22–36, 41–2, 45–8, 53, 64–6, 69–70, 74, 77, 87, 93, 96, 105–6, 120–2, 124–5, 154, 156, 163, 172 n31, 173 n46, 174 n51–2, 175 n80, 176 n90, 177 n94, n96, 178 n103, n115, 180 n15, 185 n63, 188 n12, n13, 191 n50, 193 n74, 198 n22, 200 n66, 203 n3, 205 n43, 206 n55, n58, n61, n64, 211 n124, 218 n112, 219 n132

Avicenna, 69, 83, 195 n112

Bacon, Roger: biographical information, 68, 73, 187 n2, 192 n65, 207 n67; on signs, 75, 193 n83; on sin and the senses, 21, 103–4, 202 n103, 203 n3; on vision, 63–4, 68, 72–93, 95–107, 111, 122–4, 131, 134, 137, 139, 149, 193 n71, 195 n111–n112, 196 n116, 197 n18, 200–1 n69

Bartholomaeus Anglicus, 194 n101

basilisk, 51–2, 183 n53, n55

'beholdenness', Heidegger's theory of, 8, 168 n33

Belting, Hans, 133–4, 138, 144–7, 211 n1–n2, 212 n10, 216 n76, n88, 217 n91

Bernard of Clairvaux: and iconophobia, 208 n89; *On Conversion*, 23, 34–6, 54, 114–20, 129–30, 178 n103, 204 n23, 206